IN THE TRENCHES
Customizing and Upgrading Linux

Linda McKinnon
and Al McKinnon

Gearhead Press

Delivering technical information to IT professionals

MEMORIAL LIBRARY
500 N. DUNTON
ARLINGTON HEIGHTS, IL 60004

PUBLISHED BY
Gearhead Press
a unit of Gearhead Group Corporation
2760 East W.T. Harris Boulevard
Charlotte, North Carolina 28213

© 2000 Gearhead Press

All rights reserved. No part of this book may be reproduced or transmitted in any form or by any means, electronic or mechanical, including photocopying, recording, or by any information storage and retrieval system, without written permission from the publisher.

Library of Congress Control No.: 00-134951
ISBN 1-930713-01-0

Printed in Canada
1 2 3 4 5 6 7 8 9 10
First printing, October 2000

Gearhead Press books are distributed in the United States and Canada by Publishers Group West. For ordering information, call 510-528-1444 or visit PGW's Web site *(http://www.pgw.com)*. For information about corporate sales or international editions, contact Gearhead Press at 704-598-6262 (phone), 704-598-6207 (fax), or by visiting its Web site, *www.gearheadpress.com*.

"Red Hat" is a registered trademark of Red Hat, Inc. Used with permission. All other brand names and product names mentioned herein are trademarks, registered trademarks, or trade names of their respective holders.

The authors and publisher have taken care in the preparation of this book, but make no express or implied representations or warranties of any kind, and assume no responsibility for errors or omissions. In no event shall the authors or publisher be liable for incidental or consequential damages in connection with or arising out of the use of the information or programs contained herein.

Acknowledgments

First and foremost, thanks to Linda for the inspiration to write this book. It was your observations about the demands of Linux/UNIX professionals that led to the development of this reference. Thanks also to National Public Radio in the U.S. and the Canadian Broadcasting Corporation in Canada for keeping us company while we wrote: may your flow of ideas never be stemmed. Finally, I dedicate this book to the memory of Keeler, our beloved old dog and faithful companion who spent her last few months watching us pound out thousands of words and trace out miles of mouse lines. She is sorely missed.

—Al McKinnon

Thanks to all the folks that came to me and said, "Please write that down for us." Without you, I never would have embarked on this literary tour. A special thanks to my peers who shared their views, and my students who shared their ideas and needs. During the last five years, I have taught both basic and advanced Linux/UNIX curriculum to more than 1200 individuals. You know who you are; you guided my choice of topics. This book is dedicated to those who we have yet to convert from that other operating system.

—Linda McKinnon

Contents

INTRODUCTION xi

CHAPTER 1: PREPARING FOR INSTALLATION: CHRONICLING
YOUR EQUIPMENT 1
Do Not Be Afraid—Just Do Your Homework! 1
Discovering and Chronicling Your System's Equipment 4
Exercise 7
Quiz 8

CHAPTER 2: HARD-DISK-PARTITION PLANNING AND PREPARATION ... 9
Swap Space Options 10
How Much Swap Space Is Required? 11
Hard-Disk Partitioning 12
   Master Boot Record and Partition Table(s) 13
   Boot Process 14
   Linux and LILO 16
   Disk Partitioning: Example of a Simple Approach 21
   Disk Partitioning: Example of a Complex Approach 22
Exercise 25
Quiz 25

CHAPTER 3: INSTALLING LINUX FROM A CD-ROM 27
Creating a Linux Install Boot Disk 28
   Creating the Install Boot Disk from a DOS/Windows System ... 29
   Creating the Install Boot Disk from a UNIX System 31

v

Installing Linux on a SCSI System 32
   Invoking the Linux Installation Program 33
   Inputting Information in the Installation Program 33
   Forcing Linux to Recognize Your SCSI Controller and Drives . . 34
   Stepping through the Installation 36
Installing Linux on an IDE System 63
   Invoking the Linux Installation Program 63
   Inputting Information in the Installation Program 64
   IDE Drive Geometry 65
   Stepping through the Installation 66
Quiz 90

CHAPTER 4: INSTALLING LINUX USING NFS **91**
Quick Review of NFS 91
Preparing the NFS Server 93
   Step 1. Insert Linux CD-ROM in NFS Server 93
   Step 2. Log In as Regular User and su to Root 94
   Step 3. Record IP Address and Netmask of NFS Server 94
   Step 4. Add an Entry for the CD-ROM to Server's /etc/fstab File . 94
   Step 5. Mount CD-ROM as File System on NFS Server 95
   Step 6. Export CD-ROM File System to Access It without Security. 95
Start Target Installation System 96
   Step 1. Create Floppy Disks 97
   Step 2. Boot Target System 97
   Step 3. Choose NFS Image Option 98
   Step 4. Provide Networking Information 98
   Step 5. Provide Information about NFS Server 99
   Step 6. Proceed with Otherwise "Normal" Installation 100
Quiz 101

CHAPTER 5: CONFIGURING THE VIDEO **103**
Video Signal Generation 104
   Video-Adapter Memory 104
   Basic Video-Adapter Bus 107
Video Display 110
   Basic Monitor Design 110
   Video Frame and Synchronization 112
   How HSPs and VSPs Are Related 116

Contents

Monitor Performance and Capabilities 121
   Monitor Age 121
   Bandwidth 122
   Vertical Frequency 125
   Horizontal Frequency 125
   Dot Pitch 126
   The Bottom Line: Match Video Hardware and
      Monitor to Your Expectations 129
Interlacing 129
Getting Ready for Video Configuration 132
   The XF86Config File: Heart of the X Server 133
   Using SuperProbe to Obtain Video Information 135
   Using Xconfigurator to Create the Basic XF86Config File 137
Exercise 138
   Step 1. Invoking SuperProbe 138
   Step 2. Invoking Xconfigurator 139
   Step 3. Initiating Xconfiguration 139
   Step 4. Probing for Hardware 140
   Step 5. Specifying Video-Adapter Hardware 141
   Step 6. Specifying Monitor Type 142
   Step 7. Custom Monitor Setup 143
   Step 8. Indicating Horizontal-Sync Range 144
   Step 9. Indicating Vertical-Sync Range 146
   Step 10. Setting Resolution and Color Depth 147
   Step 11. Probing with X Server Configured Thus Far 147
   Step 12. If Results of Xconfigurator Probe Are Successful 148
   Step 13. If Results of Xconfigurator Probe Are *Not* Successful . . 149
   Step 14. Selecting Video Modes 151
   Step 15. Starting X to Test the Chosen Configuration 152
   Step 16. Can You See This Message? 153
   Step 17. Do You Want to Automatically Boot into X? 153
   Step 18. Reviewing the Configuration File Prior to Running X . 154
   Step 19. Problems with Chosen Configuration. 155
Quiz 157

Chapter 6: Configuring Printers 159
Basic Commands and Utilities 159
Configuring Local Printing 163
Configuring Remote Printing 168
   Prerequisites 168
   The Configuration 169
Quiz 174

Chapter 7: Adding, Replacing, and Upgrading RPM Packages 175
RPM Definition and Package Management 176
RPM Naming Convention 177
SRPM versus RPM 178
A Package's Function and Contents 178
Replacing and Upgrading the XFree86 Package 181
   Step 1. Identify RPM Packages to Replace 182
   Step 2. Obtain Necessary Files and Place on System 183
   Step 3. Make Notes on Packages to be Upgraded versus
      Packages to be Installed 184
   Step 4. Query the RPM Database to Confirm the Upgrade 186
Using Packages to Install XF86Setup 187
Exercise 189
Quiz 192

Chapter 8: Upgrading the Kernel Using RPM Packages 193
Why Upgrade or Patch the Kernel? 194
The Security Advisory 194
Suggested Upgrade Procedure 196
   Step 1. Check Disk Space 196
   Step 2. Identify Packages Already Installed 197
   Step 3. Organize Packages and Perform Integrity Check 199
   Step 4. Compare Existing Packages to Downloaded Packages 199
   Step 5. Record Current Version 200
   Step 6. Create an Emergency Boot Diskette 201
   Step 7. Proceed to Upgrade or Install Packages 202
   Step 8. Optional: Create RAM Disk Support File 203

CONTENTS

Step 9. Setting up LILO to Boot from New Kernel 203
Step 10. Shut Down and Reboot to Test New Kernel 204
Exercise 206
Quiz 211

CHAPTER 9: CONFIGURING THE KERNEL 213
Linux Kernel Configuration Menu 214
   Code maturity level options 216
   Processor types and features 217
   Loadable module support 218
   General setup 219
   Plug and Play support Option 223
   Block devices 223
   Networking Options 230
   Network Device Support 231
   SCSI Support 235
   SCSI low-level drivers 236
   Filesystems 237
   Save and Exit 238
Quiz 239

CHAPTER 10: INSTALLING A NEW KERNEL BY BUILDING A NEW SOURCE TREE 241
Finding a New Kernel 242
Installing a New Kernel 243
   Step 1. Record Current Kernel Level and Create
      Boot and Rescue Diskettes 244
   Step 2. Obtain the Source Code in tar File Format 245
   Step 3. Check Space Requirements for New Kernel and
      New Source Tree 247
   Step 4. Preserve Old Source Tree 248
   Step 5. Unpack Archived tar Files 249
   Step 6. Create Link to New Linux Source Tree 250
   Step 7. Check for .o Files and Dependencies in Source Tree . . . 250
   Step 8. Check Software Requirements 252
   Step 9. Configure Kernel 254
   Step 10. Prepare for Compilation: make dep and make clean . . 255

Step 11. Compile Kernel: make bzImage 256
Step 12. Make Modules: make modules and
   make modules_install 258
Step 13. Copy bzImage Kernel and System.map Files
   to Correct Directories 259
Step 14. Optional: Create RAM Disk File 261
Step 15. Modify /etc/lilo.conf File to Point to
   New Kernel without and with a RAM Disk File 262
Step 16. Update Master Boot Record 263
Step 17. Shut Down and Test System: Rescue if Necessary 264
Step 18. Check New Kernel 265
Exercise 266
Quiz 273

APPENDIX A: PATCHING KERNELS 275

APPENDIX B: QUIZ ANSWERS 279

INDEX 289

Introduction

THIS BOOK IS FOR SYSTEM PROFESSIONALS who want to improve their Linux skills, and gain a thorough understanding of installing and upgrading the Linux operating system, the kernel, and applications. Thus, readers should have a basic knowledge of Linux or other UNIX-based operating systems (such as SCO UNIX, HP/UX, Solaris, or AIX), plus a working knowledge of information and networking technologies.

We have organized the book in a way that has proven to be most useful to our students, and most successful when undertaking a Linux installation or upgrade. In preparation for installing Linux, Chapter 1 begins with chronicling our equipment. Then, because Linux administrators encounter disk partitioning and swap space issues almost immediately when beginning an install, we cover these next in Chapter 2. Chapter 3 takes you step by step through a Linux install, first on SCSI hardware and then on IDE hardware. Understanding that you might install Linux over a network connection, Chapter 4 steps you through installing Linux using an NFS connection.

Chapter 5 provides an in-depth section on video, discussing video signal generation, monitor performance and capabilities, the advantages and disadvantages of interlacing, and, finally, how to configure your video setup. Then, in Chapter 6, we guide you through the printer configuration process. In Chapter 7, we show you how to work with and manage RPM packages. Building upon what we've learned in Chapter 7, Chapter 8 shows you how to upgrade a kernel using RPM packages. In Chapter 9, we configure a kernel and, finally, in Chapter 10 we show you how to install a new kernel from scratch.

Audience

Readers should be familiar with UNIX-based operating systems and commands, computer networking concepts, and the Internet. This book is suitable for anyone requiring comprehensive skills in the installation or upgrading of a Linux operating system and applications. It is also an excellent primer for individuals pursuing system administration training and certification.

Objectives

This book will teach you to perform a Linux installation and configuration on SCSI and IDE systems, to configure the X video system on any system with a CRT-based monitor, to add or upgrade applications, and to upgrade or install a new kernel for the Linux operating system. The book can be used as a companion to *In the Trenches: Installing and Administering Linux* (Gearhead Press, 2000). It also serves as an excellent primer and resource for professionals familiar with Microsoft, Novell, or other UNIX platforms who wish to become more familiar with Linux, a UNIX/POSIX platform.

After studying this book and performing the exercises, you should be able to:

▲ Investigate and chronicle the equipment in a given system

▲ Understand swap space and swap space options

▲ Partition a hard disk

- Describe the boot process
- Create Linux boot and rescue disks
- Install and configure Linux on SCSI and IDE systems
- Configure local or remote printing
- Discuss video signal generation
- Discuss the video display on a CRT monitor
- Explain the structure and function of an *XF86Config* file
- Configure video settings with the `Xconfigurator` program
- Briefly describe NFS
- Install and configure Linux via an NFS connection
- Manage, install, and upgrade RPM packages
- Upgrade and install applications with RPM packages
- Upgrade a Linux kernel using RPM packages
- Download a kernel source file from the Internet
- Uncompress a `tar` file
- Configure basic and crucial kernel options
- Modify LILO to boot from the new kernel

Typographical Conventions

A monospaced font in regular text is used to highlight command names, command options, and programs (for example, utilities). Examples appear below:

- ▲ We recommend recording the output from the `uname -a` command.

- ▲ The *bz2* files are simply files compressed with `bzip2`, which means you need the `bzip2` utility to unzip them.

Italics are used to indicate file names, directory and path names, variable names, new concepts, and general emphasis in regular text, as well as variable strings in command lines. Examples follow:

- ▲ Rename the *linux* directory to *linux.revision_number* and link the directory back to *linux*.

- ▲ The revision number indicates the *patch* level of the respective kernel.

- ▲ You will need an *additional* 55 MB or so if you want to add the new kernel and source tree without touching the existing one.

The following monospaced font is used for examples of command statements and dialog box options; bold monospaced type is used for operating system responses.

```
# cd /usr/src/linux
# make mrproper
make[1]: Entering directory '/usr/src/linux-2.2.13/
    arch/i386/boot'
rm -f tools/build
rm -f setup bootsect bzImage compressed/bvmlinux.out
```

Named keys on the keyboard and key sequences in regular text and elsewhere are enclosed in angle brackets, such as <Enter>, <Tab>, <Space>, and so on.

 TIP: *The occasional tip is intended to save you time and trouble.*

NOTE: *The notes are brief asides and issues related to the subject at hand.*

 WARNING: *The warnings appearing in this book are intended to help you avoid disaster or unanticipated results.*

Chapter 1

Preparing for Installation: Chronicling Your Equipment

CHRONICLING YOUR EQUIPMENT BEFOREHAND can prove to be very important to a Linux installation. If you've heard a horror story or two about a Linux installation (overblown, in our opinion), chances are the source of the horror was a lack of complete knowledge of the target system.

In this chapter, you may be doing one or more of the following: using a hardware investigation utility, checking the system BIOS (basic input/output system), or even pulling the cover off the system to look inside. It all will be in the name of (eventually) knowing what you're doing and moving ahead in a deliberate manner, with everything under control.

Do Not Be Afraid— Just Do Your Homework!

Linux installation is not a horror story—it's just a different kind of operating system installation. Any horror stories you may have heard are just myths, and generally originate from one of the following two circumstances:

- ▲ The storytellers either did not investigate or did not chronicle their equipment for quick and easy reference prior to beginning their Linux installation.
- ▲ Perhaps their equipment was too new. Their version of the Linux kernel may not yet have had the necessary drivers for their new hard disk, video card, and the like.

Keep in mind that messy installation experiences happen with "that other GUI (graphical user interface) operating system," too, for the same reasons. To prevent such horrors during your installation, you need only to do your homework. Identify and chronicle all the equipment on your system for reference during Linux installation. This first chapter will show you what to look for.

Where Are You Starting From?

You may be building a brand new system or trying to install Linux on an older system. We will try to draw your attention to, and comment on, all the issues that pertain to both scenarios.

Using Recently Purchased Equipment

If you are installing on recently purchased equipment, you must take the time to do some research on the Internet to learn which systems are or are not supported by Linux. Yes, some play better than others. It is not so much the system in general as the interface and adapter cards that are inside them. There are some very good Web sites that specialize in this information, including the "nitty gritty stuff" on hard drives, controllers, modems, network cards, sound cards, ports, memory, and video chips, including the monitor. The definitive hardware reference site is *www.redhat.com*. From there you can follow links to the hardware compatibility lists. Be meticulous.

Chapter 1: Preparing for Installation

You should be obsessed with ensuring that you receive from vendors all technical booklets on all parts within the system. At the risk of sounding redundant, this includes all detailed information on the hard drive, controllers, modems, network cards, sound cards, ports, memory, and video chips, including the monitor. We cannot emphasize enough the importance of knowing the exact details of video and monitor technical specifications. If your system is being assembled by a dealer, make sure that you get all the booklets and utility disks that shipped with every card inside your system before you leave the premises.

The "bench guys" that work on these systems like to collect utilities in case they ever have to solve an issue with customers' systems. If at all possible, you should try to deal with a company that is willing to give you copies of any new drivers or utilities that it has had to acquire in order to correctly set up your system. The drivers and utilities that ship with the interfaces are often obsolete, so the technicians have to acquire and use their own. Needless to add, the dealers and technicians that share this information are worth their weight in gold.

Using Existing Equipment

Regarding installation on older or existing equipment: generally the more established and better supported the system, the better off you'll be. However, there are some exceptions to this, too. We recommend that you perform the same checks on hardware, drivers, and utilities that you'd make on any new system. You may end up replacing unsupported hardware. As a result of the new interest in Linux, valuable Web sites have emerged that specialize in assisting you with acquiring documentation on systems, interfaces, and adapters. Again, the premier reference site is *www.redhat.com*. You may have to take the cover off of the system and start by identifying the various adapters and video cards (right down to their chip sets). Information on monitors can be tough to come by, in which case you may have to rely upon Linux support groups that have taken the time to share their experiences.

In general, Linux will run on a 386 or 486 with 16 MB of memory. Do not, however, expect to get a decent X Window System desktop, such as KDE (The K Desktop Environment), to perform unless you have at least 32 MB of memory. Having said that, these systems will work very well at the command line, if that is sufficient for your needs.

Discovering and Chronicling Your System's Equipment

There are many good tools available on the market that can help you to discover what is inside your system. The trick is to find one that does not require the installation of another operating system first. Ideally, you could find a utility that works on a system that has just been booted by a single operating system diskette. It seems silly and unproductive to have to load another operating system on a machine just to be able to run probing utilities.

We have provided an example component list in Table 1-1. The necessary components are listed in the first column; the names, specifications, and settings in column two derive from our example system. You can use this list directly as a sort of template, or you can create your own customized list. The list will likely change a little depending on the system that you have and what you use to discover system attributes. Meanwhile, we provide a similar template in Table 1-2 to help you list the required system information in the chapter exercise.

Incidentally, we gathered the information about the example system using the utility `winmsd`, because the system had Microsoft Windows 95 installed on it prior to the Linux installation. We could also have used the Device Manager found in the Control Panel under System. As you can see, the example system is hardly brand new. It has proven to be a very good Linux system nonetheless.

Table 1-1: Components of the Example System

Components	Names/Specifications/Settings
System BIOS/Bus	Award Modular BIOS v4.51PG, AT/AT-compatible EISA/ISA HAL
CPU	x86 Family 5 Model 4 Stepping 3, Genuine Intel, 199 MHz
Monitor	TTX CPS-1760, multi-frequency
Display type	Mbyte Video Memory, Shared Memory BIOS v1.04e, 10-01-97
Video adapter type	SiSV-compatible display adapter
Video adapter settings/specs	Settings: 640 x 480, 16 bpp Horizontal: 30–65 KHz Vertical: 50–90 Hz
Video chip type/video memory	SiS 5597/5598/4 MB
Digital-to-analog converter (DAC)	SiS
Sound card	None
Mouse type/no. of buttons	Microsoft Serial/2
HDD capacity/controller type	3.2 GB/SCSI
Driver that Windows uses for reference	SiSV/sys v4.00
RAM size/type	64 MB/SDRAM
CD-ROM type/speed	SCSI/24x
Keyboard type	US-102
HDD/peripheral interface type/controller	SCSI Adaptec 1522B; I/O Port 340; IRQ 11; BIOS address CC000h

Continued

Table 1-1: Components of the Example System (continued)

Components	Names/Specifications/Settings
Networking details	Standalone IP 192.168.6.35 Mask 255.255.255.0
Printer	HP LaserJet 6
Modem type/specs	None

CHAPTER 1: PREPARING FOR INSTALLATION

Exercise

Appearing below is a template of system components you can use to check the equipment on your system. The component names and their corresponding specifications and settings may differ from system to system.

Table 1-2: Template for Chronicling Equipment

Components	Names/Specifications/Settings
System BIOS/Bus	
CPU	
Monitor	
Display type	
Video adapter type	
Video adapter settings/specs	
Video chip type/video memory	
Digital-to-analog converter	
Mouse type/no. of buttons	
HDD capacity/controller type	
Driver OS uses for reference	
RAM size/type	
Sound card	
CD-ROM type/speed	
Keyboard type	

Continued

Table 1-2: Template for Chronicling Equipment (continued)

Components	Names/Specifications/Settings
HDD/peripheral interface type; IRQ; port address; memory addresses	
Networking details (interface card name/specs; addresses; mask; host names; domain name; name servers; default gateway)	
Printer name/model no./specs	
Modem type/specs	

Quiz

1. What two scenarios are most likely to cause problems in a new Linux installation?

2. For what two system components are hardware details critical to Linux installation?

3. If you are going to be installing Linux on a newly built system, what information and documentation is necessary?

4. If you are going to be installing Linux on an older system, what will you need to do before installing?

5. What types of utilities can be used to gather system information?

See Appendix B for answers.

Chapter 2

Hard-Disk-Partition Planning and Preparation

THREE MAJOR ISSUES FACE USERS WHO ARE NEW to the installation and configuration of UNIX-like platforms. One of them is how to handle hard-disk partitioning, the topic of this chapter. The other two issues are dual booting (also covered in this chapter) and video configuration (which is discussed in detail in Chapter 5).

Linux users encounter the disk-partitioning issue almost immediately upon beginning an installation. The first topic we address in this chapter is swap space options, because the decision to create a swap *partition* versus a swap *file* must be made before installation. Both options work, but one may be more appropriate than the other, depending on performance requirements and other criteria discussed in the following section.

After covering swap space options, we turn to hard-disk partitioning. We then illustrate the roles of partitions and other software during the boot process. Finally, we present examples of simple and complex disk-partitioning strategies.

Swap Space Options

Before we begin this discussion, it is useful to note that swap space is sometimes referred to as "disk paging." Linux will write "pages" of memory to the hard disk when RAM (random access memory) is full. You should try to prevent the operating system from writing pages to the hard disk, because system performance will suffer. Swap space is never a fix for the lack of system RAM.

Swap space can be a dedicated swap partition or, alternatively, a swap file. The partitioning can be simple or complex. There are pros and cons in the use of each option. The issues are two: (1) Which option do you need or want? (2) How large should you make the partition(s) or file(s)?

We recommend a dedicated swap partition because you will get better performance. Swap partitioning must be planned before installation so that you can create the necessary partition types and sizes during the installation. The three types of partitions are primary, extended, and logical (discussed later in the chapter). Our swap partition is an extended partition within the (primary and extended) Linux operating system partition. Figure 2.1 shows a simple illustration of the swap partition.

You should not entirely rule out the use of swap files, however. Swap files can be created after the installation is complete for use in "emergency" situations. They will work in conjunction with the rest of your computer memory configuration(s). But swap files should be deactivated and removed as soon as possible after emergencies have been resolved. If longer-term solutions are required, consider adding RAM or repartitioning the hard disk (that is, once a proper system backup has taken place). Do not rely on using the comparatively inefficient swap files for anything beside the short term.

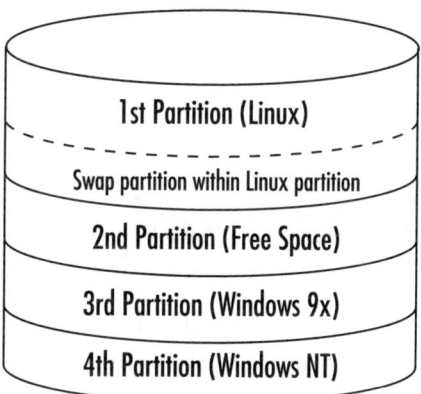

Figure 2.1. Hard-disk partitioning.

How Much Swap Space Is Required?

If your system has only 16 MB of RAM or less, a swap partition is mandatory. In such cases the swap partition has to be at least 16 MB. If you are going to run X (the Linux X Window System), however, performance will be quite unacceptable if you only have 16 MB of RAM.

The amount of swap space you choose to create depends on your system—that is, on how much RAM you have and the number of applications you will typically be running. A reasonable, albeit rough, estimate is a size equal to twice the amount of physical RAM. For example, if you have 32 MB of RAM in the system and the system is going to be running two or three applications, you are well advised to configure 64 MB of swap space. You can start with this amount and then monitor your system and application performance and make adjustments later as necessary. For systems with 64 MB of RAM or more, a swap partition equal to the RAM installed is a good starting point. We consider a swap partition in excess of 200 MB to be wasteful.

The amount of swap space is worth thinking about before proceeding with your installation. Any adjustments to increase the size of the swap partition after installation will involve backing up and restoring file systems and applications, repartitioning, and reformatting.

Hard-Disk Partitioning

As mentioned previously, the three types of partitions are primary, extended, and logical. You can create only four primary partitions on a drive, but only one primary partition can be an extended partition. An extended partition can hold a maximum of 12 logical partitions.

Theoretically, you can put a different operating system in each primary partition, as seen in Figure 2.1. If your Linux system is going to be part of a production system, placing different operating systems on the hard disk is generally not recommended. If you are installing Linux on a test or home system, however, you may wish to install other operating systems for many reasons.

If you are just starting out and are using a Red Hat-based distribution, we recommend that you use `Disk Druid`. The `Disk Druid` tool will walk you through the creation of partitions. If you are somewhat experienced with partitioning, you may want to use `fdisk`. If you are an expert, you can download a tool called `FIPS` (First nondestructive Interactive Partition Splitting program), which will allow you to manipulate your existing partitions without damaging your data (providing you use the tool correctly). A product called Partition Magic is also a popular utility for disk partitioning.

CHAPTER 2: HARD-DISK-PARTITION PLANNING

WARNING: *The four tools mentioned here are not identical, and they have very different default behaviors. For example, if you use* `fdisk` *to create a set of multiple file-system partitions for Linux, you have to specifically create a primary partition or extended/logical partitions. In contrast, if you create the file-system partitions using the* `Disk Druid` *tool, Linux automatically organizes each individual file-system partition into logical partitions for you.*

Be careful when placing different partitions for different operating systems on the hard disk. For example, if you wish to create four partitions containing DOS, Windows 9x, OS/2, and Linux, use each operating system's respective disk-partitioning tool. Use the `fdisk` (or equivalent) tool that shipped with the product. This will ensure compatibility between the partition and the operating system. The exception here may be the OS/2 version of `fdisk`. You can use it to create *all* the partitions, but then you'll have to go back to Linux `fdisk` to change the partition type to Linux.

When starting with a blank disk, you should always begin with the least sophisticated partition manager first and work your way up. The customary sequence follows: Windows 9x, Windows NT/2000, OS/2, and then Linux's `fdisk` or `Disk Druid`.

At the end of the partitioning process, you will have created the "partition table," a map of the drive partitions. The partition table is placed in sector 0 of cylinder 0 of the physical hard disk. With respect to the physical disk, the partition table resides at the same location, along with the master boot record (MBR).

Master Boot Record and Partition Table(s)

The MBR is always on the first sector of the physical hard disk (Figure 2.2). That first sector is numbered or called, somewhat idiosyncratically, "sector 0." The partition table is always located in the MBR as

13

well. In case you've heard the term "partition boot record," it is synonymous with the MBR.

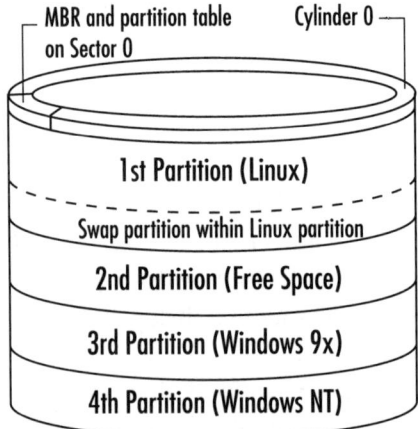

Figure 2.2. The MBR and the partition table(s).

Boot Process

Our intent in this section is to explain how the MBR and the partition table work together to contribute to booting the system. Most PC architectures behave in the manner we are about to describe. The process is fairly generic—that is, regardless of the operating system installed, the process is much the same. Only the last few steps of the process, involving the "root file system" and init, can be considered unique to Linux.

When a PC is turned on, a small boot program (which resides on the PC's ROM [read-only memory] BIOS chips) performs a POST (power-on self-test). A POST tests the basic hardware, CPU, memory, and other system components. Immediately after the POST, the boot program (also called "the BIOS") sets off in a quest for an operating system to copy to its RAM; it will eventually turn over control of the PC to the operating system in RAM.

If the PC's CMOS (complementary metal-oxide semiconductor) is configured such that the BIOS is to search the hard disk first (as opposed to a floppy disk or a CD-ROM), then the BIOS will begin by searching the first sector of the first cylinder (the first cylinder is called "cylinder 0," just as the first sector of the cylinder is called "sector 0") for further instructions.

When it finds a small program called the "boot manager" (also called the "bootstrap loader"), the BIOS loads a copy of the MBR/boot manager into RAM and then "branches" to it (that is, passes control to it) so the boot manager can take over. The boot manager within the copy of the MBR reads the partition table, which points to the boot sector within what the partition table calls the "active partition" (a holdover from the DOS days; "active" means "bootable"). The boot manager then reads the boot sector, and the boot sector takes over.

The boot sector then reads the compressed operating system kernel into RAM, and a small program at the beginning of the kernel uncompresses the kernel. The kernel takes over and continues the boot process by (1) checking for other installed hardware and installing appropriate drivers; (2) mounting the root file system; and (3) invoking the `init` (initialization) process, which in turn invokes other processes and daemons, depending on its configuration. The `init` process also switches to the default or specified run-level mode and invokes `getty`. (Getty opens tty lines and sets their modes, prints the log-in prompt and gets the user's name, and initiates a log-in process for the user.) At this point, the PC is finished booting and is ready for log-in. This process is summarized in Figure 2.3.

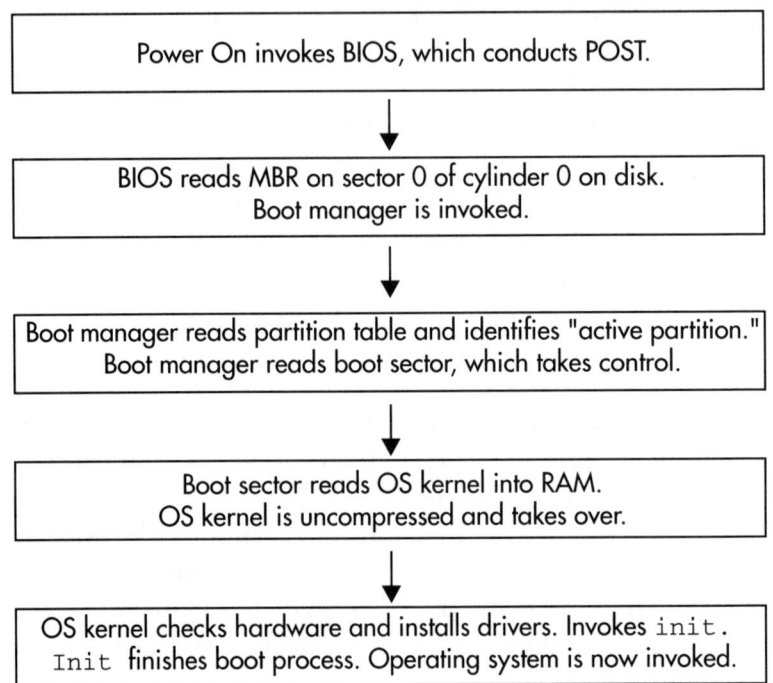

Figure 2.3. The boot process.

We admit that we have simplified the boot process, but in summary, the MBR generally houses the boot manager, and the boot manager reads the partition table to find the location of each partition installed on the physical drive. If each partition contains a unique operating system, then each will also probably contain a boot sector and kernel for its operating system.

Linux and LILO

You have probably inferred from our discussions thus far that most operating systems boot off of a primary partition, not a logical partition. In reality, Linux is an exception to this general rule.

Chapter 2: Hard-Disk-Partition Planning

LILO (LInux LOader) is a small boot-manager program that can be configured to reside in one of three places: inside the MBR, on a floppy disk or other external medium, or on the Linux partition block (Figure 2.4). Other available boot-manager programs that do the same tasks as LILO are OS/2's Boot Manager and Partition Magic (which uses OS/2's Boot Manager). You should not use more than one of these programs because they do not work together. If you contemplate booting with OS/2, then we suggest you use the OS/2 Boot Manager instead of LILO.

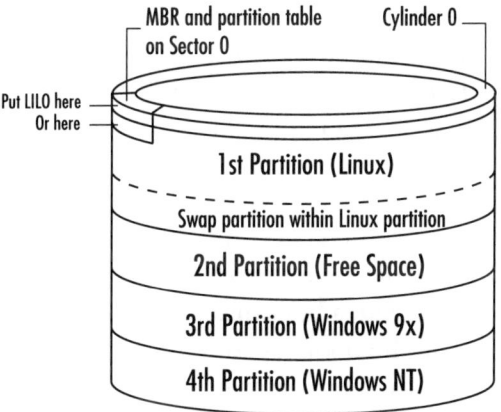

Figure 2.4. Linux and LILO, the Linux Loader.

Thus, LILO is not your only option for a boot manager. You can do without it or use some other boot manager. On any system that doesn't "multi-boot" with OS/2, however, we recommend using LILO. Thus, if and when you choose LILO to be the boot manager, it can be configured to boot Linux by default or allow you to choose (via a small and simple procedure) which partition you wish to boot from (that is, which operating system you wish to use). Another decision you have to make in a multi-OS configuration (in which you are using LILO) is where to install LILO.

Where to Install LILO

The MBR is the recommended place to install LILO, unless the MBR already starts another boot manager that loads the operating system, such as OS/2's Boot Manager, or an operating system loader, such as System Commander. The MBR is a special area on your hard drive that is automatically loaded by your computer's BIOS and is the earliest point at which LILO can take control of the boot process. If you install LILO in the MBR, when your machine boots, LILO will present a `boot:` prompt. You can then boot Red Hat Linux or any other operating system you configure LILO to boot.

If your system will use only Red Hat Linux, you should install LILO in the MBR. For systems running Windows 9x along with Linux, you also should install LILO in the MBR so that LILO can boot both operating systems.

If you have Windows NT (and you want to install LILO), you should install LILO on the first sector of the root partition, not in the MBR. Be sure to create a boot disk. In a case such as this, you will either need to use the boot disk or configure the NT system loader to boot LILO from the first sector of the root partition.

If you have chosen to use a boot manager other than LILO (such as OS/2's Boot Manager), then put LILO in the first sector of the boot partition so that the other boot manager can find it. How? Answer `First sector of the boot partition` when presented with the LILO install menu.

In this case, your other boot manager will take control first. You can then configure that boot manager to start LILO (which will then boot Red Hat Linux). Ultimately, to boot Linux, you will still have to invoke LILO, but LILO will not be the boot manager.

Without LILO

If you choose not to install LILO for any reason, you will not be able to boot your Red Hat Linux system directly and will need to use another boot method (such as a boot diskette). Use this option only if you are sure you have another way of booting your Red Hat Linux system!

Using LILO

If you have chosen to let LILO manage the disk, then you can access the boot sequence by using the <Tab> key precisely at the `boot:` prompt during initialization. If your timing is correct, a list of available operating systems, as configured in the */etc/lilo.conf* file, will appear.

The following sample */etc/lilo.conf* file creates two boot choices, Linux or DOS:

```
boot=/dev/hda
map=/boot/map
install=/boot/boot.b
prompt=
timeout=50
image=/boot/vmlinuz-2.2.5-15
    label=linux
    root=/dev/hda7
    read-only
other=/dev/hda1
    label=dos
    table=/dev/hda
```

During initialization, you might use the <Tab> key to display these options. Then you can choose which operating system to boot and enter it at the `boot:` prompt, as shown here.

```
LILO boot: <Tab>
linux dos
boot: dos
```

You have got to be quick or LILO will default to using the first entry (in this example, Linux).

LILO Configuration

If you wish to add other options to the LILO boot process as part of the command, enter them into the kernel parameters field presented during the LILO configuration. The parameters required are similar to those discussed in the Chapter 3 subsection, "Forcing Linux to Recognize Your SCSI Controller and Drives."

▲ Bootable partition: Every bootable partition is listed, including partitions used by other operating systems.

▲ The "Boot label" column: This column will be filled in with the word `linux` on the partition holding your Red Hat Linux system's root file system. Other partitions may also have boot labels. If you would like to add boot labels for other partitions (or change an existing boot label), click once on the partition to select it. Once selected, it will present a screen that will allow you to change the boot label.

Managing LILO

Assume that you had a perfectly functioning Linux operating system until last night when you decided to add a Windows NT partition to the disk. Now nothing will boot. What happened? Windows has overwritten the master boot record area.

How do you fix this problem? You must have a bootable DOS floppy at hand with `fdisk` available. Then you use the DOS command `fdisk /mbr`. Many experienced administrators and users know when to do this, but often they do not know why. The `fdisk /mbr` command will replace (not fix, but replace) the entire MBR with a clean DOS one. Yes, this means that the little LILO program that lives inside the MBR is gone. The deletion is easily remedied, however, by

CHAPTER 2: HARD-DISK-PARTITION PLANNING

recreating LILO in two easy steps. First, edit the */etc/lilo.conf* file, and then run `/sbin/lilo` to replace or copy the code to the MBR.

By the way, *never* use any DOS version older than version 5.0.

Disk Partitioning: Example of a Simple Approach

You can dedicate the entire hard-drive space to Linux with one file-system partition and one swap partition, as illustrated in Figure 2.5. This approach is obviously not the same as creating multiple file-system partitions to accommodate specific file systems. Nevertheless, there is nothing wrong or incorrect about this simple approach. The advantages to this approach are that it is simple to install and maintain, and each file-system directory is allowed to grow freely.

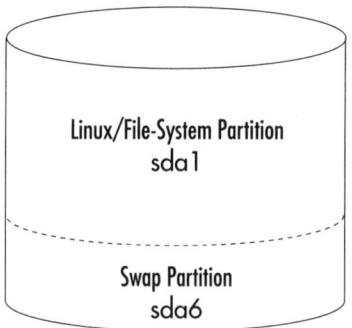

Figure 2.5. Simple example of disk partitioning.

Assuming that you are configuring for a SCSI (small computer system interface) system, the entire disk, as represented in Figure 2.5, will be known as *sda* (SCSI disk a). The two partitions on the *sda* disk will be known as *sda1* and *sda6*, representing the root (/) and file-system partitions, and the swap partition, respectively. When the system initializes, the boot process will display these entities using the following format *sda*: <sda1 <sda6>>. This illustrates their relationship and

21

dependencies. (We discuss IDE [integrated device electronics] technology in the next section. With IDE, the disk partitions are called *hda* [hard disk a], *hda1*, and so on, instead of *sda*.)

Thus, *all* of the following directories will be under the root directory (/), and *all* will be within a single file-system partition.

```
drwxr-xr-x    2 root root     2048 Jun 13 06:56 bin
drwxr-xr-x    2 root root     1024 Jun 13 07:09 boot
drwxr-xr-x    5 root root    34816 Jun 17 16:36 dev
drwxr-xr-x   29 root root     3072 Jun 19 08:25 etc
drwxr-xr-x    5 root root     1024 Jun 17 09:05 home
drwxr-xr-x    4 root root     3072 Jun 13 06:48 lib
drwxr-xr-x    2 root root    12288 Jun 13 06:22 lost+found
drwxr-xr-x    4 root root     1024 Jun 13 06:23 mnt
dr-xr-xr-x   73 root root        0 Jun 17 10:36 proc
drwxr-x---   18 root root     1024 Jun 19 12:12 root
drwxr-xr-x    3 root root     2048 Jun 13 07:00 sbin
drwxrwxrwt   14 root root     1024 Jun 19 12:22 tmp
drwxr-xr-x   20 root root     1024 Jun 13 06:41 usr
drwxr-xr-x   16 root root     1024 Jun 13 07:00 var
```

Disk Partitioning: Example of a Complex Approach

Assume that you wish to separate the file systems described below by assigning each one to its own partition. Figure 2.6 illustrates an example of a complex disk partitioning scheme. Assume also that you have the following reasons for using this configuration.

▲ To keep the / (root) partition inside the 1023 cylinder range (that is, to observe the "1024 cylinder rule," as there are 1024 cylinders although the numbering runs from 0 to 1023) and thus, facilitate system booting. The root partition only needs to be between 80 MB and 100 MB. It need only contain files necessary to boot the system as well as some configuration files. Do not keep applications and data here.

▲ To give */usr* its own logical file-system partition so that, if more applications are installed than you had originally expected, you will be able to easily back up and restore this file-system partition, and then increase its size without having to touch the / (root) file-system partition. This is where most of the application software should be kept, so be generous. Some system planners will also further separate */usr/local* to keep their own scripts and customized software separate from, say, Red Hat's Package Manager (RPM) software. Further, they may separate */usr/src* to isolate the Linux kernel sources and RPM software sources.

▲ To give */home* its own logical file-system partition to protect the / (root) file system from being accidentally filled to 100% capacity, which could halt the system.

▲ To use a separate, logical, swap partition for performance and maintenance reasons.

▲ To have separate partitions for */usr/local/* and */tmp* because they can fill up quickly and, in so doing, jeopardize the operating system partition.

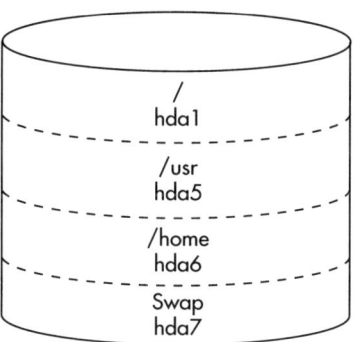

Figure 2.6. Complex example of disk partitioning.

Using the above configuration, the files and directories are divided and placed according to the following listing. Assuming this hard disk is IDE technology, the hard disk is generally called *hda*, and its partitions are called *hda1* for the root (/), *hda5* for /*usr*, *hda6* for /*home*, and *hda7* for the swap partition. The boot process shows *hda: <hda1 <hda5 hda6 hda7>>*, respectively. The following directories are in / (root).

```
drwxr-xr-x   2 root root  2048 Jun 13 06:56 bin
drwxr-xr-x   2 root root  1024 Jun 13 07:09 boot
drwxr-xr-x   5 root root  4816 Jun 17 16:36 dev
drwxr-xr-x  29 root root  3072 Jun 19 08:25 etc
drwxr-xr-x   4 root root  3072 Jun 13 06:48 lib
drwxr-xr-x   2 root root 12288 Jun 13 06:22 lost+found
drwxr-xr-x   4 root root  1024 Jun 13 06:23 mnt
dr-xr-xr-x  73 root root     0 Jun 17 10:36 proc
drwxr-x---  18 root root  1024 Jun 19 12:12 root
drwxr-xr-x   3 root root  2048 Jun 13 07:00 sbin
drwxrwxrwt  14 root root  1024 Jun 19 12:22 tmp
drwxr-xr-x  16 root root  1024 Jun 13 07:00 var
```

In the /*usr* partition, you will find a directory of the same name:

```
drwxr-xr-x  20 root root 1024 Jun 13 06:41 usr
```

In the /*home* partition, you will find a directory that also has the same name as the partition:

```
drwxr-xr-x   5 root root 1024 Jun 17 09:05 home
```

Exercise

Planning partitions is fundamental to planning for a Linux installation. This exercise may or may not be straightforward, depending on whether you have to propose and configure a simple or more complex system. You may wish to use your results from this exercise in one or the other of the installation exercises in Chapter 3, so keep them handy.

Plan the basics of a Linux installation, based on the parameters and specifications that you wish to use. Make sure that you include a logical picture of your suggested partitions. Try to anticipate, and then write down, their respective Linux logical labels, partition sizes, contents, and so forth, such as *hda* (or *sda*) and *hda1* through *hda7* (or *sda1* though *sda7*), and so on.

Quiz

1. What are the two key parts of the Linux kernel?
2. What are the similarities and differences between a swap partition and a swap file?
3. How much space should be created for swap space, and what are some of the considerations?
4. What are the three types of disk partitions available in Linux, and what are their numeric limits per drive?
5. What are the four tools available for disk partitioning and manipulation?
6. What is the primary consideration for disk partitioning on multi-boot (multiple OS) configurations, and in what order should the partitions be created?

7. What are the steps of the generic boot process?

8. What is LILO, and where can it be configured to reside?

9. Where should LILO be installed on single and multi-boot systems?

10. How do you access the boot sequence with LILO to boot to another operating system?

See Appendix B for answers.

Chapter 3

Installing Linux from a CD-ROM

IN THIS CHAPTER, WE DISCUSS THE NECESSITY for a boot disk and then walk through Linux installations on two different system architectures: SCSI (small computer system interface) and IDE (integrated drive electronics). First, you will need a copy of Linux. Linux can be obtained from several sources, including your local software vendor, the Internet (via download or mail order), or on the CD-ROM included with this book's companion, *In the Trenches: Installing and Administering Linux* (Gearhead Press, 2000).

If you have Red Hat Linux version 5.2 through 6.1, the menus will look similar to those shown here but may be presented in a slightly different order. The newer Red Hat 6.2 version has a different look and feel to the installation. Red Hat 6.2 offers a GUI installation option (which is new). However, we are going to bypass the GUI installation and run you through the text-menu installation for three reasons. First, a high video-failure rate has been reported for the GUI install method. Second, our objective is to present you with a more consistent view of the Red Hat installation procedure that has been in place since the earlier versions. And finally, the text-menu installation includes some menus that you would not normally see in the GUI install, and thus gives you a more technical view of the overall procedure.

By definition, "Linux is a UNIX-like operating system kernel that is freely distributable." Technically, Linux is not freeware nor in the public domain. The GNU Public License (GPL) covers Linux. This means that you cannot change the source code of the kernel and release it under a more restrictive license. Any changes or modifications made to Linux are covered by the GPL as well.

Creating a Linux Install Boot Disk

Technically, all Linux CDs are bootable. Whether your Linux CD will boot from your system depends on whether this option is available on your PC. If not, you will have to create the necessary boot and supplemental diskettes. You can create these diskettes either from a UNIX/Linux session or a DOS/Windows session. You should have at least two diskettes available to accomplish this task.

In versions previous to Red Hat 6.*x*, you might have required support for PCMCIA (Personal Computer Memory Card International Associates) and SMB (Session Message Block) installation, so you would have had to create additional diskettes for such support ahead of time. The Linux installation procedure would, at some point(s), prompt you to insert these diskettes. At such times, you would insert the diskettes or you would be forced to stop the installation; you wouldn't be given a chance to create the diskettes in the heat of the moment. With newer versions of Red Hat Linux, the installation procedure has been changed, so this is no longer an issue.

Meanwhile, toward the end of this installation, you will be prompted to insert a blank diskette which will be used to create a rescue diskette. We highly recommend that you do so. For now, though, let's return to our discussion of boot disks.

The method for creating a Linux install boot disk depends on the operating system you have to begin with, and whether you want to use that operating system to create the boot disk. We discuss two methods: (1) creation from within a DOS/Windows operating system (that is, when the system on which you will install Linux is already a DOS/Windows system); and (2) creation from within a UNIX system (that is, when your target system is already UNIX-based). Boot diskettes made using DOS/Windows or Linux behave the same; thus, choosing one or the other for the boot diskettes makes no difference.

Creating the Install Boot Disk from a DOS/Windows System

To create the boot disk from DOS/Windows, we will use a program called `rawrite`. In this example session, we insert the Red Hat Linux product CD into the CD drive and list the contents of the *images* directory. Your list may not be identical, but it should resemble the following. The file you are looking for is called *boot.img*.

```
E:\>cd images
E:\images>dir
 Volume in drive E is Red Hat Linux_i3
 Volume Serial Number is 0B2C-F104
 Directory of E:\images

03/08/00  05:51p       <DIR>          .
03/08/00  06:02p       <DIR>          ..
03/08/00  01:37p                  348 <translation table>
03/08/00  03:38p            1,474,560 boot.img
03/08/00  03:39p            1,474,560 bootnet.img
03/08/00  05:51p       <DIR>          de
03/08/00  05:51p       <DIR>          drivers
03/08/00  05:51p       <DIR>          es
03/08/00  05:51p       <DIR>          fr
03/08/00  05:51p       <DIR>          it
03/08/00  03:39p            1,474,560 pcmcia.img
             11 File<s>      4,424,028 bytes
                                     0 bytes free
```

Customizing and Upgrading Linux

The `rawrite` program is in the *dosutils* directory, and the image files are in the *images* directory. Run the `rawrite` program for each of the image files that you need from this directory—for example:

```
E:\>cd images

E:\images>\dosutils\rawrite
Enter disk image source file name: boot.img
Enter target diskette drive: a:
Please insert a formatted diskette into drive A: and
 press -ENTER- :
```

Then, boot the system with the diskette.

```
E:\images>dir a:
 Volume in drive A is LINUX BOOT
 Volume Serial Number is 2410-07EF

 Directory of A:\
```

Appearing below are the resulting contents of the new boot image diskette.

```
03/08/00  03:38p         5,860  LDLINUX.SYS
03/08/00  03:38p       587,970  VMLINUZ
03/08/00  03:38p           393  SYSLINUX.CFG
03/08/00  03:38p           749  BOOT.MSG
03/08/00  03:38p           653  EXPERT.MSG
03/08/00  03:38p           859  GENERAL.MSG
03/08/00  03:38p           860  PARAM.MSG
03/08/00  03:38p           506  RESCUE.MSG
03/08/00  03:38p           545  SNAKE.MSG
03/08/00  03:38p       854,091  INITRD.IMG
          10 File<s>  1,452,486 bytes
                          2,560 bytes free
```

Creating the Install Boot Disk from a UNIX System

In a UNIX-based environment, you can use the dd utility to create a set of boot and related image diskettes. First, mount the Red Hat CD and list the CD contents to locate the images directory.

```
# mount /dev/cdrom
# mount
/dev/hda1 on / type ext2 (rw)
none on /proc type proc (rw)
/dev/hda6 on /home type ext2 (rw)
/dev/hda5 on /usr type ext2 (rw)
none on /dev/pts type devpts (rw,gid=5,mode=620)
# cd /mnt/cdrom
# ls -l
total 67
-rw-r--r--    8 root     root        18385 Sep  7  1999 COPYING
-rw-r--r--    9 root     root         3400 Mar  8 08:42 README
-rw-r--r--   18 root     root        16300 Mar  8 12:10 RELEASE-NOTES
-rw-r--r--    8 root     root         1908 Sep 25  1999 RPM-GPG-KEY
drwxrwxr-x    5 root     root         2048 Mar  8 15:51 RedHat
-r--r--r--    1 root     root          544 Mar  9 11:07 TRANS.TBL
-rwxr-xr-x    9 root     root          538 Sep 25  1999 autorun
-rwxr--r--    1 root     root         2048 Mar  8 16:02 boot.cat
drwxrwxr-x    5 root     root         2048 Mar  9 10:40 doc
drwxrwxr-x    6 root     root         4096 Mar  8 15:51 dosutils
drwxrwxr-x    7 root     root         2048 Mar  8 15:51 images
drwxrwxr-x    4 root     root         2048 Mar  8 15:51 misc
dr-xr-xr-x   51 root     root         8192 Dec 31  1969 rr_moved
```

Once you've located the *images* directory, list its contents as follows:

```
# cd /mnt/cdrom/images
# ls -l
total 4343
```

```
-r--r--r--    1 root    root         348 Mar  9 11:37  TRANS.TBL
-rw-rw-r--    8 root    root     1474560 Mar  8 13:38  boot.img
-rw-rw-r--    8 root    root     1474560 Mar  8 13:39  bootnet.img
drwxrwxr-x    2 root    root        2048 Mar  8 15:51  de
drwxrwxr-x    2 root    root        2048 Mar  8 15:51  es
drwxrwxr-x    2 root    root        2048 Mar  8 15:51  fr
drwxrwxr-x    2 root    root        2048 Mar  8 15:51  it
-rw-rw-r--    8 root    root     1474560 Mar  8 13:39  pcmcia.img
```

Run the dd program for each of the image files that you need from the *images* directory. This procedure will yield a diskette from which you can boot the system and start the installation program.

```
# dd if=boot.img of=/dev/fd0
```

WARNING: *Red Hat has reported certain problems with boot images. Consider downloading the latest recommended boot images from* http://www.redhat.com/errata. *If you are determined to perform a GUI-assisted install, these more recent boot images may resolve the video problems experienced at the beginning of the installation. The bad boot images do get parsed and appear to work, but create problems later in the process when passing information to the* lilo.conf *files.*

Installing Linux on a SCSI System

In this section, we install Linux on a SCSI (rhymes with "fuzzy") system. SCSI was originally developed for Macintosh and UNIX equipment. Its data transfer rates are generally considered fast and reliable. However, it's a little more expensive and its installation and configuration are a bit more complicated than IDE hardware. The information we present in the preamble to this section is repeated at the beginning of the IDE installation section, so you can skip directly to "Installing Linux on an IDE System" if that's your goal.

For this installation, we use SCSI hard-disk and CD-ROM drives. The SCSI controller card is part of the Adaptec 152x family. The hard-disk partitioning is quite simple—three native Linux partitions and one swap partition. The system we are installing is connected to a network, and we have a serial mouse with two buttons.

Invoking the Linux Installation Program

The Linux installation program consists of a series of dialog boxes, sometimes called "screens" or "windows." These dialog boxes present information to you, and request information and decisions from you. The two most common methods used to invoke the installation program follow:

▲ Inserting the Linux CD-ROM into the CD drive and booting the system (provided, of course, that the system's CMOS is configured to allow booting from the CD-ROM drive).

▲ Inserting a Linux-bootable floppy disk into the floppy-disk drive and booting the system (provided that the system's CMOS is configured to allow booting from the floppy-disk drive).

The installations chronicled in this section and in the IDE installation section presume that you will use the first method (using the Linux CD-ROM). In fact, you will eventually see a dialog box that instructs you to insert the CD.

Inputting Information in the Installation Program

As you install Linux, you will notice several different ways of inputting information in the installation program. These methods are summarized below:

▲ *Text input.* You will encounter dialog boxes wherein you will be requested to type information, usually on a dashed line. This information insertion method is often used in conjunction with other methods (buttons, toggles, and so on).

▲ **Check boxes.** These are spaces defined by brackets or boxes, which you either select or deselect by pressing the <Space> bar.

▲ **Buttons.** These are generally square boxes that you access with the <Tab> key, and then select by pressing the <Enter> key.

▲ **Scroll and select.** Some dialog boxes contain lists of components, packages, or default services, from which you will have to choose by scrolling up or down and selecting. You will use combinations of <Tab> and <Space> keys, followed by pressing <Enter> at the end of the dialog boxes.

We present the above list here for two reasons. First, these are the insertion methods you have to use, and the above listing serves as a guide. Second, and more importantly, the list helps you focus on the input methods so that you can prevent mistakes. If you occasionally make a mistake, take heart—you won't be the first or the last to do so.

Insert your CD-ROM and boot the system. If all goes well you should see the operating system on the boot disk load into RAM. If this boot-disk image recognizes and interprets the geometry of your SCSI controller, you should see the Welcome to Linux 6.2! installation screen, and you can proceed to the next step. If not, read the next section for information on how to force Linux to recognize your SCSI controller and drives (providing, of course, that your SCSI hardware is supported by Linux).

Forcing Linux to Recognize Your SCSI Controller and Drives

You will have to specify the SCSI controller's IRQ (interrupt request) and base address. For systems that do not store drive geometry in the CMOS, you will have to specify drive geometry as well. Knowing the drive geometry is useful, because if the drive geometry is in CMOS and you are experiencing detection problems, then you should review your configuration for conflicts and test the individual components using utilities.

Appearing below are examples of the format that Linux is looking for, but your specific parameters must be determined by reading your documentation and perhaps using the utilities that shipped with the controller. The secret here is that all hex values must use the prefix 0x, as illustrated in the examples. Once the system is up and running, you can make these entries available to the system so that you do not have to supply them at boot time.

- ▲ *aha152x=port,irq,scsi_id,1*
  Specify port, IRQ, and SCSI ID for BIOS-less AIC-6260 controllers. Included are Adaptec 1510 and 152x, and Soundblaster-SCSI controllers.

  ```
  Boot:linux aha152x=0x340,11,7,1
  ```

- ▲ *tmc8xx=memaddr,irq*
  Specify address and IRQ for BIOS-less Future Domain TMC-8xx SCSI controller.

  ```
  Boot: linux tmc8xx=0xca000,5
  ```

- ▲ *hd*=cylinders,heads,sectors*
  Specify the drive geometry. This is required for systems such as the IBM PS/1, ValuePoint, and ThinkPad. An example here is drive c: with 683 cylinders, 16 heads, and 32 sectors per track.

  ```
  Boot:linux hdc=683,16,32
  ```

Documented issues about the use of ICP Vortex controllers with certain SCSI devices are available on the Red Hat Web site *(www.redhat.com)*. Documented solutions are available, although they are not for the uninitiated.

If you have trouble locating information on your equipment, check the hardware compatibility listings on the Red Hat site before wasting too much time *(http://www.redhat.com/hardware)*. Next, ensure that your configurations for SCSI controller IDs, SCSI device IDs, and terminations of all devices in the SCSI chain are correct. Most problems revolve around these issues. Be careful not to mix SCSI types such as fast and wide drives on old SCSI controllers. These types of combinations will stop any operating system cold, including Linux.

Stepping through the Installation

Installing Linux on a SCSI system is a 26-step process that begins with the Welcome screen.

Step 1. Welcome!

If you were to walk away from the first screen without making a selection, the installation program would proceed to boot the system on its own and default to the GUI Install mode. If the system were to detect a problem, however, it would change to Text Install mode. As mentioned previously, problems with GUI installations have been reported. Consequently, we demonstrate the following installations using the fail-safe, text-menu method.

```
                   Welcome to Red Hat Linux 6.2!

  • To install or upgrade a system running Red Hat Linux 2.0 or later,
      press the <ENTER> key.

  • To install or upgrade a system running Red Hat Linux 2.0 or later
      in text mode, type: text <ENTER>.

  • To enable expert mode, type: expert <ENTER>. Press <F3> for
      more information about expert mode.

  • To enable rescue mode, type: linux rescue <ENTER>. Press <F5>
      for information on rescue mode.

  • If you have a driver disk, type: linux dd  <ENTER>.

  • Use the function keys listed below for more information.

      [F1-Main] [F2-General] [F3-Expert] [F4-Kernel] [F5-Rescue]
```

CHAPTER 3: INSTALLING LINUX FROM A CD-ROM

We'll elaborate here on the main bullet points in the preceding dialog box.

▲ **Bullet 1**. *Install or upgrade a system running Red Hat Linux 2.0 or later.* This choice will access a GUI install panel. However, be aware that this choice has a high video-failure or misconfiguration rate, as it does not interpret all video cards and monitors correctly. If you choose this option and it fails, we recommend that you immediately reboot and use the text-installation option. If you do manage to install Linux with the use of the GUI install panel, you may experience problems with the GUI log-in panel. A Red Hat "Alert" is reproduced here.

```
           Red Hat Alert: Graphical Login doesn't work during installation
Problem:

During the installation process, if you selected graphical login and
either the "customize" button or "test this configuration" button,
Red Hat Linux will start in text console mode rather than the
graphical environment, in many cases.

Fix:

If you haven't already installed, use the latest boot images from
http://www.redhat.com/support/errata/RHEA1999045-01.html.

If you are not dropped into text mode automatically, just type text
at the boot: prompt on the next try.

If you've already installed, reboot, and at the boot: prompt, type
linux single. Then edit your /etc/inittab and change this line:
          id:3:initdefault:
to
          id:5:initdefault:

Save your changes and type: shutdown -r now. On reboot, your system
will be in the graphical environment.
```

▲ **Bullet 2**. *Install or upgrade a system running Red Hat 2.0 or later in text mode* is necessary if using the GUI install panel is not successful. For practical reasons and in order to facilitate the installation for the majority of users, we have chosen to use text mode.

▲ **Bullet 3.** *Enable expert mode* is not for the faint of heart but is sometimes necessary—for example, in the event that `Autoprobe` does not appear to find your cards with correct settings. Choosing expert mode means that you must be prepared to supply all necessary information for all settings, such as the IRQ, I/O, and DMA (direct memory access) settings.

▲ **Bullet 4.** *Enable rescue mode* is a recent feature added to the installation start-up that allows you to boot your system if LILO or the boot sectors get trashed. There is also a procedure here that allows you to create a rescue disk after the fact if circumstances dictate that this should be done. However, you do not have to use this install menu to create a rescue disk. If your system boots normally into Red Hat 6.2, for example, you can create a post-installation rescue disk at any time by going back to the */lib/modules* directory and using the following command:

```
mkbootdisk --device /dev/fd0 kernel_number
```

where `kernel_number` is of a format similar to 2.2.*x-yy*. When you choose which kernel you want to install, you will insert the appropriate numbers for the *x* and the *yy*.

However, for versions of Red Hat Linux previous to 6.2, you can create post-installation rescue disks by going to the */images* directory on the installation CD-ROM and using this command instead:

```
dd if=rescue.img of=/dev/fd0 bs=1440 count=1
```

The next screen presumes that you have chosen Bullet 2, the text mode of installation.

Step 2. Select Language

This screen asks you what language you wish to use to perform the installation, and as a first-time system default. Linux is a multilingual operating system; you can install support for other languages at a later date and then change the default.

```
                    Choose a Language

 What language should be used during the installation process?
                    Czech            ↑
                    English          ¬
                    French           ¬
                    German           ¬
                    Hungarian        ¬
                    Icelandic        ¬
                    Italian          ¬
                    Norwegian        ¬
                    Romanian         ↓

                         OK
```

Step 3. Specify Keyboard

You cannot afford to get creative here. This is a technical question about keyboard drivers. If you answer this question incorrectly, then issues may arise when you try to enable and remap the keys. Not all keyboards are created equal. You can, however, choose the closest one here and adjust it later when the system is up and running.

```
                      Keyboard Type

          What type of keyboard do you have?
                    slovene          ↑
                    tr_f-latin5      ¬
                    tr_q-latin5      ¬
                    tralt            ¬
                    trf              ¬
                    trq              ¬
                    uk               ¬
                    us               ↓

                         OK
```

In the GUI-assisted installation, it is possible to choose a specific "layout" and either disable or enable "dead keys." A dead key is a key that, when pressed, does not produce a result (an alphanumeric character or symbol) until another key is pressed. We recommend that you choose to adjust the layout and dead keys later. The default layout is `U.S. English w/ISO9995-3`, and the dead-keys default is `Enable dead keys`. Enable dead keys is required for key composing or what is known as "keyboard character mapping." For a technical discussion of issues related to dead keys in Linux, refer to *http://www.tux.org/~balsa/linux/deadkeys/*.

Step 4. Welcome

Press OK at the next screen.

```
              Welcome to Red Hat Linux!

   This installation process is outlined in detail in the Official
   Red Hat Linux Installation Guide available from Red Hat Software.
   If you have access to this manual, you should read the
   installation section before continuing.

   If you have purchased Official Red Hat Linux, be sure to
   register your purchase through our web site,
   http://www.redhat.com.

                  OK                    Back
```

Step 5. Specify Installation Type

One of the most popular features of contemporary Linux systems is the new desktops, GNOME and KDE. The one you choose should ultimately depend on what you want to do. If you are experimenting, try to install one and then the other. It is not the case that if you choose GNOME you cannot run KDE applications. Consider your choice between the two as making one dominant over the other. Of course,

CHAPTER 3: INSTALLING LINUX FROM A CD-ROM

the industry is somewhat political, and the KDE development group has different mandates than the GNOME development group.

If you just need TCP/IP (Transmission Control Protocol/Internet Protocol) connectivity with all the necessary `ftp`, `telnet`, and `rlogin` options, choosing `Install Server System` may save you some work; you could then add a desktop later.

Choose `Install Custom System` here, because we are going to define the environment.

```
                        Installation Type

            What type of system would you like to install?

                    Install GNOME Workstation
                    Install KDE Workstation
                    Install Server System
                    Install Custom System
                    Upgrade Existing Installation

                         OK            Back
```

In response to the next screen, insert the Linux CD-ROM and select OK.

```
                              NOTE

            Insert your Red Hat CD into your CD drive now.

                         OK        Back
```

Step 6. Configure for a SCSI System

The object of this process is to install Linux on a SCSI system. So choose Yes.

```
                    SCSI Configuration

            Do you have any SCSI adapters?

              No           Yes          Back
```

Assume that you have a driver from the Adaptec 152x family and select that option.

```
                       Load Module

                 Which drive should I try?

                 Adaptec 152x    #
                 Adaptec 1542
                 Adaptec 1740
                 Adaptec 2740, 2840, 2940
                 AdvanSys Adapters
                 Always IN2000
                 . . . more

                 OK                     Back
```

At first we tried the Autoprobe option shown in the next screen, but it failed. Specify options worked, though. It is very important that you use the hexadecimal representations where appropriate. When we tried to define the I/O port parameter as 340, and then as 340h, neither worked. We did not get a response until we used the correct hexadecimal representation of 0x340.

The only reference we found that provided the necessary information on SCSI devices was *http://metalab.unc.edu/LDP/HOWTO*

/BootPrompt-HOWTO.html. Remember the string and format suggestions we gave you in the "Forcing Linux to Recognize Your SCSI Controller and Devices" section earlier in this chapter, and apply them when you are following the HOW-TOs.

```
                         Module Options

      In some cases, the aha152x driver needs to have extra
      information to work properly, although it normally works
      fine without. Would you like to specify extra options for
      it or allow the driver to probe your machine for the
      information it needs? Occasionally, probing will hang a
      computer, but should not cause any damage.

                            Autoprobe
                          Specify options

            OK                                     Back
```

An example of the exact syntax used follows.

```
                         Module Parameters

             Module options: aha152x=0x340,11,7,1

             OK                                    Back
```

In response to the query in the next screen, we select No.

```
                         SCSI Configuration
          I have found the following types of SCSI adapters on your
          system:

                            Adaptec 152x

          Do you have any more SCSI adapters on your system?

                 No              Yes              Back
```

In the next screen, we select `SCSI` because the entire system is SCSI.

```
                        CDROM type
            What type of CDROM do you have?
                           SCSI
                        Other CDROM

            OK                              Back
```

Step 7. Partition Disk using Disk Druid

We are going to choose `Disk Druid` instead of `fdisk` for partitioning. Be aware that both `Disk Druid` and `fdisk` are destructive to existing partitions.

```
                           Disk Setup

   Disk Druid is a tool for partitioning and setting up mount points.
   It is designed to be easier to use than Linux's traditional disk
   partitioning software, fdisk, as well as more powerful. However,
   there are some cases where fdisk may be preferred.

               Which tool would you like to use?

         Disk Druid            fdisk              Back
```

Step 8. View Hard-Disk Attributes

The next screen indicates that we have an 8.2 GB SCSI hard disk called drive *sda*, which is the correct designation for the first SCSI hard disk in the machine. You will now proceed to create the filesystem partitions. Select `Add`.

```
                    Current Disk Partitions

   Mount Point      Device          Requested    Actual  Type


   Drive Summaries
   Drive Geom [C/H/S]               Total        Used    Free
   sda  [ 1046/255/63]              8205M        0M      8205M  [          ]


            Add            Edit           Delete       OK        Back
```

Step 9. Add or Edit Partitions

The Edit New Partition dialog box, shown next, will appear whenever you select Add or Edit in the Current Disk Partitions dialog box. In this example, you will be creating a couple of primary partitions: a Linux Native partition containing several logical partitions (namely, the root partition, the /*usr* partition, and the /*home* partition); and a Linux swap partition. So you will see the Edit New Partition dialog box for each of those partitions. After each partition is created, clicking on the OK button in Edit New Partition will update the Current Disk Partitions and return you to that box. To continue creating partitions, you have to click Add again.

When creating the root, /*usr* and /*home* partitions, in turn, you'll have to enter their mount points (/, /*usr*, and /*home*, respectively), enter the desired size of the partition, and set the type to Linux Native. When creating the swap partition, do not enter a mount point (that is, leave that entry blank), enter the desired size, and set the type to Linux Swap.

Customizing and Upgrading Linux

```
                       Edit New Partition

         Mount Point: /_ _ _ _ _ _ _ _ _ _ _ _ _ _ _ _ _

         Size (Megs): 800            Type: Linux Swap
                                           Linux Native
         Grow to fill disk? [   ]          DOS 16 bit <32M
                                           DOS 16 bit >=32M
         Allowable Drive: [   ] sda

                    OK                     Cancel
```

If you are editing existing partitions, then the above dialog box will be slightly different. For example, the Type will already be specified. There will be an Allocation Status field, which will read Successful or Unsuccessful, rather than the Allowable Drive specification. Again, clicking on OK will return you to the (updated) Current Disk Partition screen.

Step 10. Create New Hard-Disk Partitions

The next screen shows the configuration we recommend for this installation. If you are configuring your hard disk according to the exercise in Chapter 2, then consult your planning sheet, and create, add, and edit the partitions until they match what you need.

Note that every time you add, delete, or edit partitions, you will be returned to this dialog box. And every time it will show you how you are progressing, with new or different partitions or other specifications. Remember that none of the changes will take effect until you select OK at the very end of the partitioning process.

Once you have the configuration you want, select OK to save these changes to your configuration tables.

```
              Current Disk Partitions

Mount Point    Device      Requested   Actual    Type

/              sda1         800M       3631M     Linux native
/usr           sda5         700M       3200M     Linux native
/home          sda6         268M       1239M     Linux native
               sda7         128M        133M     Linux swap

Drive Summaries
Drive Geom [C/H/S]         Total       Used      Free
sda  [ 3067/ 64/32]        8205M       8204M     1M  [              ]

         Add         Edit         Delete         OK        Back
```

Step 11. Format New System Partitions

For this installation you are going to format all of the partitions to ensure that they are clean. The partition tables were replaced by `Disk Druid`; the installation program actually removes and replaces the existing data blocks. You should select the `Check for bad blocks during format` option. In fact, if you are installing Linux on a production system, we highly recommend that you select this option, even though the process may take a while on some large or (heaven forbid) damaged disks.

It should go without saying that all newly created partitions should be formatted. If you have preserved partitions from a previous configuration and you do not mind removing data in them, then they too should be formatted again. On the other hand, don't format existing partitions containing files or data that you want to preserve. Remember that preserving partitions applies most if you are upgrading Linux.

```
                    Partitions to Format

   What partitions would you like to format? We strongly suggest
   formatting all of the system partitions, including /, /usr, and
   /var. There is no need to format /home or /usr/local if they have
   already been configured during a previous install.

                  [ * ] /dev/sda1  /
                  [ * ] /dev/sda6  /home
                  [ * ] /dev/sda5  /usr

                  [ * ] Check for bad blocks during format

                    OK                      Back
```

Step 12. LILO Configuration

The following LILO Configuration screen asks about using linear mode (required by some SCSI hard drives). When we installed Linux without this option, the system failed to boot. Once this option was added, the system booted correctly. There is very little information available on linear mode other than it is required for some drive types. It would be appreciated if Red Hat would provide information regarding this requirement, to facilitate installation in systems that use SCSI technology solely, or that use SCSI in combination with IDE technology. We found only one fairly plausible explanation for linear mode on the Web: it was described as a code support mechanism, or last chance, to pass to the system any information it still needed in order to boot. In other words, when BIOS finishes its POST and tries to read sector 0 of the first cylinder, it may need additional information to boot. You can plug in additional parameters by choosing linear mode.

We are from the school of thought that wants to know when options are being passed to the kernel and when they are not. Therefore, we tested linear mode, required it, and implemented it. Otherwise, we would not have used it. If you have sufficient information on the drives you are using, then you can probably predict this behavior.

```
                    LILO Configuration

    A few systems will need to pass special options to the kernel at
    boot time for the system to function properly. If you need to
    pass boot options to the kernel, enter them now. If you don't need
    any or aren't sure, leave this blank.

    [ * ]   Use linear mode (needed for some SCSI drives)


                    OK      Skip      Back
```

We plan to use LILO to manage the disk. Therefore, at the next screen choose the Master Boot Record option.

```
                    Lilo Installation

        Where do you want to install the bootloader?

        /dev/sda        Master Boot Record
        /dev/sda1       First sector of boot partition

                    OK              Back
```

```
                    LILO Configuration
    The boot manager Red Hat uses can boot other operating systems as
    well. You need to tell me what partitions you would like to be
    able to boot and what label you want to use for each of them.

    Device          Partition       Default         Boot label
    /dev/sda1       Linux Native    *               linux

                    Okay    Edit    Back
```

For this installation, we are only installing Linux. Thus, we will select OK for the default */dev/sda1* partition which has been highlighted for us by the installation process. If there were already another operating system installed on another partition, then we would have more than one selection here. Eventually, when the system booted up, we would have to choose which operating system to boot. We highly recommend, if you are installing Linux on a production system, that no other operating systems be installed. In other working environments, however, such as at home, you might appreciate having more than one operating system.

Step 13. Host Name and Basic TCP/IP Configurations

In the next screen, you will be prompted for a host name for your computer. Input the host name that you select. You can change it later if necessary.

```
                    Hostname Configuration
    The hostname is the name of your computer. If your computer is
    attached to a network, this may be assigned by your network
    administrator.

                        Hostname: HostB

              OK                              Back
```

Next, you will be prompted for TCP/IP networking addresses. It may be necessary to consult with your Internet service provider (ISP) or system administrator, as necessary, for information to fill in the next dialog box. We'll enter and explain some examples in the next paragraph.

For this installation, let's say our lab consists of a simple network and that our system requires only a static IP address to communicate. So we enter 192.168.6.34 as our IP address. The installation program will automatically put in the Class C Netmask 255.255.255.0, which is correct and acceptable for us. The default gateway IP address is the first interface card on the proxy server that connects us to the outside world via a cable or other service. In this case, our lab doesn't have one, so the default 192.168.6.254 supplied by the installation program is also acceptable. The primary nameserver entry here is also not relevant to our lab. Normally, it might be ignored anyway because a proxy server would handle all Internet name resolution requests, so it could, in that case, be left null. For us here, though, the 192.168.6.1 supplied by the installation program is also acceptable

```
                    Network Configuration
         [ ] Use bootp/dhcp
         IP address:                192.168.6.34
         Netmask:                   255.255.255.0
         Default gateway (IP):      192.168.6.254
         Primary nameserver:        192.168.6.1

                         OK         Back
```

Step 14. Configure the Mouse

The program immediately asks you to configure the mouse if it finds one. If you have a three-button mouse, you will be better equipped to take advantage of the X Window System. If your mouse only has two buttons, then you should select Emulate 3 Buttons in the following dialog box. Once you are configured for it, to emulate the third button (that is, the middle button on a three-button mouse), press both the left and right buttons at the same time. If you ever wish to change the mouse configuration, you can use the */usr/sbin/mouseconfig* command, linuxconf, or */usr/sbin/setup*. This last command displays a menu of choices of which mouseconfig is one.

Customizing and Upgrading Linux

```
                          Mouse Selection
           Which model of mouse is attached to this computer?

                     ALPS - GlidePoint (PS/2)
                     ASCII - MieMouse (PS/2)
                     ASCII - MieMouse (serial)
                     ATI - Bus Mouse
                     Generic - 2 Button Mouse (PS/2)
                     Generic - 2 Button Mouse (serial)
                     Generic - 3 Button Mouse (PS/2)
                     Generic - 3 Button Mouse (PS/2)
                     [*] Emulate 3 Buttons?

                           OK       Back
```

Step 15. Configure the Time Zone

During the development of this installation exercise, we chose Canada/Mountain time zone. Choose whichever is appropriate to your present location. If you ever wish to change the time configuration, use the */usr/sbin/timeconfig* command.

```
                         Configure Timezones
                 Format machine time is stored in:

                    [   ] Hardware clock set to GMT

                         Africa/Abidjan
                              .
                              .
                         Canada/Mountain  #
                              .
                              .
                         Zulu

                           OK       Back
```

Chapter 3: Installing Linux from a CD-ROM

Step 16. Set Root Password

Remember to choose a good password and then make sure you remember it. Linux has rules and guidelines for proper passwords. It would pay to review them in the man pages and Red Hat online documentation.

```
                        Root Password

    Pick a root password.  You must type it twice to ensure you
    know what it is and didn't make a mistake in typing. Remember
    that the root password is a critical part of system security!

        Password:
        Password (again):

                OK                              Back
```

The installation process allows you to add other users at this time. You need not add all users now, though, because you can revisit this task at any time after completing the installation. The reason the Add User dialog appears here is to allow you to log in to the system for the first time as a user and switch to a root user to perform the first set of system administration tasks, which is considered proper form.

```
                        Add User

        Enter the information for the user.

        User ID:        dbadmin
        Full name:      Database Administrator
        Password:
        Password (confirm):

                     OK        Cancel
```

53

Step 17. Configure Authentication

Accept the following defaults to use shadow passwords and allow the use of MD5 encryption.

```
                     Authentication Configuration

           [ * ] Use Shadow Passwords
           [ * ] Enable MD5 Passwords
           [   ] Enable NIS

           NIS Domain:    _____
           NIS Server:    [ ] Request via Broadcast
           or use:        _____


                   OK                         Back
```

Step 18. Choose Components to Install

Components are groups of software packages that provide a service or feature to the system. The components list in our next screen does not display all the possible selections; rather, only the ones we suggest installing for this exercise. You may note that the dialog box on your screen is a little smaller than the one shown next; by following the arrows, you will eventually reveal all the components.

To see the packages that comprise the components, choose `Select individual packages`. Before you do so, be prepared: this will slow down the installation process. You also run the risk of mistakenly installing parts of components or packages that will not work because other packages they depend on have not been installed. Nevertheless, if you have the time, go ahead and browse through the list during the installation.

CHAPTER 3: INSTALLING LINUX FROM A CD-ROM

```
                Package Group Selection

       [ * ]  Printer Support              ↑
       [ * ]  X Window System              ¬
       [ * ]  GNOME                        ¬
       [ * ]  KDE                          ¬
       [ * ]  DOS/Windows Connectivity     ¬
       [ * ]  Networked Workstation        ¬
       [ * ]  NFS Server                   ¬
       [ * ]  Anonymous FTP Server         ¬
       [ * ]  Kernel Development           ¬
       [ * ]  Utilities                    ↓

       [   ]      Select individual packages

             OK                       Back
```

If you are performance-minded, you may want to be somewhat selective at this stage. If performance is not a primary consideration, you may want to choose all components and, thus, all of the packages. As you scroll down through this dialog box, you will eventually see the Everything choice at the bottom of the component list.

WARNING: *The installation program will tell you if you have inadequate disk space. In the meantime, do not forget your planning and do not make disk space too tight in the root (/) and /usr file-system partitions. Finally, be sure to avoid removing mandatory packages, such as the kernel and certain libraries and their respective support packages.*

Try to resolve all package dependencies before continuing. (As mentioned earlier, one package or component may not work unless its companion package or packages are also installed.) However, if any dependencies are inadvertently missed, the installation program will warn you of that as well. You can still add them at any time after installation.

Step 19. Find Video Adapter

The installation program has conducted a probe using the `PCI Probe` and found the video adapter. Select `OK`.

```
                     X probe results

              Video Card: Generic Mach64
              X Server   : Mach64

                  OK              Back
```

Once you have selected `OK`, you will briefly see an Install Status box while the installation program loads the appropriate video-adapter server.

Step 20. Create Install Log

Select `OK` on the next screen. Note that the *install.log* file can come in very handy, helping to bail you out of unforeseen trouble.

```
                    Installation to begin
     A complete log of your installation will be in /tmp/install.log
     after rebooting your system. You may want to keep this log for
     future reference.

              OK                              Back
```

Step 21. Search for Overlapping Files

Next, the installation program looks for any overlapping files—that is, files that would be duplicated during the new installation process. The pertinent screen appears only in cases where you are trying to preserve at least some part of your previous system. You can ignore these messages if they do appear unless you are checking to see if a specific file is being installed. You cannot remedy overlapping files at this time, however. Should you wish to do so, you can rectify overlapping files later by uninstalling and reinstalling specific RPM packages.

Step 22. Install Status

Throughout the installation process, you will see an installation status box called Package Installation, which will show you the progress of the installation of individual packages and programs (top half), as well as the overall progress of the total Linux installation (bottom half). Note in the top half that as the individual packages are installed, the installation program will provide the package name, the size of the package, and a brief description of the package.

On the bottom, the installation program keeps track of the space used by the installed packages, as well as the remaining space required. Moreover, it tracks the total, elapsed, and remaining installation time. This might be a good time for you to take a break while the installation proceeds.

```
                  Package Installation
       Name    : nameofpackage
       Size    : 1234k
       Summary : Description of package being installed
       vvvvvvvvvvvvvvvvvvvvvvvvvvvvvvvvvvvvvvvvvvv
                 Packages    Bytes      Time
       Total     :    370    587M       0:08:35
       Completed :    220    427M       0:06:18
       Remaining :    150    160M       0:02:17

       vvvvvvvvvvvvvvvvvvvvvvvvvvvvvvvvvvvvvvvvvvv
```

Step 23. Create Boot Disk

Creating a boot disk is a good idea. Select `Yes`. However, you can always do this after you have installed Linux by using the `mkbootdisk` command.

```
┌─────────────────────────────────────────────────────────────────┐
│                          Bootdisk                               │
│                                                                 │
│   A custom bootdisk provides a way of booting into your Linux   │
│   system without depending on the normal bootloader. This is useful │
│   if you don't want to install lilo on your system, another     │
│   operating system removes lilo, or lilo doesn't work with your │
│   hardware configuration. A custom bootdisk can also be used with │
│   the Red Hat rescue image, making it much easier to recover from │
│   severe system failures.                                       │
│                                                                 │
│   Would you like to create a bootdisk for your system?          │
│                                                                 │
│            Yes               No              Back               │
└─────────────────────────────────────────────────────────────────┘
```

In response to the next screen, insert a blank floppy disk and then press OK.

```
┌─────────────────────────────────────────────────────────────────┐
│                          Bootdisk                               │
│                                                                 │
│   Insert a blank floppy in the first drive. All data on this disk │
│   will be erased during creation of the bootdisk.               │
│                                                                 │
│                         OK     Skip                             │
└─────────────────────────────────────────────────────────────────┘
```

Upon pressing OK, the installation program will respond with the following screen.

```
┌─────────────────────────────────────────────────────────────────┐
│                          Bootdisk                               │
│                                                                 │
│                      Creating bootdisk ...                      │
│                                                                 │
└─────────────────────────────────────────────────────────────────┘
```

Step 24. Set Up Monitor

Although scores of monitor names appear in this box, our monitor was not listed. Consequently, we selected Custom here. By choosing Custom, you have to fill in more information.

```
                         Monitor Setup

What type of monitor do you have? If you would rather specify
the sync frequencies of your monitor, choose "Custom" from the list.

                    Custom                    ↑
                    ADI DMC-2304              ¬
                        .                     ¬
                        .                     ¬
                        .                     ¬
                    ViewSonic VPA 150         ↓

              OK                         Back
```

Click OK in the next screen.

```
                      Custom Monitor Setup

Now we want to set the specifications of the monitor. The two
critical parameters are the vertical refresh rate, which is the
rate at which the whole screen is refreshed, and most importantly
the horizontal sync rate, which is the rate at which scan lines
are displayed.

The valid range for horizontal sync and vertical sync should be
documented in the manual of your monitor. If in doubt, check the
monitor database /usr/X11R6/lib/X11/doc/Monitors to see if your
monitor is there.

              OK                         Back
```

Our monitor is capable of up to 60 Hz, so we selected the generic Super VGA @ 56 Hz to be safe in the next screen. Monitor specifications can also be adjusted later using the Xconfigurator program.

Customizing and Upgrading Linux

```
┌──────────────────────────────────────────────────────────────────┐
│                  Custom Monitor Setup (Continued)                │
│                                                                  │
│   You must indicate the horizontal sync range of your monitor. You │
│   can either select one of the predefined ranges below that      │
│   corresponds to industry-standard monitor types, or give a      │
│   specific range. It is VERY IMPORTANT that you do not specify a │
│   monitor type with a horizontal sync range that is beyond the   │
│   capabilities of your monitor.                                  │
│                                                                  │
│           Standard VGA, 640 x 480 @ 60 Hz                        │
│           Super VGA, 800 x 600 @ 56 Hz                           │
│                       .                                          │
│                       .                                          │
│                       .                                          │
│           Monitor that can do 1600 x 1200 @ 76 Hz                │
│                                                                  │
│           OK                                           Back      │
│                                                                  │
└──────────────────────────────────────────────────────────────────┘
```

In the next screen, we chose 50–90 Hz (vertical sync range) because our monitor operates in this range.

```
┌──────────────────────────────────────────────────────────────────┐
│                  Custom Monitor Setup (Continued)                │
│                                                                  │
│   You must indicate the vertical sync range of your monitor. You │
│   can either select one of the predefined ranges below that      │
│   corresponds to industry-standard monitor types, or give a      │
│   specific range. For interlaced modes the number that counts is │
│   the high one (e.g., 87 Hz rather than 43 Hz).                  │
│                                                                  │
│                       50 -  70                                   │
│                       50 -  90                                   │
│                       50 - 100                                   │
│                       40 - 150                                   │
│                                                                  │
│           OK                                           Back      │
│                                                                  │
└──────────────────────────────────────────────────────────────────┘
```

The installation program now invokes the `Xconfigurator` program. Press OK.

```
                        Probing to begin


    Xconfigurator will now run the X server you selected to probe
    various information about your video card. It is normal for the
    screen to blink several times.
                              OK
```

Step 25. Start X

In the next screen, select `Skip`. If something went wrong now, it would be an inconvenience. In any event, we discuss video configuration in great detail in Chapter 5.

```
                           Starting X

       Xconfigurator will now start X to test your configuration.
                   OK                      Skip
```

The X installation procedure will also ask you about the mouse it found. Again, if you have a three-button mouse, you will be better equipped to take advantage of the X Window System. However, if your mouse only has two buttons, then you should select `Emulate 3 Buttons`. Meanwhile, if you ever wish to change the mouse configuration, you can use the */usr/sbin/mouseconfig* command or `linuxconf`.

```
                        Mouse Selection
        Which model of mouse is attached to this computer?

                ALPS  - GlidePoint (PS/2)
                ASCII - MieMouse (PS/2)
                ASCII - MieMouse (serial)
                ATI   - Bus Mouse
                Generic - 2 Button Mouse (PS/2)
                Generic - 2 Button Mouse (serial)
                Generic - 3 Button Mouse (PS/2)
                Generic - 3 Button Mouse (PS/2)
                [*] Emulate 3 Buttons?

                        OK         Back
```

The next screen is fairly straightforward. Select Yes.

```
                    Update X Configuration

    Mouseconfig can now update your Xfree86 configuration file to
    reflect your new mouse settings. Would you like mouseconfig to
    make these changes now?

              Yes                              No
```

Step 26. Installation Complete

Select OK at this screen.

```
                            Complete

    Congratulations, installation is complete.

    Remove the boot media and press return to reboot. For information
    on fixes which are available for this release of Red Hat Linux,
    consult the Errata available from http://www.redhat.com.

    Information on configuring your system is available in the
    post install chapter of the Official Red Hat Linux manuals.

                              OK
```

Installing Linux on an IDE System

In this section, Linux is installed on a system with integrated drive electronics (IDE) architecture. IDE was originally based on IBM PC Industry Standard Architecture (ISA). It's generally less expensive than SCSI, and it's simpler to configure. We alter the hard-disk configuration a bit for you to gain more experience and practice.

Much of the information we present here repeats the information in the previous SCSI installation. The differences are in the IDE-specific information. We repeat the information here for completeness, and in case this is the only installation exercise you do, or you are doing it at a time considerably later than the first exercise.

For this installation, we use IDE hard-disk and CD-ROM drives. The system to be installed is connected to a network, and we have a PS/2 mouse with two buttons.

Invoking the Linux Installation Program

The Linux installation program consists of a series of dialog boxes, sometimes called "screens" or "windows." These dialog boxes present information to you, and request information and decisions from you. The two most common methods used to invoke the installation program are as follows:

▲ Inserting the Linux CD-ROM into the CD drive and booting the system (provided, of course, that the system's CMOS is configured to allow booting from the CD-ROM drive).

▲ Inserting a Linux-bootable floppy disk into the floppy-disk drive and booting the system (provided that the system's CMOS is configured to allow booting from the floppy-disk drive).

The installations chronicled in this section and in the previous SCSI installation exercise presume that you will use the first method. In fact, you will eventually see a dialog box that instructs you to insert the CD-ROM.

Inputting Information in the Installation Program

As you install Linux, you will notice several different ways of inputting information in the installation program. These methods are summarized as follows:

- ▲ **Text input.** You will encounter dialog boxes wherein you will be requested to type information, usually on a dashed line. This information insertion method is often used in conjunction with other methods (buttons, toggles, and so on).

- ▲ **Check boxes.** These are spaces defined by brackets or boxes, which you either select or deselect by pressing the <Space> bar.

- ▲ **Buttons.** These are generally square boxes that you access with the <Tab> key, and then select by pressing the <Enter> key.

- ▲ **Scroll and select.** Some dialog boxes contain lists of components, packages, or default services, from which you will have to choose by scrolling up or down and selecting. You will use combinations of <Tab> and <Space> keys, followed by pressing <Enter> at the end of the dialog boxes.

We present this list here for two reasons. First, these are the insertion methods you have to use, and the above listing serves as a guide. Second, and more importantly, the list helps you focus on the input methods so that you can prevent mistakes. If you occasionally make a mistake, take heart—you won't be the first or the last to do so.

Insert your CD-ROM and boot the system. If you have trouble booting, read the following paragraphs. If you do not experience trouble booting the system, proceed to Step 1.

Sometimes Linux has trouble seeing IDE CD-ROMs. If this occurs, you should try to determine why Linux cannot see the IDE device. It is possible that the BIOS cannot see or read an IDE channel because the BIOS is limited, a legitimate problem. Or it may be a misconfigured master/slave jumper issue, which is not legitimate. If the latter is the case, then you should address this problem first.

The syntax for dealing with a CD-ROM that will not load automatically appears below. Type the following command sequence at the boot or LILO prompt:

```
linux hdx=cdrom
```

where *x* is the IDE letter that Linux specifies for the drive, depending on which IDE bus the drive is on. This scenario may also cause you some problems during boot time. Make a note of it, and if the system also fails to boot after the installation, then revisit the linear-drive option. Enable the linear-drive option to see if that will correct the problem. If the problem persists, you may want to check your equipment with Red Hat's compatibility charts as suggested in Chapter 1.

IDE Drive Geometry

The naming conventions for the IDE drives and devices shown in Table 3-1 indicate respective behaviors, which in turn are reflections of how they are installed in the target system. New IDE device-configuration rules allow up to four channels in a single system, each with two devices attached. The devices do not have to be configured consecutively, but this practice is helpful in understanding how the system works. Problems may occur with older or existing systems in which older IDE devices are attached to newer IDE controllers, and vice versa. Remember to test and document what you have done to avoid installation headaches.

Table 3-1: IDE Drive Geometry

Channel	Jumper	hdx
ide0	master	hda
ide0	slave	hdb
ide1	master	hdc
ide1	slave	hdd
ide2	master	hde
ide2	slave	hdf
ide3	master	hdg
ide3	slave	hdh

Note: ide0 = primary; ide1 = secondary; ide2 = tertiary; and ide3 = quarternary.

The partition number follows an old PC standard in which each hard drive was limited to four primary partitions. One of the four partitions can be designated as an extended partition. Within the extended partition, up to 12 logical partitions can be specified.

Stepping through the Installation

Installing Linux on an IDE system is a 26-step process that begins with the Welcome screen.

Step 1. Welcome!

If you were to walk away from the first screen without making a selection, the installation program would proceed to boot the system on its own and default to the GUI Install mode.

CHAPTER 3: INSTALLING LINUX FROM A CD-ROM

```
                    Welcome to Red Hat Linux 6.2!

 • To install or upgrade a system running Red Hat Linux 2.0 or
     later, press the <ENTER> key.

 • To install or upgrade a system running Red Hat Linux 2.0 or
     later in text mode, type: text <ENTER>.

 • To enable expert mode, type: expert <ENTER>. Press <F3> for
     more information about expert mode.

 • To enable rescue mode, type: linux rescue <ENTER>. Press <F5>
     for information on rescue mode.

 • If you have a driver disk, type: linux dd  <ENTER>.

 • Use the function keys listed below for more information.
 [F1 - Main] [F2 - General] [F3 - Expert] [F4 - Kernel] [F5 - Rescue]
```

Let's summarize what the most important bullets in the preceding dialog box mean.

▲ **Bullet 1.** *Install or upgrade a system running Red Hat Linux 2.0 or later* will access a GUI install panel. However, be aware that this choice has a high video-failure or misconfiguration rate, as it does not interpret all video cards and monitors correctly. If you choose this option and it fails, we recommend that you immediately reboot and use the text-installation option.

▲ **Bullet 2.** *Install or upgrade in text mode* is necessary if the previous installation method was not successful. For practical reasons and in order to facilitate the installation of the majority of users, we have chosen to use text mode in this installation because it is fail-safe.

▲ **Bullet 3.** *Enable expert mode* is not for the faint of heart but is sometimes necessary—for example, when `Autoprobe` does not appear to find your cards with correct settings. You would have to supply the necessary information for all settings, such as IRQ, I/O, and DMA.

▲ **Bullet 4.** *Enable rescue mode* is a recent feature of the installation start-up that allows you to boot your system if LILO or the boot sectors get trashed. There is also a procedure that allows you to create a rescue disk after the fact if circumstances dictate that this should be done. However, you do not have to use this install menu to create a rescue disk. If your system boots normally into Red Hat 6.2, for example, you can create a post-installation rescue disk at any time by going back to the */lib/modules* directory and using the following command:

```
mkbootdisk --device /dev/fd0 kernel_number
```

where `kernel_number` is of a format similar to 2.2.*x-yy*. When you choose which kernel you want to install, you will insert the appropriate numbers for the *x* and the *yy*.

However, for versions of Red Hat Linux previous to 6.2, you could create post-installation rescue disks by going to the */images* directory on the installation CD-ROM and using this command instead:

```
dd if=rescue.img of=/dev/fd0 bs=1440 count=1
```

The next screen presumes that you have chosen Bullet 2, the text mode of installation.

Step 2. Select Language

Whatever language you choose here will become the default language used for the system. You can add other language sets later.

```
                    Choose a Language
What language should be used during the installation process?
                    Czech           ↑
                    English         ¬
                    French          ¬
                    German          ¬
                    Hungarian       ¬
                    Icelandic       ¬
                    Italian         ¬
                    Norwegian       ¬
                    Romanian        ↓
                          OK
```

Step 3. Specify Keyboard

You cannot afford to get creative here. This is a technical question about keyboard drivers. If you answer this question incorrectly, then issues may arise when you try to enable and remap keys. Not all keyboards are created equal. You can, however, choose the closest one here and adjust it later when the system is up and running.

```
                    Keyboard Type
            What type of keyboard do you have?
                    slovene         ↑
                    tr_f-latin5     ¬
                    tr_q-latin5     ¬
                    tralt           ¬
                    trf             ¬
                    trq             ¬
                    uk              ¬
                    us              ↓
                          OK
```

Step 4. Welcome

Press OK at the next screen.

Customizing and Upgrading Linux

```
┌─────────────────────────────────────────────────────────────────┐
│                    Welcome to Red Hat Linux!                    │
│   This installation process is outlined in detail in the Official │
│   Red Hat Linux Installation Guide available from Red Hat Software. │
│   If you have access to this manual, you should read the        │
│   installation section before continuing.                       │
│                                                                 │
│   If you have purchased Official Red Hat Linux, be sure to register │
│   your purchase through our web site, http://www.redhat.com.    │
│                                                                 │
│              OK                              Back               │
└─────────────────────────────────────────────────────────────────┘
```

Step 5. Specify Installation Type

One of the most popular features of contemporary Linux systems is the new desktops, GNOME and KDE. The one you choose should depend on what you want to do. If you are experimenting, try to install one and then the other. It is not the case that if you choose GNOME you cannot run KDE applications. Consider your choice between the two as making one dominant over the other. Of course, as the industry is somewhat political, the KDE development group has different mandates than the GNOME development group.

If you want TCP/IP connectivity with all the attendant `ftp`, `telnet`, and `rlogin` options, choosing `Install Server System` may save you some work; you could then add a desktop later.

Choose `Install Custom System` here, because we are going to define the environment.

```
┌─────────────────────────────────────────────────────────────────┐
│                       Installation Type                         │
│             What type of system would you like to install?      │
│                                                                 │
│                      Install GNOME Workstation                  │
│                      Install KDE Workstation                    │
│                      Install Server System                      │
│                      Install Custom System                      │
│                      Upgrade Existing Installation              │
│                                                                 │
│                  OK                       Back                  │
└─────────────────────────────────────────────────────────────────┘
```

Insert the Linux CD-ROM next and select OK.

```
                            Note
         Insert your Red Hat CD into your CD drive now.
                         OK      Back
```

Step 6. Specify Initial or Upgrade Installation

In this exercise, you are installing a new installation, so choose `Install` in the next screen. Remember, `Install` will not preserve any information. `Upgrade` will preserve existing configuration files by renaming them and giving them a specific file-name extension (for example, *filename.rpmsave*). This dialog box may appear if the installation program sees remnants of a previous install on the target hard drive. In other words, the Installation Path dialog box may not always appear.

```
                       Installation Path
       Would you like to install a new system or upgrade a system
          which already contains Red Hat Linux 2.0 or later?
              Install                          Upgrade
```

Step 7. Partition Disk Using Disk Druid

Select `Disk Druid`. Be aware that both `Disk Druid` and `fdisk` are destructive to existing partitions.

Customizing and Upgrading Linux

```
                         Disk Setup
   Disk Druid is a tool for partitioning and setting up mount points.
   It is designed to be easier to use than Linux's traditional disk
   partitioning software, fdisk, as well as more powerful. However,
   there are some cases where fdisk may be preferred.

   Which tool would you like to use?

           Disk Druid              fdisk              Back
```

Step 8. View Hard-Disk Attributes

The next screen indicates that you have an 8.2 GB IDE hard disk that it calls drive *hda*, which is correct for an IDE drive. We now proceed to create the file-system partitions. Select Add.

```
                        Current Disk Partitions

     Mount Point     Device      Requested    Actual    Type




     Drive Summaries
     Drive Geom [C/H/S]          Total     Used       Free
     hda [ 1046/255/63]          8205M      0M        8205M [        ]


           Add          Edit         Delete       OK         Back
```

Step 9. Add or Edit Partitions

The Edit New Partition dialog box, shown next, will appear whenever you select Add or Edit in the Current Disk Partitions dialog box. In this example, you will be creating a couple of primary partitions: a Linux Native partition containing several logical partitions (namely, the root partition, the */usr* partition and the */home* partition); and a Linux swap partition. So you will see the Edit New Partition dialog

Chapter 3: Installing Linux from a CD-ROM

box for each of those partitions. After each partition is created, clicking on the OK button in Edit New Partition will update the Current Disk Partitions and return you to that box. To continue creating partitions, you have to click Add again.

When creating the root, */usr* and */home* partitions, in turn, you'll have to enter their mount points (/, */usr* and */home*, respectively), enter the desired size of the partition, and set the type to Linux Native. When creating the swap partition, do not enter a mount point (that is, leave that entry blank), enter the desired size, and set the type to Linux Swap.

```
                      Edit New Partition
        Mount Point: /_ _ _ _ _ _ _ _ _ _ _ _ _ _ _ _ _

        Size (Megs): 800                Type: Linux Swap
                                              Linux Native
        Grow to fill disk?  [   ]             DOS 16 bit <32M
                                              DOS 16 bit >=32M
        Allowable Drive:    [   ] hda

                    OK                        Cancel
```

If you are editing existing partitions, then this dialog box will be slightly different. For example, the Type will already be specified. There will be an Allocation Status field, which will read Successful or Unsuccessful, rather than the Allowable Drive specification. Again, clicking on OK will return you to the (updated) Current Disk Partition screen.

Step 10. Create New Hard-Disk Partitions

Appearing in the next screen is the configuration we suggest using for this installation. If you are configuring your hard disk according to the exercise in Chapter 2, then consult your planning sheet and create, add, and edit the partitions until they match what you need.

73

Customizing and Upgrading Linux

Note that every time you add, delete, or edit your partitions you will be returned to this dialog box. Every time it will show you how you are progressing, with new or different partitions or other specifications. Remember that none of the changes will take effect until you select OK at the very end of the partitioning process.

Once you have the configuration you want, select OK to save these changes to your configuration tables.

```
                       Current Disk Partitions

         Mount Point     Device      Requested     Actual    Type

         /               hda1           800M        3631M    Linux native
         /usr            hda5           700M        3200M    Linux native
         /home           hda6           268M        1239M    Linux native
                         hda7           128M         133M    Linux swap

         Drive Summaries
         Drive Geom [C/H/S]            Total       Used      Free
         hda  [ 3067/ 64/32]           8205M       8204M      1M  [              ]


                 Add           Edit         Delete         OK          Back
```

Step 11. Format New System Partitions

For this installation, you are going to format all of the partitions to ensure that they are clean. The partition tables were replaced by `Disk Druid`; the installation program actually removes and replaces the existing data blocks. You should select the `Check for bad blocks during format` option. In fact, if you are installing Linux on a production system, we highly recommend that you select this option, even though the process may take a while on some large or (heaven forbid) damaged disks.

It should go without saying that all newly created partitions should be formatted. If you have preserved partitions from a previous configuration and you do not mind removing the data in them, then they too

CHAPTER 3: INSTALLING LINUX FROM A CD-ROM

should be formatted again. On the other hand, don't format existing partitions containing files or data that you want to preserve. Remember that preserving partitions applies most if you are upgrading Linux.

```
                    Partitions to Format

What partitions would you like to format? We strongly suggest
formatting all of the system partitions, including /, /usr, and
/var. There is no need to format /home or /usr/local if they have
already been configured during a previous install.

              [ * ] /dev/hda1   /
              [ * ] /dev/hda6   /home
              [ * ] /dev/hda5   /usr

              [ * ] Check for bad blocks during format

                     OK              Back
```

Step 12. LILO Configuration

A LILO Configuration screen appears, which asks about use of linear mode (required by some SCSI hard drives). We do not have SCSI hard drives. If you were to choose to enable this feature it would have no effect, nor would it cause any problems.

```
                       LILO Configuration

A few systems will need to pass special options to the kernel at
boot time for the system to function properly. If you need to
pass boot options to the kernel, enter them now. If you don't
need any or aren't sure, leave this blank.

    [ ]  Use linear mode (needed for some SCSI drives)


           OK              Skip              Back
```

We plan to use LILO to manage the disk. Therefore, at the next screen choose the `Master Boot Record` option and then press OK.

```
                    Lilo Installation

        Where do you want to install the bootloader?

        /dev/hda         Master Boot Record
        /dev/hda1        First sector of boot partition

                     OK          Back
```

For this installation, we are only installing Linux. Thus, we will select OK for the default */dev/hda1* partition which has been highlighted for us by the installation process. If there were already another operating system installed on another partition, then we would have more than one selection here. Eventually, when the system booted up, we would have to choose which operating system to boot. We highly recommend, if you are installing Linux on a production system, that no other operating systems be installed. In other working environments, however, such as at home, you might appreciate having more than one operating system.

```
                        LILO Configuration

        The boot manager Red Hat uses can boot other operating systems
        as well. You need to tell me what partitions you would like to be
        able to boot and what label you want to use for each of them.

        Device          Partition       Default         Boot label

        /dev/hda1       Linux Native    *               linux

                        Okay        Edit        Back
```

Step 13. Host Name and Basic TCP/IP Configurations

In the next screen, you will be prompted for a host name for your computer. Input the host name that you select. You can change it later if necessary.

```
                      Hostname Configuration
      The hostname is the name of your computer. If your computer is
      attached to a network, this may be assigned by your network
      administrator.

                         Hostname: HostB

                    OK                    Back
```

Next, you will be prompted for TCP/IP networking addresses. It may be necessary to consult with your Internet service provider (ISP) or system administrator, as necessary, for information to fill in the next dialog box. We'll enter and explain some examples in the next paragraph.

For this installation, let's say our lab consists of a simple network and that our system requires only a static IP address to communicate. So we enter 192.168.6.60 as our IP address. The installation program will automatically put in the Class C Netmask 255.255.255.0 which is correct and acceptable for us. The default gateway IP address is the first interface card on the proxy server that connects us to the outside world via a cable or other service. In this case, our lab doesn't have one, so the default 192.168.6.254 supplied by the installation program is also acceptable. The primary nameserver entry here is also not relevant to our lab. Normally, it might be ignored anyway because a proxy server would handle all Internet name resolution requests, so it could, in that case, be left null. For us here, however, the 192.168.6.1 supplied by the installation program is also acceptable.

```
            Network Configuration

        [ ] Use bootp/dhcp
        IP address:              192.168.6.36
        Netmask:                 255.255.255.0
        Default gateway (IP):    192.168.6.254
        Primary nameserver:      192.168.6.1

                    OK        Back
```

Step 14. Configure the Mouse

The program immediately asks you to configure the mouse if it finds one. If you have a three-button mouse, you will be better equipped to take advantage of the X Window System. However, if your mouse only has two buttons, then you should select `Emulate 3 Buttons`. If you ever wish to change the mouse configuration, you can use the */usr/sbin/mouseconfig* command or `linuxconf`.

```
                       Mouse Selection

       Which model of mouse is attached to this computer?

              ALPS - GlidePoint (PS/2)
              ASCII - MieMouse (PS/2)
              ASCII - MieMouse (serial)
              ATI - bus Mouse
              Generic - 2 Button Mouse (PS/2)
              Generic - 2 Button Mouse (serial)
              Generic - 3 Button Mouse (PS/2)
              Generic - 3 Button Mouse (PS/2)
              [*] Emulate 3 Buttons?

                    OK        Back
```

Step 15. Configure the Time Zone

During the development of this installation exercise, we chose `Canada/Mountain` time zone. Choose whichever is appropriate to your present location. If you ever wish to change the time configuration, you can use the /usr/sbin/`timeconfig` command.

```
                        Configure Timezones
               Format machine time is stored in:
                  [   ] Hardware clock set to GMT
               Africa/Abidjan
               .
               .
               Canada/Mountain   #
               .
               .
               Zulu

                         OK          Back
```

Step 16. Set Root Password

Remember to choose a good password and then ensure that you remember it. Linux has rules and guidelines for proper passwords. Reviewing them would be worthwhile. Check the `man` pages and the Red Hat online documentation.

```
                           Root Password
            Pick a root password.  You must type it twice to ensure you
            know what it is and didn't make a mistake in typing. Remember
            that the root password is a critical part of system security!

                 Password:
                 Password (again):

                         OK                         Back
```

The installation process will allow you to add users at this time. You need not add all users now, though, because you can revisit this task at any time after completing the installation. The reason the Add User dialog appears here is to allow you to log in to the system for the first time as a user and switch to a root user to perform the first set of system administration tasks, which is considered proper form.

```
                          Add User

         Enter the information for the user.

         User ID:          dbadmin
         Full name:        Database administrator
         Password:
         Password (confirm):

                    OK              Cancel
```

Step 17. Configure Authentication

In the next screen, you will use shadow passwords and MD5 encryption and configure NIS.

```
                 Authentication Configuration
         [ * ] Use Shadow Passwords
         [ * ] Enable MD5 Passwords
         [   ] Enable NIS
         NIS Domain: _____
         NIS Server: [   ] Request via Broadcast
         or use:     _____

                    OK                         Back
```

Step 18. Choose Components to Install

Components are groups of software packages that provide an overall service or feature to the system. The components list in our next screen does not display all the possible selections; rather, only the ones we suggest installing for this exercise. You may note that the

CHAPTER 3: INSTALLING LINUX FROM A CD-ROM

dialog box on your screen is a little smaller than the one shown next; by following the arrows, you will eventually reveal all the components.

To see the packages that comprise the components, choose `Select individual packages`. Before you do so, be prepared: this will slow down the installation process. You also run the risk of mistakenly installing parts of components or packages that will not work because other packages they depend on have not been installed. Nevertheless, if you have the time, go ahead and browse through the list during the installation.

```
                    Package Group Selection
              [ * ] Printer Support              ↑
              [ * ] X Window System              ¬
              [ * ] GNOME                        ¬
              [ * ] KDE                          ¬
              [ * ] DOS/Windows Connectivity     ¬
              [ * ] Networked Workstation        ¬
              [ * ] NFS Server                   ¬
              [ * ] Anonymous FTP Server         ¬
              [ * ] Kernel Development           ¬
              [ * ] Utilities                    ↓

              [   ] Select individual packages

                    OK                    Back
```

If you are performance-minded, you may want to be somewhat selective at this stage. If performance is not a primary consideration, you may want to choose all components and, thus, all of the packages. As you scroll down through this dialog box, you will eventually see the `Everything` choice at the bottom of the component list.

81

WARNING: *The installation program will tell you if you have inadequate disk space. In the meantime, do not forget your planning and do not make disk space too tight in the root (/) and /usr file-system partitions. Finally, be sure to avoid removing mandatory packages, such as the kernel and certain libraries and their respective support packages.*

Try to resolve all package dependencies before continuing. As mentioned earlier, one package or component may not work unless its companion packages are also installed. However, if any dependencies are inadvertently missed, the installation program will warn you of that as well. You can still add them at any time after installation.

Step 19. Find Video Adapter

The installation program has conducted a probe using the `PCI Probe` and found the video adapter. Select OK.

```
                    X probe results

            Video Card: Generic Mach64
            X Server  : Mach64

                  OK            Back
```

Once you have selected OK, you will briefly see an Install Status box while the installation program loads the appropriate video-adapter server.

Step 20. Create Install Log

Select OK here. As careful as you may be, you can never tell when the *install.log* file might be needed to bail you out of unforeseen trouble.

```
                    Installation to begin

    A complete log of your installation will be in /tmp/install.log
    after rebooting your system. You may want to keep this log for
    future reference.

              OK                              Back
```

Step 21. Search for Overlapping Files

Next, the installation program looks for any overlapping files—that is, files that would be duplicated during the new installation process. The pertinent screen appears only in cases where you are trying to preserve at least some part of your previous system. You can ignore these messages if they do appear unless you are checking to see if a specific file is being installed. You cannot remedy overlapping files at this time, however. Should you wish to do so, you can rectify overlapping files later by uninstalling and reinstalling specific RPM packages.

Step 22. Install Status

Throughout the installation process, you will see an installation status dialog box called Package Installation, which will show you the progress of the installation of individual packages and programs (top half), as well as the overall progress of the total Linux installation (bottom half). Note in the top half that as the individual packages are installed, the installation program will provide the package name, the size of the package, and a brief description of the package.

On the bottom, the installation program keeps track of the space used by the installed packages, as well as the remaining space required. Moreover, it tracks the total, elapsed, and remaining installation time. This might be a good time for you to take a break while the installation proceeds.

```
                    Package Installation
         Name    : nameofpackage
         Size    : 1234k
         Summary : Description of package being installed
         vvvvvvvvvvvvvvvvvvvvvvvvvvvvvvvvvvvvvvvvvvvvv
                    Packages   Bytes    Time
         Total      :    370    587M    0:08:35
         Completed  :    220    427M    0:06:18
         Remaining  :    150    160M    0:02:17

         vvvvvvvvvvvvvvvvvvvvvvvvvvvvvvvvvvvvvvvvvvvvv
```

Step 23. Create Boot Disk

Creating a boot disk is a good idea. Select Yes. However, you can always do this after you have installed Linux as well, by using the mkbootdisk command.

```
                              Bootdisk
       A custom bootdisk provides a way of booting into your Linux system
       without depending on the normal bootloader. This is useful if you
       don't want to install lilo on your system, another operating system
       removes lilo, or lilo doesn't work with your hardware configuration.
       A custom bootdisk can also be used with the Red Hat rescue image,
       making if much easier to recover from severe system failures.

       Would you like to create a bootdisk for your system?

                  Yes              No              Back
```

In response to the next screen, insert a blank floppy disk and then press OK.

Chapter 3: Installing Linux from a CD-ROM

```
                          Bootdisk

   Insert a blank floppy in the first drive. All data on this disk
   will be erased during creation of the bootdisk.

                          OK    Skip
```

The program will proceed to create the boot disk.

```
                          Creating

                       Creating bootdisk …
```

Step 24. Set Up Monitor

Although scores of monitor names appear in the next screen, our monitor was not listed. Consequently, we selected `Custom` here. By choosing `Custom`, you have to fill in more information.

```
                       Monitor Setup
   What type of monitor do you have? If you would rather specify the
   sync frequencies of your monitor, choose "Custom" from the list.

                   Custom                    ↑
                   ADI DMC-2304              ¬
                     .                       ¬
                     .                       ¬
                     .                       ¬
                   ViewSonic VPA 150         ↓

                   OK                      Back
```

Click OK in the next screen.

```
                    Custom Monitor Setup

 Now we want to set the specifications of the monitor. The two
 critical parameters are the vertical refresh rate, which is the rate
 at which the whole screen is refreshed, and most importantly the
 horizontal sync rate, which is the rate at which scan lines are
 displayed.

 The valid range for horizontal sync and vertical sync should be
 documented in the manual of your monitor. If in doubt, check the
 monitor database /usr/X11R6/lib/X11/doc/Monitors to see if your
 monitor is there.

                  OK                              Back
```

Our monitor is capable of up to 60 Hz, so in the next screen we selected the generic `Super VGA @ 56 Hz` to be safe. This can also be adjusted later using the `Xconfigurator` program.

```
              Custom Monitor Setup (Continued)

 You must indicate the horizontal sync range of your monitor. You can
 either select one of the predefined ranges below that correspond to
 industry-standard monitor types, or give a specific range. It is
 VERY IMPORTANT that you do not specify a monitor type with a
 horizontal sync range that is beyond the capabilities of your monitor.

              Standard VGA, 640 x 480 @ 60 Hz
              Super VGA, 800 x 600 @ 56 Hz
              .
              .
              .
              Monitor that can do 1600 x 1200 @ 76 Hz

              OK                              Back
```

In the next screen, we chose 50–90 Hz (vertical sync range) because our monitor operates in this range.

```
                  Custom Monitor Setup (Continued)

    You must indicate the vertical sync range of your monitor. You
    can either select one of the predefined ranges below that
    corresponds to industry-standard monitor types, or give a
    specific range. For interlaced modes the number that counts is
    the high one (e.g., 87 Hz rather than 43 Hz).

                              50 -  70
                              50 -  90
                              50 - 100
                              40 - 150

          OK                                           Back
```

The installation program now invokes the `Xconfigurator` program. Press OK.

```
                         Probing to begin

    Xconfigurator will now run the X server you selected to probe
    various information about your video card. It is normal for the
    screen to blink several times.

                                OK
```

Step 25. Start X

Next, select `Skip`. If something went wrong now, it would be an inconvenience. In any event, we discuss video configuration in great detail in Chapter 5.

```
                            Starting X

    Xconfigurator will now start X to test your configuration.

                        OK          Skip
```

Customizing and Upgrading Linux

The X installation procedure will also ask you about the mouse it found. Again, if you have a three-button mouse, you will be better equipped to take advantage of the X Window System. However, if your mouse only has two buttons, then you should select `Emulate 3 Buttons`. Meanwhile, if you ever wish to change the mouse configuration, you can use the */usr/sbin/mouseconfig* command or `linuxconf`.

```
                          Mouse Selection

         Which model of mouse is attached to this computer?

                  ALPS  - GlidePoint (PS/2)
                  ASCII - MieMouse (PS/2)
                  ASCII - MieMouse (serial)
                  ATI   - bus Mouse
                  Generic - 2 Button Mouse (PS/2)
                  Generic - 2 Button Mouse (serial)
                  Generic - 3 Button Mouse (PS/2)
                  Generic - 3 Button Mouse (PS/2)
                  [*] Emulate 3 Buttons?

                          OK        Back
```

The next screen is straightforward. Select `Yes`.

```
                       Update X Configuration

   Mouseconfig can now update your Xfree86 configuration file to
   reflect your new mouse settings. Would you like mouseconfig to make
   these changes now?

                     Yes                    No
```

Step 26. Installation Complete

Select OK at this next screen.

```
                          Complete

  Congratulations, installation is complete.

  Remove the boot media and press return to reboot. For information on
  fixes which are available for this release of Red Hat Linux, consult
  the Errata available from http://www.redhat.com.

  Information on configuring your system is available in the post
  install chapter of the Official Red Hat Linux manuals.

                              OK
```

If you are having trouble with the installation, stop and research what you are doing. Based on our experience, most problems involve hard drive configuration or compatibility, followed by network cards and drivers.

With respect to drives, the problem is often a lack of documentation, on the jumper or termination settings. If it is the latter, perhaps you should consider purchasing a new network card. The last network card that we purchased was a D-Link Ethernet card for $20 (Canadian), and the drivers were flawless. We have had tremendous luck finding Linux drivers for some cards by visiting *http://www.driversguide.com*. However, spending a lot of time looking for a driver may not be worthwhile compared with simply replacing your card with one that you know works.

We also know that diverse video hardware issues can cause installation difficulties. Consequently, we have dedicated an entire chapter to video configuration. Consult Chapter 5 for details.

Quiz

1. What two methods are most commonly used for installing Linux?
2. What information needs to be specified to force Linux to recognize your SCSI controller and drive if they are not detected?
3. In what format must you specify the previous values in order for Linux to accept them?
4. What four options are available for installation at the Welcome screen?
5. What two options are available if your SCSI devices are not detected by `Autoprobe`?
6. If Linux cannot see an IDE CD-ROM, what should you check?
7. What is the naming syntax for IDE drives?
8. If you choose not to create a boot disk during installation, how can the disk be created later?

See Appendix B for answers.

Chapter 4

Installing Linux Using NFS

IN CHAPTER 3, WE COVERED INSTALLING LINUX on SCSI and IDE systems. For both installations, we used a CD-ROM as the source for the operating system files, as though both installations were on stand-alone systems. In this chapter, we install Linux again, but now the target is known as 192.168.6.36 on the network, and the binary files for the Linux installation are on another system on the network known as 192.168.6.34. The binary files may be on that system's hard disk, or on a CD-ROM accessible through that system's CD-ROM drive. The target system will be an NFS (Network File System) client, and the system with the binary files will be an NFS server. Basically, there are two major tasks in this type of installation: (1) prepare the NFS server, and (2) prepare the NFS client (that is, the system that is to receive the new Linux operating system).

You may be surprised by the fact that the NFS system need not be a Linux- or even a UNIX-based system. It only has to house the Linux files and be able to function as an NFS server. Of course, in our example, the NFS server is another Red Hat Linux system.

Quick Review of NFS

Sun Microsystems developed NFS in the 1980s and courteously shared it with the industry, such that NFS became a standard way for sharing disk resources across a network. Its primary strength is its interoperability—you can find NFS support in every UNIX-related operating system, and for just a few dollars (comparatively), you can get NFS support for other operating systems as well. (Microsoft has recently announced support for NFS on Windows 2000 server operating systems.) Its second strength is its ability to make file systems on remote systems appear to be local on client systems on the network.

There are a couple of network requirements, however, and here we are going to rely on the classic non-UNIX definitions of "server" and "client." Specifically, a server is a system that responds to commands from clients, providing services such as data management, network administration, and security. A client is a standalone system that accesses shared network resources provided by a server. (Be careful, because these are not Linux/UNIX definitions.)

Referring to Figure 4.1, the network requirements are as follows:

▲ HostA and HostB must be able to communicate via the TCP/IP protocol stack.

▲ HostA, which is the system with the exportable binary files already installed either on its hard disk or on a CD-ROM in its CD-ROM drive, has to share access to the HDD directory or the CD-ROM. HostA and its sharable/exportable files will be known as the NFS server (using the classic networking definition of server, not the UNIX/Linux definition). This is somewhat analogous to a "net share" in Microsoft Windows.

▲ HostB is the system that needs to access HostA's exportable directories. HostB will, thus, be known as the NFS client (here, again, using the classic networking, but non-UNIX/Linux, definition). The NFS client will mount the exportable HDD directory or CD-ROM drive from the NFS server. This is somewhat analogous to a "net use" or "net share" scenario in Microsoft Windows.

▲ Certain configuration files must be modified. We will walk through this configuration in the next section.

CHAPTER 4: INSTALLING LINUX USING NFS

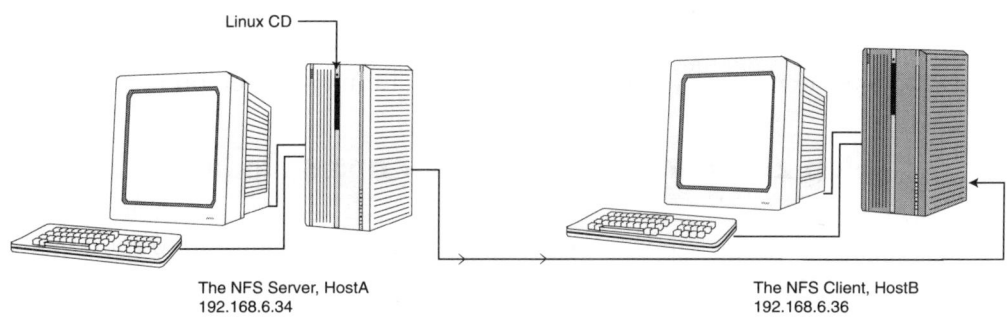

Figure 4.1. An NFS connection.

NFS has a concept of security and ownership. For purposes of this exercise, we are not going to configure security on the NFS server. We will export the file system in such a way that it can be accessed by any NFS client on the network. If you are going to share file systems on a routine basis with other users on other systems, you have to ensure to the best of your ability that they are trustworthy and are set up using the basic security features of NFS. Otherwise, you might want to consider a non-NFS protocol, to provide better security. For our example Linux installation, NFS's drawbacks are really of no concern. In fact, imperfect security is advantageous as we mention in the next section.

Preparing the NFS Server

Set up an NFS server by following these six steps. Note that these instructions assume that you are on HostA, which is going to be your NFS server.

Step 1. Insert Linux CD-ROM in NFS Server

Put the Linux operating system CD-ROM into the CD-ROM drive of your network's designated NFS server. As discussed previously, this could be any system on which NFS is supported regardless of the installed operating system—Linux, another UNIX flavor, DOS, OS/2, and so on—as long as the system can function as an NFS server. The system in our example is a server with Linux installed on it.

Step 2. Log In as Regular User and su to Root

Log in to the Linux NFS server as a regular user and su to root, because you will have to modify the *tcp* files in the */etc* directory.

```
Login: username
Password: xxxxxxxx
Last login: Day Month Date Time on ttyx
$ su
Password: xxxxxxxx
```

Step 3. Record IP Address and Netmask of NFS Server

You will need this information later to provide the target installation system, so that it can locate the exported CD-ROM. Use the following ifconfig command syntax:

```
# ifconfig eth0
```

Step 4. Add an Entry for the CD-ROM to Server's /etc/fstab File

Make sure that the CD-ROM is mounted as a file system every time the system boots. To do this, you have to check the */etc/fstab* file and ensure that the */dev/cdrom* line, as it appears in the example, is inserted into the file. The entry directs the system to mount the physical device called */dev/cdrom* as an ISO 9660 file system called */mnt/cdrom*. Do not make it automatic at boot; do make it read-only.

CHAPTER 4: INSTALLING LINUX USING NFS

```
# cat /etc/fstab
/dev/sda1      /              ext2      defaults       1 1
/dev/sda6      /home          ext2      defaults       1 2
/dev/sda5      /usr/local     ext2      defaults       1 2
/dev/sda7      swap           swap      defaults       0 0
/dev/fd0       /mnt/floppy    msdos     user,noauto    0 0
/dev/cdrom     /mnt/cdrom     iso9660   noauto,ro      0 0
none           /proc          proc      defaults       0 0
none           /dev/pts       devpts    mode=0622      0 0
```

If this line is not present, then add it using the text editor of your choice.

Step 5. Mount CD-ROM as File System on NFS Server

This step must be done manually because we have asked to use the `noauto` option. Therefore, you will issue the `mount` command. The mount command refers to the */etc/fstab* file and sees that */mnt/cdrom* is */dev/cdrom* and will handle it accordingly.

```
# mount /mnt/cdrom
```

Now, if you wish, you can test whether the file system has been mounted. Just change to the */mnt/cdrom* directory using the `cd` command, and you should be able to list all the files on the CD-ROM.

Step 6. Export CD-ROM File System to Access It without Security

Having no security here is important. If security was enabled, the client that is going to be the Linux installation target (known as HostB) would have no way of authenticating itself to make the initial connection to the NFS server. In other words, any kind of security would stop you dead in your tracks at this point. To tell the NFS server to export the files on its CD-ROM, start by adding the following entry

95

Customizing and Upgrading Linux

to the server's /etc/exports file. First, cat the file to see what's in it. If the CD-ROM entry /mnt/cdrom (ro) does not appear, use your text editor to add it. Using (ro) without options tells the system there is no need for security here. Therefore, if you have more entries than shown below, remove them.

```
# cat /etc/exports
# This is the exports file for HostA
#
/mnt/cdrom     <Tab>(ro)
```

You're not quite finished yet. Now you have to export the CD-ROM file system and make sure that it is properly exported with no security options enabled. Because you have created an /etc/exports file with the above syntax in it, you can use the exportfs -a command to export all directories. Doing so will not enable the server's default security options. You may have to use the command's absolute path name, because the directory it's in (/usr/sbin) may not be in your path.

```
# /usr/sbin/exportfs -a
# /usr/sbin/exportfs
/mnt/cdrom     <world>
```

The NFS server should now be ready. If you see <world>, consider your efforts successful. Just keep in mind that <world> is not what you want on the Internet, or even some intranets or extranets.

Start Target Installation System

Set up an NFS client by following these six steps.

CHAPTER 4: INSTALLING LINUX USING NFS

Step 1. Create Floppy Disks

If you are using Red Hat 5.2, you will have to create three floppies, each with a specific file. You can do this at the NFS server that you configured because the CD-ROM is already mounted. The floppies are listed below according to their respective files.

- ▲ *boot.img*. In this version, the *boot.img* serves for all installations.
- ▲ *supp.img*. This is needed only if you require PCMCIA (Personal Computer Memory Card International Association) support—for example, for the network PC card.
- ▲ *rescue.img*. It is always a good idea to create this one.

If you are using Red Hat Linux 6.X, you will also have to create three floppies, but they have slightly different files, listed below.

- ▲ *boot.img*. For CD installations; this floppy disk would be bootable.
- ▲ *bootnet.img*. For NFS, FTP (File Transfer Protocol), and HTTP (Hypertext Transfer Protocol) installations; this floppy disk would also be bootable.
- ▲ *pcmcia.img*. For CD, NFS, FTP, and HTTP installations involving PCMCIA (that is, "PC Card") devices; this floppy disk would be bootable, too.

Step 2. Boot Target System

Go to the target installation system, HostB, which is going to be the NFS client. Insert the Linux boot diskette and proceed to the Installation Method screen. Note that this screen may vary slightly (that is, present a slightly different list of installation media selections), depending on whether you have booted with the Red Hat 5.2 or 6.*x* versions. The `NFS Image` selection appears regardless of the version you are using.

```
                    Installation Method
   What type of media contains the packages to be installed?

                      Local CDROM
                      NFS Image
                      Hard Drive
                      FTP


                           OK
```

Step 3. Choose NFS Image Option

In the Installation Method screen, select the `NFS Image` option.

Step 4. Provide Networking Information

You'll be prompted next for networking information for the target system. This is the IP address for the NFS client system known as HostB—that is, the IP address for the system from which you are initiating the installation. Do *not* enter the IP address of the NFS server yet; this will come later.

You can use DHCP (Dynamic Host Configuration Protocol) or enter a hard IP address. We suggest a designated IP address because using one will be less complicated and permit you to follow what is going on. The network addresses below are used only as examples. The installation procedure will ask you if want to change these values later anyway.

```
IP address:              192.168.6.36
Netmask:                 255.255.255.0
Default gateway (IP):    192.168.6.254
Primary nameserver:      192.168.6.1
```

CHAPTER 4: INSTALLING LINUX USING NFS

We used the suggested defaults for the default gateway and the primary nameserver because these two systems are on the same segment, and what you use for their addresses will not make any difference at this point. The only two entries that you need are the IP address and the netmask; the default gateway (IP) and primary nameserver, if entered, will be ignored.

After providing the preceding information, you'll be asked for the following:

```
Domain name:
Host name:   HostB
Secondary nameserver (IP):
Tertiary nameserver (IP):
```

We enter only the host name here because our NFS server or network is not configured for name services; we are using flat */etc/hosts* files. At this point, you should be able to `ping` the target installation system from the NFS server. You will have to use the `<Alt>-<F1>` and `<Alt>-<F2>` keys to toggle back and forth between the screens to get a command line that will allow you to issue a `ping`.

Step 5. Provide Information about NFS Server

Next, you'll be asked for information on the NFS server that you set up. This is the IP address for the NFS server that you recorded in the above set of steps. What it will do here is construct a `mount` command using the IP address you give it and the name of the exported file system. In other words, it will mount */mnt/cdrom* on system 192.168.6.34 and start reading from it as if it were local.

```
NFS server name:       192.168.6.34
Red Hat directory:     /mnt/cdrom
```

At this point the target installation system will use the above information to construct a mount to the NFS server. If things do not go well, use the <Alt>-<F1>, <Alt>-<F2>, and <Alt>-<F3> keys to toggle back and forth between screens and a command line that will allow you to issue a `ping` command.

Step 6. Proceed with Otherwise "Normal" Installation

The rest of the installation will continue normally as if it were from a local CD-ROM, with the exception of the one screen that will prompt for changes in networking addresses. Imagine all the information and data being communicated between the two systems that would normally be read from the local CD-ROM drive.

CHAPTER 4: INSTALLING LINUX USING NFS

Quiz

1. What are the network requirements to install Linux using NFS?
2. What are the steps to prepare the NFS server?
3. What are the steps to install the target system?

See Appendix B for answers.

Chapter 5

Configuring the Video

IN CHAPTER 3 DURING THE TWO INSTALLATION scenarios, we took a shortcut for setting up the monitors. We chose a generic SVGA driver setting, intending at the time to adjust the setup later with the Xconfigurator program. A step or two later, we chose to let the installation program probe for a default screen resolution and color depth. We let the program choose the video mode and color depth and stated that, if adjustments had to be made, we would deal with them later as well with Xconfigurator.

This chapter is dedicated to the custom video configurations that were postponed in Chapter 3. We discuss the *XF86Config* file, which forms the basis of your X server, and how you can generate and modify that file with the Xconfigurator program to get the most performance out of your video adapter and display. We also briefly discuss another program, SuperProbe, which can help you investigate some of your video system information prior to tackling Xconfigurator.

Before we discuss the video configuration topics, we lay a quasi-technical groundwork for understanding TV and video display. Be prepared, for there are several names that describe the same concepts. Although you may feel that one or another term is better suited, all are legitimate names, depending on the situation or context. We focus here only on displays of the CRT (cathode-ray tube) variety.

Video Signal Generation

Video-Adapter Memory

When data are first generated in the CPU of the mainboard (also known as the "motherboard"), they are formatted as digital signals. The signals that are destined for display on the monitor screen are sent to the video-adapter hardware through one kind of interface or another, depending on which computer system is being employed. The signals may be sent and processed through the mainboard bus itself, or through PCI (Peripheral Component Interconnect), ISA (Industry Standard Architecture), AGP (Accelerated Graphics Port), or other slots or buses. The signals are sent to specifically designed and installed video-adapter cards. In Figure 5.1, we have drawn a very simplified (and separate) video-adapter card.

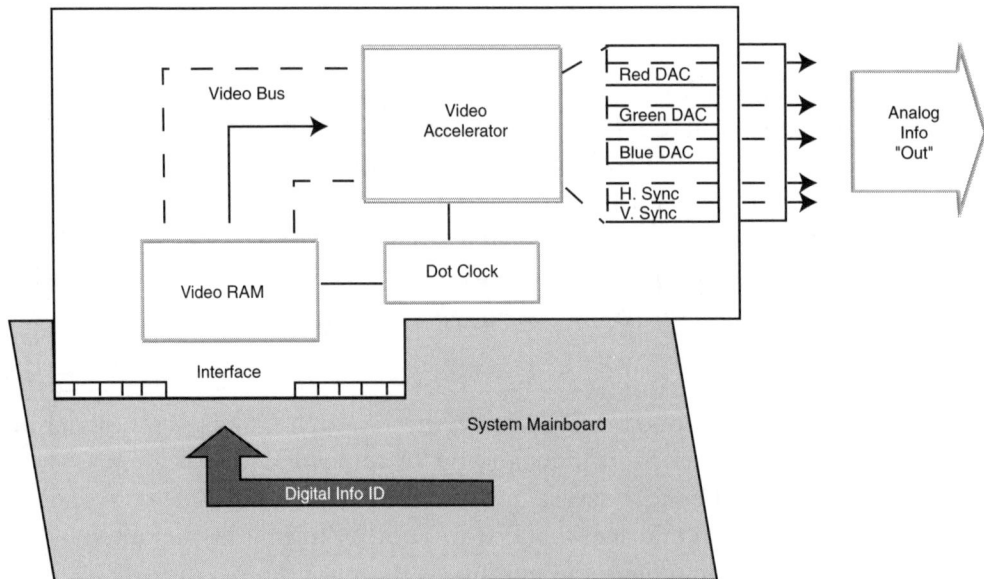

Figure 5.1. Video-adapter card.

CHAPTER 5: CONFIGURING THE VIDEO

From the interface, the digital information is likely stored, along with the video-hardware drivers, in some type of dedicated video memory. The video memory (also known as "VRAM" or the "frame buffer") is usually comprised of RAM chips separate and distinct from those used by the mainboard processor(s). Indeed, the video-memory chips are probably the more advanced (and expensive) dual-port type that allow simultaneous reception and transmission of data. In the case of AGP technology, the video hardware may also have direct access to the computer system's main RAM to supplement the otherwise separate video memory.

Regarding how much video memory you need, the amount required is a function of color depth and resolution. These concepts are defined below, mainly through the use of examples.

Looking closely at your monitor screen, you can see thousands of tiny individual dots. The dots are pixels (short for "picture elements") and result from electron beams being focused through the shadow mask onto the interior of the monitor's phosphor-coated screen. Each pixel is composed of three colors—red, green, and blue. Your screen may have as few as 480 lines of 640 pixels or as many as 1200 lines of 1600 pixels, depending on your monitor's capacity and the video hardware driving it. Each pixel represents data stored in your video memory.

How much data does each pixel represent? That depends on how many colors you want displayed on the screen. Assume that you need only 16 different colors for very basic spreadsheets, word-processing documents, or other simple images. For 16 colors, each pixel needs 4 bits (half a byte) of video memory. If you want 256 colors, on the other hand, then each pixel requires 8 bits of data (that is, 1 byte of video memory per pixel). If you want 65,536 colors (for what is commonly called "high color"), then you need 16 bits (2 bytes) of video memory per pixel, and if you want 16.78 million colors (called "true color"), then each pixel requires 24 bits (3 bytes) of memory. There is even a level of color definition based on 32 bits, or 4 bytes, of video memory per pixel, which could provide up to 4.3 billion colors! These

4-bit, 8-bit, 16-bit, 24-bit, or 32-bit (or, if you prefer, 1/2-byte, 1-byte, 2-byte, 3-byte, or 4-byte, respectively) per-pixel specifications are called the "color depths."

As mentioned a minute ago, your screen may comprise as few as 480 lines of 640 pixels or as many as 1200 lines of 1600 pixels, or somewhere in between. These dimensions, which are usually described in width in pixels by the number of lines—such as 640 x 480, 1024 x 768, or 1600 x 1200, and so on—are called the "resolution."

Another term you will encounter is "video mode." Video mode, a description of a monitor's display capacity, is the combination of resolution and color depth. For example, "16 bit, 800 x 600" is a video mode.

Later in the chapter when you are using `Xconfigurator`, you will encounter a dialog box titled Select Video Modes. This dialog box presents several mode options, from which you can select one or more, based on resolution and color depth. Table 5-1 lists the options you will find in the dialog box, plus a few more, and provides estimates of the amount of video memory required to achieve those modes. The bottom line is that if you don't have the required memory, don't expect your combination of video hardware and monitor to give you the mode you request. On the other hand, if you do have a sizable amount of video memory, then you might be surprised at how good and true a picture Linux will allow you to display.

Here's the formula we used to calculate the video memory required for each video mode in Table 5-1.

```
VRAM required = color depth x line width x number of
    lines / 1,048,576
```

where `color depth` is bytes per pixel, `line width` is pixels per line, `number of lines` is lines per screen, and `1,048,576` is number of bytes in 1MB. For example, you would calculate the amount VRAM required for 8-bit, 800 x 600 video mode as follows:

```
1 x 800 x 600 / 1,048,567 = 0.458 MB
```

Table 5-1: Video Modes

Resolution (pixels x lines)	Color depth 8 bits (1 byte/pixel, or 256 colors)	Color depth 16 bits (2 bytes/pixel, or 65,536 colors)	Color depth 24 bits (3 bytes/pixel, or 16.78 million colors)	Color depth 32 bits (4 bytes/pixel, or 4.29 billion colors)
640 x 480	0.293 MB	0.586 MB	0.879 MB	1.172 MB
800 x 600	0.458 MB	0.916 MB	1.374 MB	1.831 MB
1024 x 768	0.750 MB	1.5 MB	2.25 MB	3.0 MB
1152 x 864	0.950 MB	1.899 MB	2.848 MB	3.797 MB
1280 x 1024	1.25 MB	2.5 MB	3.75 MB	5.0 MB
1600 x 1200	1.832 MB	3.663 MB	5.493 MB	7.325 MB

You will probably want to refer back to this table later during the `Xconfigurator` process. Next, remember that your video memory must also contain your video driver software. Consequently, you may not be able to get the resolution and color depth you want from your video memory if the estimated requirement is almost equal to your video memory capacity. Something (resolution, colors) might have to be sacrificed. You might have to learn how to truly custom design your resolution, a process we discuss later.

Although `Xconfigurator`'s Select Video Modes dialog box does not contain a 32-bit color depth option, the `XF86Setup` program does. That's why we included the 32-bit column in the table.

Basic Video-Adapter Bus

It is likely that your video hardware has separate processors of its own (labeled "video accelerator" in Figure 5.1) that allow the video to be processed independently of the main system processors. The separate processors are often called "chipsets" as well, or the "RAMDAC," because some of them combine video memory and digital-to-analog converters. `Xconfigurator` and other utilities may refer to the processors using these terms. During the video configuration exercise at the end of this chapter, `Xconfigurator` will suggest that you consult beforehand some of the video-server manual pages and chipset-specific READMEs. It will also suggest that you know beforehand the name of the chipset and the amount of video memory on your video card.

How do you estimate the amount of work video processors do? Earlier we discussed the memory required to store the information that will be displayed. The video processors have to move the stored data through the video bus and to the monitor and move it there according to the vertical synchronization frequency (VSF, also known as the "screen refresh rate"). We discuss VSF in a bit more detail later in the chapter. Basically, the VSF is the rate per second at which the monitor's displays are redrawn. The range is from 40 to 160 screen refreshes per second (measured as cycles per second, or hertz, and abbreviated as Hz). To quickly summarize, the work (measured in megabytes per second) is approximately equal to the amount of data per screen multiplied by the number of screens drawn per second. Table 5-2 provides estimates of image-data transfer rate by the video processors, using example refresh rates of 50, 60, and 75 Hz.

To calculate these estimates, we used the following formula:

```
Data transfer rate = line width x number of lines x
      color depth x refresh rate / 1,048,576
```

where `line width` is pixels per line, `number of lines` is lines per screen, `color depth` is bytes per pixel, and `1,048,576` is number of bytes in 1MB.

For example, you would calculate the data transfer rate for 800 x 600 resolution, 24-bit color depth, and 60 Hz refresh rate as follows:

```
800 x 600 x 3 x 60 / 1,048,576 = 82.4 MB/second
```

CHAPTER 5: CONFIGURING THE VIDEO

Note that the Table 5-2's heading is "Image-Data Transfer Rate." The visible image is not the only data processed and transferred from the video hardware to the monitor. Later in the chapter we discuss additional information that must be transferred—the synchronization signals that govern the deflection of the electron beams. These signals add even more data. The Video Electronics Standards Association (VESA), for the sake of safety, recommends that you always add 4% to 5% to any line-rate calculation (the number of lines from a given resolution multiplied by the desired or given refresh rate) because of the overscan sync signal. There is also another 25% or so of overhead for the retrace of horizontal scan lines. We discuss and clarify these terms and concepts as we progress through the chapter.

Table 5-2: Image-Data Transfer Rate

Resolution	Color depth 8 bit			Color depth 16 bit			Color depth 24 bit			Color depth 32 bit		
	Refresh rate			Refresh rate			Refresh rate			Refresh rate		
	50 Hz	60 Hz	75 Hz	50 Hz	60 Hz	75 Hz	50 Hz	60 Hz	75 Hz	50 Hz	60 Hz	75 Hz
640 x 480	14.7	17.6	22.0	29.3	35.2	44.0	44.0	52.7	65.9	58.6	70.3	87.9
800 x 600	22.9	27.6	34.3	45.8	54.9	68.7	68.7	82.4	103.0	91.6	109.9	137.3
1024 x 768	37.5	45.0	56.3	75.0	90.0	112.5	112.5	135.0	168.8	150.0	180.0	225.0
1152 x 864	47.5	57.0	71.2	94.9	113.9	142.4	142.4	170.9	213.4	189.8	227.8	284.8
1280 x 1024	62.5	75.0	93.8	125.0	150.0	187.5	187.5	225.0	281.3	250.00	300.0	375.0
1600 x 1200	91.6	109.9	137.3	183.1	219.7	274.7	274.7	329.6	412.0	366.2	439.5	549.3

Note: The image-data transfer rate is measured in MB per second

The video processors are governed by the video hardware's onboard memory clock (also called the "dot clock" or "VGA memory clock"), which performs the same function as the mainboard bus clock but is dedicated to the video bus alone. The activity of the onboard memory clock, which we refer to as the "dot clock" henceforth, is measured in million of cycles per second (megahertz, or MHz). Meanwhile, the video hardware, especially if it is located on a separate adapter card, also probably has its own separately sized bus (likely 32- or 64-bit) to optimize the processing and movement of data through the video adapter to the monitor.

Thus, the video signals are processed and, after leaving the accelerator, the actual picture element signals are converted from digital to analog format in the three (one for each of the primary colors red, green, and blue) digital-to-analog converters (DACs) on the card (called "A/Ds" in days gone by). Why are they converted? Although this is a long story, the fundamental reason is to provide more colors and improved control of light intensity on the screen.

Only five signals leaving the video adapter are represented earlier in Figure 5.1. In reality, however, there are more. But the five we include in the illustration are the most important at this stage in the discussion: the red, blue, and green signals, plus the two synchronization signals. We discuss the importance of all the signals in the next section.

Video Display

Basic Monitor Design

As illustrated in Figure 5.2, within the monitor, the color signals (which are constantly varying voltages) are amplified and enter respective red, blue, and green electron guns. The variations of the voltages govern the intensity of the electron beams that are emitted from those guns. Meanwhile, the synchronization signals are also amplified and then enter the magnetic deflection yoke (a collection of deflection coils) wherein they govern the aiming and movement of the electron beams, as well as the size of the individual picture elements (that is, the pixels). The impact of the electrons on the phosphor-coated screen creates the pixels and, thus, the display image.

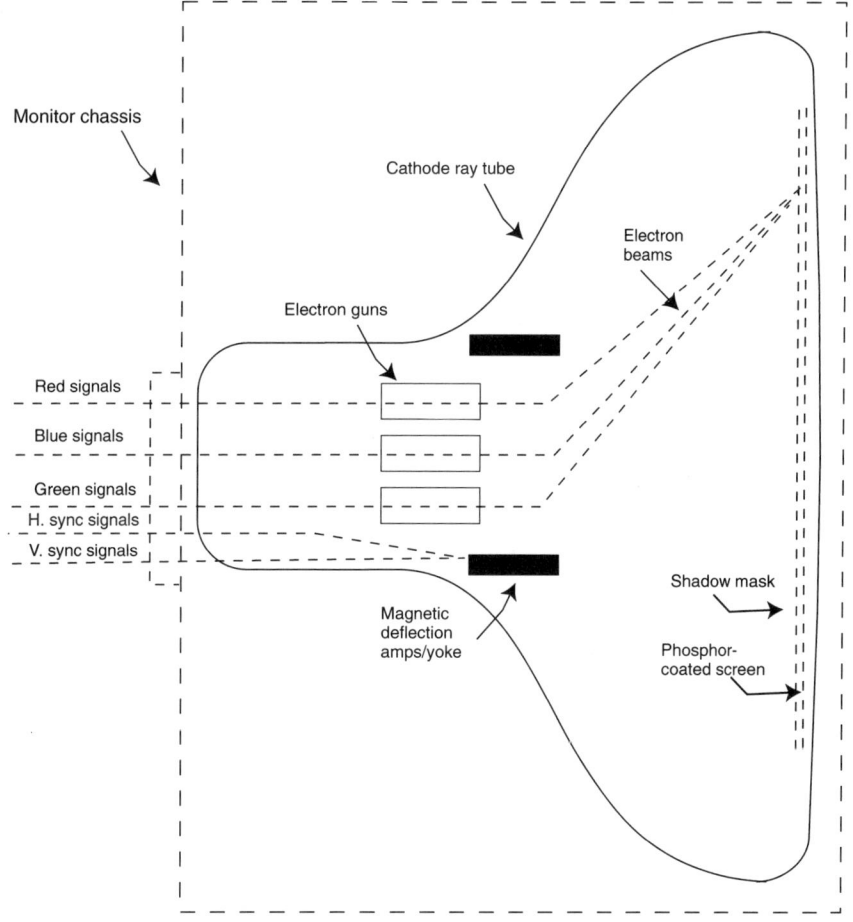

Figure 5.2. A simplified model of video-display design.

The screen is coated in stripes of phosphor material ("phosphor" is roughly defined as a material that glows when energized by electrons). Each stripe glows a different color—red, green, or blue—when energized. The stripes may be oriented vertically (as in Sony's Trinitron) or quasi-horizontally (where the three colors are arranged in a triangle). In the quasi-horizontal orientation, the left end of the stripe is higher than the right end.

The shadow mask, next to the phosphor-coated screen, keeps the red, green, and blue electron beams precisely on target within their respective color stripes on the screen. Depending on the nature of the monitor's technology, the shadow mask may have vertical slots, circular holes, elliptical holes, and so on.

The electron guns are a combination of connected high-voltage cathodes (which emit electrons) and anodes. The electron beams are also called "cathode rays," which is why monitors have historically been called "cathode ray tubes" (CRTs). In fact, a part of the monitor is actually called the cathode ray tube (on a TV, it's called the "picture tube"). The cathode ray tube is made of thick glass, and the pressure within it is less than atmospheric (that is, it's under vacuum).

If you wish to do further research on monitor design, check any elementary radio and television electronics textbook or manual.

Video Frame and Synchronization

In the three previous sections, we discussed how display signals are generated and sent to the monitor, and how electrons are emitted from guns and then impact on a phosphor-coated screen to create a display image. In this section we discuss the movement of the electron beams across and down the screen itself.

CHAPTER 5: CONFIGURING THE VIDEO

The entire display image, from the top left dot to the bottom right dot and including all of the lines in between, is called a "frame." (When we discuss the concept of interlacing, you will see how a frame is also considered to be composed of two "fields.") To create a frame, the electron beams are first aimed at the top left corner of the screen (as seen by the system user). This is called "beginning a frame." The deflection yoke then causes the beams to traverse horizontally from left to right straight across the screen, creating a "scan line." For most of the travel across the screen, the electron beams hit and activate tiny phosphor dots (because the phosphor material coats the screen in very narrow stripes, according to the colors they will produce when hit), causing them to light up. Figure 5.3 illustrates how a frame is created.

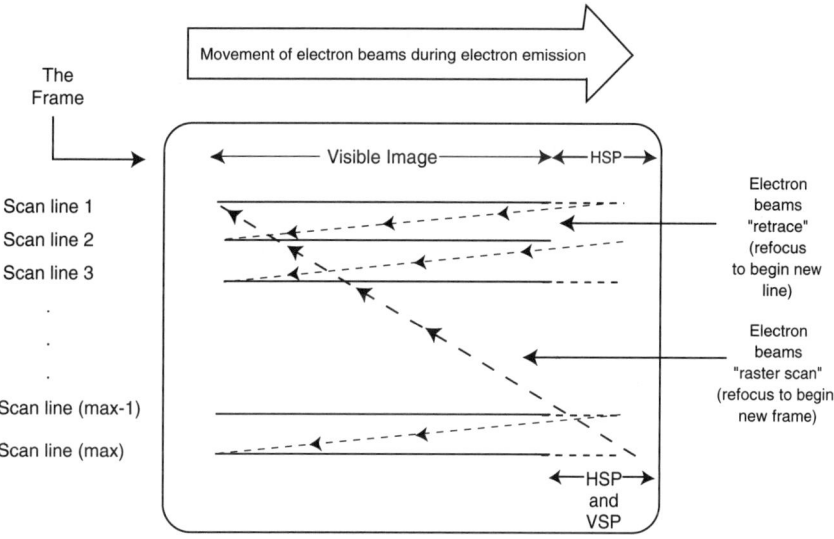

Figure 5.3. Creating a frame.

The signals (analog voltages) received at the electron guns also determine the intensity of the light emitted by the phosphors. After a beam leaves a phosphor, the phosphor continues to glow very briefly. The ability of a phosphor to continue to glow after electron impact is called its "persistence." (The phosphors would eventually fade but they are re-energized on the next return sweep of the beams—but we're getting ahead of ourselves a little.) If the phosphor persistence is too long, you will see ghost images on the screen because previous images will not have faded sufficiently before the phosphors are re-energized. If persistence is too short, the screen will be perceived to flicker, that is, to brighten during electron impact, darken immediately, brighten significantly during the next electron impact, then darken, and so on. Screen flicker is not only annoying, but can cause severe discomfort.

Near the end of each horizontal scan line, the beams from the electron guns are actually shut off very briefly just before a "horizontal synchronization pulse" (HSP) is received by the deflection yoke from the video adapter. The guns are then retraced back to the left edge of the screen, except that the deflection yoke alters the angle of the guns so that when electron-beam emission is resumed, the beams will now focus on the next lower line of the display (when we discuss interlacing, you will see the exception to this rule).

The rate of the sweeping motion of the electron beams from left to right, line by line, is called the "horizontal synchronization frequency," the "horizontal scan frequency" (HSF), or the "line rate," and it's measured in kilohertz (thousand cycles per second, or KHz; 1 Hz = one cycle per second). In other words, the horizontal scan frequency is the number of times per second that the monitor's electron guns can write a horizontal scan line. The actual calculation is the number of lines drawn per screen by the number of screens drawn per second. Customarily, HSFs are in the 30 to 70 KHz range.

The electron beams will continue to traverse from left to right across the display, and then be returned to the left side of the next lower line, until they reach the bottom line of the display. Once again, they will travel horizontally until they approach the right side. However, near the end of the very last line, the deflection yoke will receive a

CHAPTER 5: CONFIGURING THE VIDEO

slightly different signal, a vertical synchronization pulse (VSP), from the video adapter. The VSP will tell it to shut off the electron beams and, this time, focus the guns back at the left side of the display's first line. Thus, the beams end the frame, and then raster scan (that is, travel back to the upper left corner) to begin a new frame.

The number of times per second that the electron beams move from the top left dot of the frame to the bottom right dot is called the "vertical synchronization frequency" or "vertical scan frequency" (VSF). The VSF is also measured in hertz (Hz), and the customary range is from 50 to 100 Hz, although the lowest can be 40 Hz and the highest over 160 Hz.

The VSF is also called the "vertical refresh rate," or simply, "refresh rate." Remember the previous mention of refresh rate. We often generalize and say that a screen is refreshed about 60 times a second. Thus, the basic meaning of all these vertical sync or refresh terms is simply the number of times the electron beams redraw the display on the screen.

You may notice that if the refresh rate drops below 50 Hz, screen flicker may result, due to the lack of sufficient phosphor persistence. As mentioned earlier, screen flicker should be avoided because it can cause discomfort to the user.

Let's quickly review video frame and synchronization basics: HSFs are in the 30 to 70 KHz range, while VSFs are in the 40 to 160 Hz range. For every VSP (once per frame), the beams have to experience many hundreds, or even thousands, of HSPs (once per line). VSFs and HSFs are critical in designing the amplifiers used by the magnetic deflection yoke.

Another definition worth mentioning: The time it takes to stabilize and sync the vertical and horizontal movements is also referred to as "sync pulsing." In the next section, we again describe raster scanning, but we explore the actual time taken and where the pulses travel.

No doubt you've noticed that these terms and specifications can be easily confused. Take the time to understand them and their potential impacts on the configuration of your video display. The Linux-provided ability to specify and modify can be a great boon to optimizing your equipment. However, misunderstanding and misusing the concepts can lead to frustration and, occasionally, destruction of your equipment.

How HSPs and VSPs Are Related

In the previous section, we illustrated a fairly typical raster scan of the visual image on a monitor screen. We mentioned that horizontal sync pulses (HSPs) occur at the end of each line and that vertical sync pulses (VSPs) occur at the end of each frame.

Figure 5.4 shows two diagrams, each consisting of basic voltage versus time graphs for video signals and synchronization pulses. The diagrams are typical monitor timing charts provided by manufacturers. The graphs in the figure are from a TTX CPS-1760 17-inch monitor at 800 x 600 resolution. Note that the timing numbers change for different resolutions.

Horizontal Signals

Note that in the horizontal signals diagram in Figure 5.4, time is measured in microseconds (millionths of a second). Now look at the left side of the horizontal synchronization signals graph, which shows the synchronization signals that travel from the video adapter to the magnetic deflection amplifiers in the monitor along the dedicated horizontal signals line. The first event is a 2-microsecond HSP, which has occurred at the right end of a horizontal scan line. Note that the HSP signal appears to be negative with respect to the normal synchronization signal, which is the specification for this monitor at this resolution. When a multiple-frequency monitor like this one detects this signal orientation, and then reads the orientation (positive or negative) and duration of the vertical synchronization signal, it is tipped off as to what resolution and frequencies to expect.

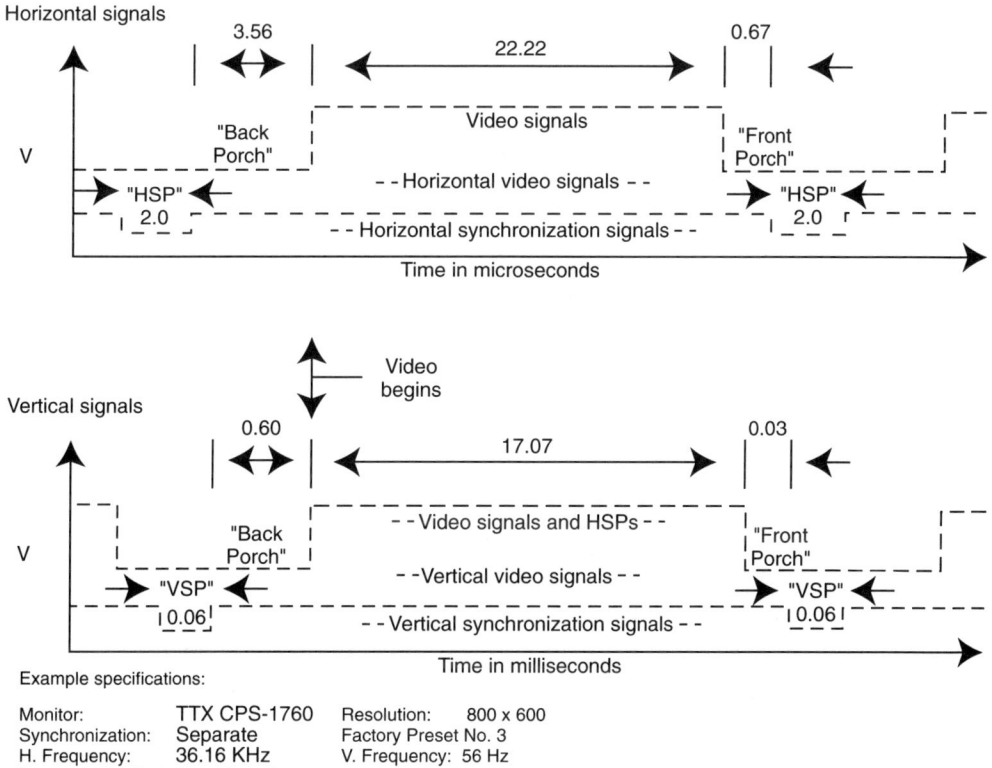

Figure 5.4. Voltage versus time graphs for video signals and synchronization pulses. (Diagrams are not to scale.)

Looking at the video signals graph immediately above that point, you see that the next event is a 3.56-microsecond back porch, which is the travel time for the electron beams to go from the right side of one line to the left side of the next lower line, and during which you see that the electron guns are turned off. Immediately after that back porch period, the electron beams are activated as analog video signals and are sent from the video adapter to the electron guns through the dedicated red, green, and blue signal lines. For 800 x 600 resolution, the video signals (which are really three sinusoidal, or wavy, signals but are simplified as one flat voltage for these timing charts) are sent for 22.22 microseconds, after which the electron guns are deactivated for a 0.67-microsecond front porch period. At the end of the front-porch period, you glance down again at the horizontal signals graph and see that another HSP comes through, which ends the scan line and begins the cycle anew.

You can see that for the total 22.22 microseconds during which the image data were sent, there has been an overhead of 6.23 microseconds of other signal activity. So each scan line took 28.45 microseconds.

Vertical Signals

In the vertical signals diagram, note first that time here is measured in milliseconds (thousandths of a second), not microseconds. A millisecond is equal to 1000 microseconds. Now let's start at the left side of the vertical synchronization graph, which shows the synchronization signals that travel from the video adapter to deflection amplifiers in the monitor, along their own dedicated vertical synchronization line. Here you see that the first event is a 0.06-millisecond VSP, which is the signal received at the bottom of a frame. Looking at the video signals graph immediately above the VSP, you see a 0.60-millisecond back porch, which is the travel time for the electron beams to go from the bottom right corner of the frame to the top left corner, and during which the electron beams are deactivated. Immediately after that back porch period, the electron beams are reactivated at a time that coincides exactly with the activation on the first horizontal scan line. Following along the video signals and HSP's portion of the vertical video signals, you see that, for the next 17.07 milliseconds, all the horizontal scan lines are drawn on the screen. If you divide 17.07 milliseconds by the total 28.45 microseconds per scan line, you'll get exactly 600 scan lines, which is an exact match for the

800 x 600 resolution specification. After the video signals and HSP period, there is an additional 0.03-millisecond front-porch period during which the electron beams are deactivated as a prelude to the next VSP, which will begin the cycle anew.

Note that there is overhead in the vertical signal cycle, just as there was for the horizontal signal cycle. This time, the vertical overhead is 0.69 milliseconds versus the 17.07 milliseconds of scan lines. The overhead is roughly equal to scanning an additional 23 or so lines (that is, an additional 4%, roughly), which is why it's often called "overscan." We mentioned before that the Video Electronics Standards Association (VESA) recommends that you always add 4% to 5% to any line-rate calculation because of the overscan sync signal. Overscan is mentioned again in the next section on monitor capabilities.

Earlier we discussed resolution, color depth, and video memory. Now that we have discussed horizontal and vertical synchronization, let's have a brief look at how the video configuration file *XF86Config* stores resolution information in modelines. The following is a typical modeline:

```
Modeline "800x600" 69.65 800 864 928 1088 600 604 610
    640 -HSync -VSync
```

The numbers and other codes in the above modeline are described in Table 5-3.

Table 5-3: Modeline Numbers and Codes

Number/Code	Description
800 x 600	Resolution
69.65	Dot Clock Frequency, in MHz
800	Pixel count at the end of the visible part of the horizontal scan line and the beginning of the HSP's front porch

Continued

Table 5-3: Modeline Numbers and Codes (continued)

Number/Code	Description
864	Pixel count at the end of the front porch and the beginning of the HSP itself
928	Pixel count at the end of the HSP and the beginning of the HSP's back porch
1088	Pixel count at the end of the back porch
600	Line count at the bottom of the visible part of the screen and the beginning of the VSP's front porch
604	Line count at the end of this front porch and the beginning of the VSP itself
610	Line count at the end of the VSP and the beginning of the VSP's back porch
640	Line count at the end of the VSP's back porch
-HSync	HSP will be a negative polarity with respect to its normal voltage level
-VSync	VSP will be a negative polarity with respect to its normal voltage level

Despite what we discussed regarding timing charts for monitors, you can see that the *XF86Config* file stores video-mode timing information according to a pixel and line convention. Note that all horizontal scan-line numbers are divisible by 8, indicating the discrete bytes of information. The vertical numbers need not be divisible by 8, because all the lines are already broken into bytes. In addition, the file treats the beginning of the visible display as zero for all counting.

Modes can be specified in a multiline format. The following is equivalent to the earlier modeline example:

```
#    Mode "800x600"
#       DotClock   69.65
#       Htimings   800 864 928 1088
#       Vtimings   600 604 610 640
#       Flags      "-HSync" "-VSync"
#    EndMode
```

Monitor Performance and Capabilities

Earlier we discussed the image-data transfer rates required for certain color depths and display resolutions, followed by the basic operations of a monitor. The impression we may have left with you thus far is that your monitor can always handle anything you send to it, assuming that you have sufficient video-adapter hardware. This impression may or may not be accurate. This issue is a bit tricky. There are several factors that can affect a monitor's performance and capabilities:

▲ Monitor age

▲ Bandwidth

▲ Vertical frequency

▲ Horizontal frequency

▲ Dot pitch

Let's consider each point individually.

Monitor Age

If the monitor is a new multiple-frequency device, then it may be capable of handling anything you send to it, especially if the video-adapter hardware and computer system predate it by a year or so. If you're trying to make use of an older and therefore less expensive monitor, however, then you should get a handle on what you *want* the monitor to do for you versus what it *can* do for you. It could become a performance bottleneck or, worse, a bit of a bomb (literally).

Bandwidth

A monitor's bandwidth is a measure of its capability to accommodate the information sent to it. If the monitor is a new model, it may reflect the modern manufacturer's expectations: namely, that video-adapter hardware will continue to become more powerful (that is, capable of sending more information via the DCF, or dot clock frequency), so monitors should be manufactured to anticipate DCF increases. That's why some systems people say, "Don't worry, it's a new monitor, so the DCF probably won't tax the monitor's bandwidth."

As we said earlier, though, if the monitor is older—perhaps a fixed-frequency color model, but with a large screen size that could be potentially beneficial to your operations—then you have to determine its capabilities as best you can.

In this book, we call the bandwidth output from the video adapter the "DCF," and the bandwidth capability of the monitor the "bandwidth." Both are measured in MHz. The higher the DCF, the more information being transmitted to the monitor in the form of refreshes per second, resolution, color depth, and line rates. The higher the bandwidth, the higher the monitor's capabilities to cope with the DCF being sent to it.

If you do not know the dot clock frequency of your video-adapter hardware, the `XF86Free - X Server` might be able to help. Try running the `startx` script, and then exit and read the output. Even if it fails, it should give you some useful information in the standard error returned. Example output from the script follows:

CHAPTER 5: CONFIGURING THE VIDEO

```
[root@hostname /home]# cat versa-video
(--) SVGA: CHIPS: probed memory clock of 31499 KHz
(--) SVGA: chipset: ct65550
(--) SVGA: videoram: 2048k
(**) SVGA: Using 16 bpp, Depth 16, Color weight: 565
(--) SVGA: Maximum allowed dot-clock: 44.098 MHz
(**) SVGA: Mode "800x600": mode clock = 40.000
(--) SVGA: Virtual resolution set to 800x600
(--) SVGA: SpeedUp code selection modified because virtualX != 1024
(--) SVGA: CHIPS: 1098752 bytes off-screen memory available
(--) SVGA: CHIPS: SpeedUps selected (Flags=0xF)
(--) SVGA: CHIPS: Memory mapped I/O selected
(--) SVGA: Using XAA (XFree86 Acceleration Architecture)
(--) SVGA: XAA: Solid filled rectangles
(--) SVGA: XAA: Screen-to-screen copy
(--) SVGA: XAA: 8x8 pattern fill
(--) SVGA: XAA: 8x8 color expand pattern fill
(--) SVGA: XAA: CPU to screen color expansion (bitmap, TE/NonTE
    imagetext, TE/NonTE polytext)
(--) SVGA: XAA: Using 6 128x128 areas for pixmap caching
(--) SVGA: XAA: Caching tiles and stipples
(--) SVGA: XAA: Horizontal and vertical lines and segments
waiting for X server to shut down
(**) Supplied
(--) Probed
```

Thus, we have a maximum allowed dot clock of 44.098 MHz. You will not be asked for this information by Xconfigurator, but it is still good to know. Remember, though, that a monitor must exceed the 44.098 MHz number, because it will have to cope with retrace and overscan signals.

If you do not know the bandwidth of your monitor, consult Table 5-4, which indicates the bandwidth that a monitor must have to cope with the respective image-data transfer rates, plus retrace and overscan.

Table 5-4: Monitor Bandwidth Requirements

Reso-lution	Color depth = 8 bit Refresh rate			Color depth = 16 bit Refresh rate			Color depth = 24 bit Refresh rate			Color depth = 32 bit Refresh rate		
	50 Hz	60 Hz	75 Hz	50 Hz	60 Hz	75 Hz	50 Hz	60 Hz	75 Hz	50 Hz	60 Hz	75 Hz
640 x 480	20.1	24.1	30.1	40.1	48.15	60.2	60.2	72.2	90.3	80.3	96.3	120
800 x 600	31.4	37.6	47	62.7	75.24	94.1	94.1	113	141	125	150	188
1024 x 768	51.4	61.6	77	103	123.3	154	154	185	231	205	247	308
1152 x 864	65	78	97.5	130	156	195	195	234	293	260	312	390
1280 x 1024	85.6	103	128	171	205.5	257	257	308	385	342	411	514
1600 x 1200	125	150	188	251	301	376	376	451	564	502	602	752

Note: Monitor bandwidth is measured in MHz; estimates assume 30% extra for overscan and retrace.

To calculate these estimates, we used the following formula:

```
Bandwidth = line width x number of lines x
    color depth x refresh rate x 1.045 x 1.25
```

where *line width* is pixels per line, *number of lines* is lines per screen, *color depth* is bytes per pixel, *refresh rate* is screen redraws per second, 1.045 is the number used to compensate for overscan, and 1.25 is the number used to compensate for retrace.

For example, you would calculate the bandwidth necessary for 800 x 600 resolution, 24-bit color depth, and 60 Hz refresh rate as follows:

```
800 x 600 x 3 x 60 x 1.045 x 1.25 = 113 MHz
```

Vertical Frequency

The maximum vertical frequency (or maximum refresh rate) sent from the video-adapter hardware to a monitor must not exceed the monitor's own vertical frequency.

Horizontal Frequency

The line rate received by a monitor must not exceed the monitor's horizontal frequency. Remember, the line rate is equal to the number of HSPs which, in turn, is equal to the number of lines in a desired or given resolution, such as the 600 in 800 x 600, multiplied by the desired or given refresh rate, such as the 60 in 60 Hz.

In previous sections we mentioned that VESA, for the sake of safety, recommends that we always add 4% to 5% to any line-rate calculation because of the overscan sync signal. This is less likely to be a problem at present ("present" being defined as from the year 2000 and into the future), because there are more and more multiple-frequency monitors being used. Multiple-frequency monitors can detect the incoming horizontal and vertical frequencies and adjust their circuits so that their amplifiers can handle them. The ways in which these monitors work are summarized as follows:

▲ Through combinations of synchronization polarities. For example, the original VGA cards used this technique to tell the monitors whether to create screens with 350, 400, or 480 lines.

▲ Through the length of the vertical synchronization pulse. The monitors measure the length of the pulse, convert it to the equivalent number of scan lines that could be drawn during that time, and then calculate the corresponding screen length and width.

▲ By using their own memory and microprocessors to analyze synchronization signals (frequencies, timings, and the like), and then calculating and setting up the corresponding resolutions.

Dot Pitch

Monitor size is a very important issue. You should ask yourself, How big a monitor do I need for the resolution(s) I want? Unfortunately, this is not a simple question to answer. It depends on the monitor capabilities we have described thus far, plus a grasp of the dot pitch of the monitor. What's the dot pitch? It's the distance on your monitor, generally measured in millimeters, between successive phosphor stripes of the same color. Dot pitches generally vary between 0.31 and 0.22 millimeters.

On any screen, the dot pitch is fairly easy to see if you use a magnifying glass. On something like a Sony Trinitron screen, it's especially easy to see, because the phosphor stripes are vertical and the shadow mask (which Sony calls its "aperture grille") is slotted so that it doesn't cover too much of the phosphor area. That said, we don't suggest you measure the dot-pitch distance yourself. It's a lot easier to consult the manufacturer's specifications in the monitor's manual.

You may notice that on older color screens, seeing the dot pitch is a little more difficult, because the shadow masks have holes, as opposed to slots, and the color stripes are slanted left to right. The dot pitch, therefore, is not measured strictly vertically or horizontally, but inclined. Your manufacturer's manual will specify horizontal and vertical measurements, but to get the true measurements, the manufacturer will have applied a correction factor to account for the angle of the phosphor stripes. While we do not recommend trying to measure the dot pitch on your monitor, it is worthwhile to take a close look to determine the type of monitor screen technology you have.

CHAPTER 5: CONFIGURING THE VIDEO

Why is dot pitch important? If you are using a monitor of a certain size and you want to obtain a certain resolution on it, then you have to be confident that your monitor's dot pitch is small enough to show that resolution. Let's use the Sony CPD-120VS 15-inch monitor as an example. The manual says that it has an aperture grille (that is, dot) pitch of 0.25 mm. Assume that you want to display the monitor's maximum-rated resolution of 1280 dots x 1024 lines. First, how big is that image? A dot pitch of 0.25 mm means that there are 101.6 dots per inch. If you divide the 1280 dots by 101.6 dots per inch, you get an image with a width of 12.6 inches (or 320 mm). Consulting the manual, we see that the screen is only 11.2 inches (284 mm) wide. If the math does not work out perfectly, read on.

At this juncture, all we can say is you have to *be careful of what you read in the manufacturer's manual.* It turns out that the dot pitch is correct. Because the manual was written for both the Sony CPD-120VS (15-inch) monitor and the CPD-220VS (17-inch) monitor, the maximum resolution for the 17-inch monitor is reproduced in the 15-inch monitor manual. The viewable image size is included for both monitors, however, and the 15-inch monitor has a viewable image size of 284 mm. If you divide 284 mm by the dot pitch of 0.25 mm, you get a pixel width of 1136. Thus, the maximum *standard* size you can display is likely 1024 x 768.

Conversely, if you had been adamant about displaying 1280 x 1024 on a 15-inch monitor, you would have needed a dot pitch of 0.22 mm (284 mm/1280 pixels = 0.22 mm). This is impossible for the Sony CPD-120VS, unfortunately, and we couldn't find a single product in the monitor specification database that could do it either. The 0.22-mm dot pitch seems only to be available in 21-inch monitors, as of this writing. The 17-inch Sony CPD-220VS monitor might actually handle 1280 x 1024, although the extra time required for horizontal sync pulses and their respective front porch and back porch timings may not allow it. Again, you have to be careful with what the manufacturer tells you in manuals. Your best bet is to check out the resolutions that can be displayed on a monitor prior to making your purchase. In the meantime, Table 5-5 may be useful. Remember, the numbers in the table may not be totally reliable, because there may be additional signal overhead (overscan and retrace) or monitor limitations (dot pitch) that prevent these resolutions from being achieved.

There are several good sources of additional information available, but none of them provides a comprehensive review of all aspects of image generation and display. One interesting source is Eric S. Raymond's XFree86 Video Timings HOWTO, wherein he describes how to customize the size of a monitor's display. It's handy and provides a detailed illustration of why the various screen widths must accommodate the actual size of information bytes. He also presents a small table of minimum bandwidth requirements per resolution.

Table 5-5: Maximum Resolution for Standard-Size Monitors

Nominal monitor size	Maximum resolution
14"	800 x 600
15"	1024 x 768; 800 x 600
17"	1024 x 768
19"	1280 x 1024
21"	1600 x 1200

You can also access *http://ms.ha.md.us/~hawks/hardware/monitor.html* for a table of monitor specifications, including bandwidth, dot pitch, display size, synchronization specifications, and so forth. The only handy column missing in that table is nominal resolution size, but this can be quickly calculated from the given display sizes. Another reasonably good discussion of video generation and display is connected to the table. Other good Internet sites are *http://www.pctechguide.com* and *http://www.zdnet.com*.

Chapter 5: Configuring the Video

The Bottom Line: Match Video Hardware and Monitor to Your Expectations

If you have expectations of your monitor (for example, you may want a huge monitor to handle high resolutions so that you can have several programs open and displayed at once), then try to ensure that your video hardware can process and send the necessary information to your monitor. You will need adequate video memory and a bus sufficient to handle the flow. Then, on the other end, try to ensure that your monitor will indeed handle everything that the video hardware sends. Its bandwidth has to be high enough to handle all the information, and its sync frequencies high enough to handle line rates and refresh rates. It would be a shame to have video hardware that is capable but too powerful for the monitor, or a monitor that is choked back to lower resolutions because the video adapter cannot send it enough information quickly enough. Most importantly, it would be a shame if you can't do the work you need to do without spending more money.

In the next section, we discuss a technique for getting high resolution out of a lower-end monitor, that is, a monitor with bandwidth that may not permit it to support high DCFs.

Interlacing

In previous sections, we examined how the electron beams create frames line by line. Some video adapters, however, send their information such that the beams scan only every second line on one pass (that is, the odd-numbered lines), and then go back for a second pass, where they scan the lines they missed on the first pass (that is, the even-numbered lines). This process is called "interlacing" and each full pass is called a "field." Thus, two complete fields will equal one frame. Figure 5.5 illustrates this technique.

Why would you want to use interlacing? Interlacing can help you by reducing the amount of new information carried with each refresh, while maintaining high resolution. This would be useful, for example, if your monitor had only a certain bandwidth capacity or if your video-adapter hardware had a limited DCF, such that you could not view a high resolution without flicker or without getting an error message announcing that you had exceeded bandwidth limits. Thus, using an interlaced mode might allow you to display higher resolutions without overtaxing the video adapter or monitor amplifiers, or you might obtain a higher resolution on a monitor that has less expensive components (amplifiers, processors, and the like) or is based on an older technology.

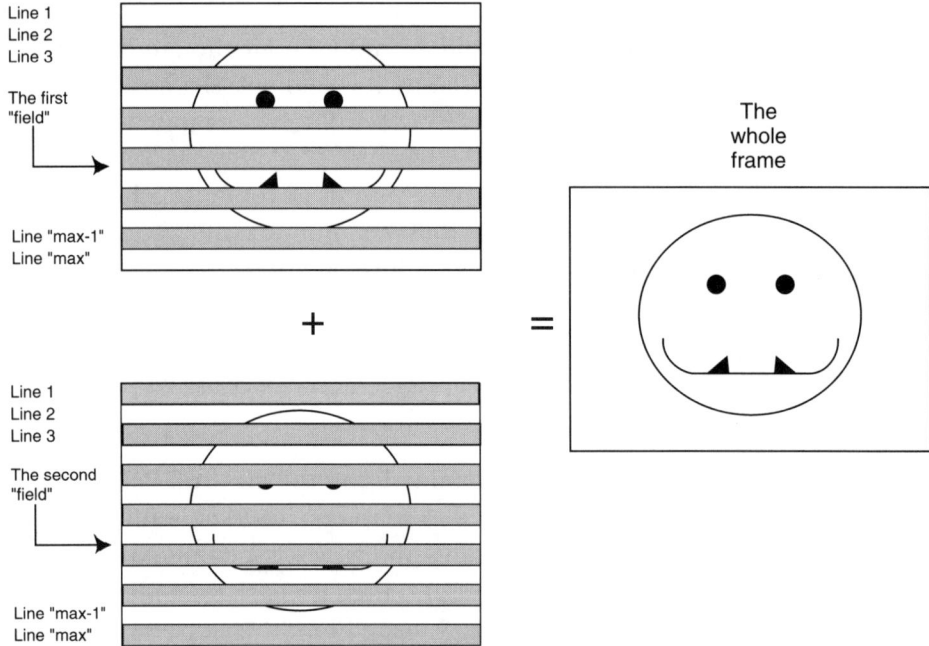

Figure 5.5. A simplified illustration of interlacing.

Let's assume that you are trying to display a high resolution with respectable color depth, but your resulting refresh rate comes out

Chapter 5: Configuring the Video

low, say at 45 Hz. The flicker could be most annoying. In this case, you could try an interlaced 90 Hz refresh rate. You get the same line rate, equivalent to 45 Hz noninterlaced, but you (probably) get no flicker.

Some guidelines for using interlacing follow:

- ▲ Don't use interlacing, except maybe for comparison purposes, when your hardware can easily handle noninterlaced displays.

- ▲ Use interlacing where, in noninterlaced mode, you are too close to or over the limits of your video hardware, monitor DCF, or bandwidth, such as in the example cited above.

- ▲ Try to use interlacing at high resolutions, so that the alternately refreshed lines are still close together.

- ▲ Don't expect miracles from interlacing. If you are exceeding your bandwidth and horizontal-scan rates (such as in the example) and pushing the limits of your vertical-scan rates, then interlacing can't help you. It can't get you past the vertical-scan limits either. Your vertical-scan rates have to be only 50% to 70% of the maximum. Even then, interlacing may not be a sure thing, but it's worth a try.

- ▲ If you are custom designing the modelines, remember to use an odd number of vertical lines.

What are the drawbacks of interlacing? If the refresh rate turns out to be too low, such that the persistence of the phosphors is too short, then the dots may noticeably lose their luminosity between electron-gun passes and give you that annoying (in extreme cases, physically sickening) flickering. In addition, interlaced displays are always going to be inferior when compared with noninterlaced displays at the same vertical-scan frequency (but don't forget that they'll use only half the bandwidth and half the horizontal-scan rate). Anyway, flicker and the loss of quality are the most common disadvantages cited against interlacing, and they are often cited by those who do not understand the whys and wherefores of this technique.

However, if the phosphor dots have enough persistence and the vertical-scan frequency is still high enough, interlacing may be a good alternative in some situations, especially if you are constrained by video bandwidth, DCF, or horizontal bandwidth. Remember that television has used interlacing since its inception. That's why picture quality (resolution) has always been acceptable based on fairly affordable components with a reasonably long useful life.

Note also that noninterlaced line-by-line horizontal scanning was developed later than TV technology. You can probably guess, now, what high-definition TV (also called "high-density TV" or "HDTV") is, and why it is so much more expensive than conventional TV.

Just keep in mind that it's always a better idea to use noninterlaced modes at any given resolution than to use interlaced modes, as long as you can establish refresh rates that are high enough to prevent flickering.

Getting Ready for Video Configuration

Having gotten some basic concepts under our belts, we'll gather the information we need to configure the video. The bandwidth and frequency ranges of the monitor, and the frequency of the video-adapter's dot clock, will determine the ultimate resolution for your display. Then, in the upcoming exercise, we'll fine-tune the video-adapter device driver, which is something we cannot do with most software programs. As you work through the exercise, we remind you of the sections to review for concepts and definitions, and to help you make various selections.

The XF86Config File: Heart of the X Server

We constantly hear references to "the X server," but we rarely hear a definition of it. Although many refer to individual video-driver packages as the X servers—and we don't really blame them, since those video-driver and attribute files are those we focus on most—the (total) X server is actually the X11R6 software you find installed in the /usr/X11R6 directory, in conjunction with other software and configuration files. The version of X11R6 ported for use on Intel-based systems is XFree86, and that's why we refer to your particular X system as XFree86.

Thus, when XFree86 is invoked, it reads the *XF86Config* file and follows the instructions found therein. *XF86Config* is a text file found in either the */etc/X11* or */usr/X11R6/lib/X11* directories (one will link to the other). *XF86Config* is composed of the following sections:

▲ Files (file path names)

▲ Module (dynamic module loading)

▲ ServerFlags (server flags)

▲ Keyboard (keyboard configuration)

▲ Pointer (pointer configuration)

▲ Monitor (monitor description)

▲ Device (graphics device description)

▲ Screen (screen configuration)

▲ XInput (extended input devices configuration)

Without going into great detail, let us simply say that the information in these sections informs XFree86 how and when to:

▲ Control and route input to the correct Linux clients

- Perform basic graphic operations on one or more screens
- Control video-related attributes such as color, color depth, screen size, and so on, and other attributes we discuss later in this chapter
- Allow or prohibit simultaneous access by other hosts or clients
- Load special software modules
- Control special system actions (such as core dumps and input device configurations)

We say that *XF86Config* is the heart of the X Window System, because it is the most fundamental and important configuration file. Once properly configured, the *XF86Config* file is unique to the system it was configured on. Unless others have absolutely identical systems (including mice, keyboards, video adapters, monitors, and so on), one system's *XF86Config* file should not be copied and passed around. In fact, doing so could be dangerous. It's always best to configure *XF86Config* for each individual system.

XF86Config can be configured in the following ways:

- *By hand*. Constructing *XF86Config* from scratch is for seasoned veterans only. We do not recommend using this method when there are others available.
- *Using* `Xconfigurator`. As we have already mentioned, this is the method we use in this chapter. It's Red Hat's graphical user interface method and runs from the command line.
- *Using* `xf86config`. This is the text-mode program available with `XFree86`. It also runs from the command line.
- *Using* `XF86Setup`, which works like a graphical utility. Once you are more familiar with video configuration, you may want to use this. On the surface, it can be quite handy. However, if you run into trouble, getting out of trouble is not very straightforward.

CHAPTER 5: CONFIGURING THE VIDEO

▲ *Using xvidtune,* another graphical utility that is usually employed after a basic X video configuration has been developed using one of the other utilities.

For further information regarding *XF86Config*, please refer to its man pages and other information sources. Meanwhile, before we discuss Xconfigurator, we have to gather some information about the video hardware on the system for which you are going to configure X. Use the SuperProbe utility to collect this information.

Using SuperProbe to Obtain Video Information

Before using the Xconfigurator program, we have to make sure we know the chipset and amount of video memory on the video card. It is also helpful if we know beforehand the video server we want to run.

SuperProbe can help. To use SuperProbe, though, you have to log in or su to be a root user (or, if you prefer, a superuser). Appearing below is the SuperProbe syntax and an example of what Super-Probe returns to the display.

[user1@hostname user1]$ su -
Password: ********

In its response, SuperProbe will present you with a warning such as the following:

```
WARNING - THIS SOFTWARE COULD HANG YOUR MACHINE.
          READ THE SuperProbe.1 MANUAL PAGE BEFORE
          RUNNING THIS PROGRAM.
          INTERRUPT WITHIN FIVE SECONDS TO ABORT!
```

Chances are that your system will not be hung by SuperProbe, but it is worthwhile to read its man page beforehand.

SuperProbe Options

The following are some options you can use with `SuperProbe`. The verbose option can be especially instructive.

- `-verbose`. `SuperProbe` will be verbose and provide lots of information as it does its work.

- `-no_dac`. Skip probing for the RAMDAC type when an (S)VGA is identified. Remember that "RAMDAC" is yet another term for the video processors (that is, chipsets, accelerators, and so on).

- `-no_mem`. Skip probing for the amount of installed video memory.

- `-info`. `SuperProbe` will print out a listing of all the video hardware that it knows how to identify.

There are other options listed in the `man` pages.

SuperProbe Results

`SuperProbe`'s output is reproduced below. It has identified the exact chip on the video adapter. In addition, `SuperProbe` is suggesting that the SVGA X Server (in the `First video` field) is compatible for the identified chipset. We know that it is the video adapter that generates the signals to set the monitor's display. It is important that we get the correct video adapter (or chipset) here, so that all signals sent to the display (that is, to the monitor) are correct.

```
# SuperProbe

First video: Super-VGA
   Chipset: Chips & Tech F65550 (Port Probed)
   Memory: 2048 Kbytes
   RAMDAC: Generic 8-bit pseudo-color DAC
           (with 6-bit wide lookup tables (or in 6-bit
           mode))
```

At this point, you could invoke `Xconfigurator` to begin the video setup, but first we'll use it to create an *XF86Config* file.

Using Xconfigurator to Create the Basic XF86Config File

Now that we know how `SuperProbe` can help us obtain some basic video information, we can focus on the main video configuration program, `Xconfigurator`. `Xconfigurator` is the program used here to create your basic *XF86Config* file. That file will be based on menu selections made after the `Xconfigurator` program has been invoked. As with `SuperProbe`, you have to be a root user (superuser) to use `Xconfigurator`.

The syntax for the `Xconfigurator` program is:

> **[root@*hostname* /root]#** Xconfigurator [*-options*]

The *XF86Config* file typically resides in */usr/X11R6/lib/X11*. A sample *XF86Config* file is supplied with `XFree86`. That sample file is configured for a standard VGA card and a monitor with 640 x 480 resolution, which may not be optimal.

You can either take the sample *XF86Config* as a base and edit it for your configuration or let the `Xconfigurator` program produce a customized base *XF86Config* file for your configuration, and then fine-tune it. We will not go into a detailed description of the configuration process, but you can review */usr/X11R6/lib/X11/doc/README.Config* for a detailed description of the configuration process.

For accelerated servers (including accelerated drivers in the SVGA server), there are many chipset and card-specific options and settings. The `Xconfigurator` program does not know about these, and on certain configurations, these settings must be specified. For further details on specific systems, refer to the server man pages and chipset-specific READMEs.

Exercise

This 19-step exercise focuses on configuring your video system by modifying the *XF86Config* file using the `Xconfigurator` program. This exercise may or may not be straightforward, depending on how much you learn about your video system and how well you communicate that information to the `Xconfigurator` program. You start out using `SuperProbe` to get information about the video hardware. Then, armed with that information, you will invoke `Xconfigurator`.

Meanwhile, we comment on each `Xconfigurator` screen. The screens you encounter, and the order in which you encounter them, will depend on the choices you make along the way. If you are doing this exercise with another system at another time in another place, you may not see all of the dialog boxes shown here. We hope, but can't guarantee, that you will not see dialog boxes that are not shown here.

We will assign just one exercise step to each screen, after presenting information, comments, or warnings.

Step 1. Invoking SuperProbe

Remember, to use `SuperProbe`, you must log in as root. If you are already logged in as an ordinary user, use the `su` command to become a root user. Then use the `SuperProbe` syntax, this time without any additional arguments or options.

```
$ su -
Password: ********
# SuperProbe
```

Record the following video information that `SuperProbe` returned to your screen:

- ▲ Video server
- ▲ Chipset
- ▲ Memory
- ▲ RAMDAC

Step 2. Invoking Xconfigurator

As a root user, invoke `Xconfigurator`.

```
# Xconfigurator
```

Follow and respond to the dialog boxes, beginning with the next step.

Step 3. Initiating Xconfiguration

This next dialog box tells you where the *XF86Config* file is located: usually it is found in the */etc/X11* directory; the *XF86Config* file found in the */usr/X11R6/lib/X11* directory is linked to */etc/X11*. This dialog box also warns you to know the chipset and amount of video memory.

You will likely have the name of the chipset if you have used `Super-Probe`. Other ways to find it involve removing the cover of your computer and examining the mainboard (if the video hardware is located there) or the video-adapter card (if you are using one and so bypassing the mainboard). The chipset type may be printed on the chipset itself. The advice in this screen regarding accelerated servers is well worth heeding.

```
                                   Welcome
This program will create a basic XF86Config file based on menu selections you make.

The XF86Config file usually resides in /usr/X11R6/lib/X11 or /etc/X11. A sample
XF86Config file is supplied with XFree86; it is configured for a standard VGA card and
monitor with 640 x 480 resolution.

You can either take the sample XF86Config file as a base and edit it for your configuration,
or let this program produce a base XF86Config file for your configuration and
fine-tune it. Refer to /usr/X11R6/lib/X11/doc/README.Config for a detailed overview
of the configuration process.

For accelerated servers (including accelerated drivers in the SVGA server), there are
many chipset and card-specific options and settings. This program does not know about
these. On some of these configurations some of these settings must be specified. Refer
to the server man pages and chipset-specific README'S.

Before continuing with this program, make sure you know the chipset and amount of
video memory on your video card. SuperProbe can help with this. It is also helpful if
you know what server you want to run.

                       OK                          Cancel
```

Locating the video memory also may mean you have to remove the cover of the computer to determine if you have a video-adapter card or if the video hardware is on the mainboard. You may even have to check the system's BIOS (that is, enter the CMOS Setup Utility and examine the Chipset Features Setup, when it boots up). Needless to say, manuals and Internet Web sites can prove invaluable in collecting this information. In the meantime, acknowledge the message and continue with the configuration by using your <Tab> key to select OK, and then pressing <Enter>.

Step 4. Probing for Hardware

After you initiate the program, Xconfigurator will automatically probe to identify your video hardware. As you can see in the figure here, it found video-adapter hardware requiring a ViRGE/DX or ViRGE/GX driver. It also suggests using the SVGA video server.

Chapter 5: Configuring the Video

```
                    PCI Probe

    PCI probing found a:

        PCI Entry  :    ViRGE/DX or /GX
        X Server   :    SVGA

                        OK
```

Has the probe found something in your system? If it has, accept what it found and continue by selecting OK, and then pressing <Enter> to continue to the next screen.

Sometimes the probe is unsuccessful, and the program asks for your help. The next section shows you the screen it presents in this event.

Step 5. Specifying Video-Adapter Hardware

If you do not encounter this next dialog box, you can move on to Step 6.

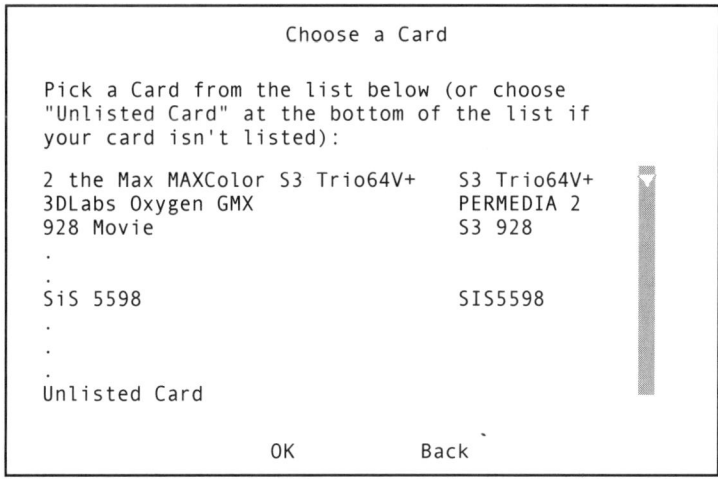

As we said earlier, `Xconfigurator` will automatically probe for your video hardware as soon as you initiate the program. However, there are times when it cannot easily determine your hardware. Then it will present this dialog box. Note how it presents the name of the card in the left column and the respective driver in the right column. You can select your card (that is, your video-adapter hardware, which may or may not be a separate card). Select your video hardware or, if it's not listed, select `Unlisted Card`, and then <Tab> to OK and press <Enter>.

Step 6. Specifying Monitor Type

At this point, you are asked for the type of monitor attached to your system. The Linux database contains specifications for over 200 monitors, so it's often worthwhile to scroll down through the listing presented to you. If you find your monitor listed there, you won't have to do a lot of the manual configuration. However, if you scroll down the list and you don't find your particular monitor, you must select `Custom`.

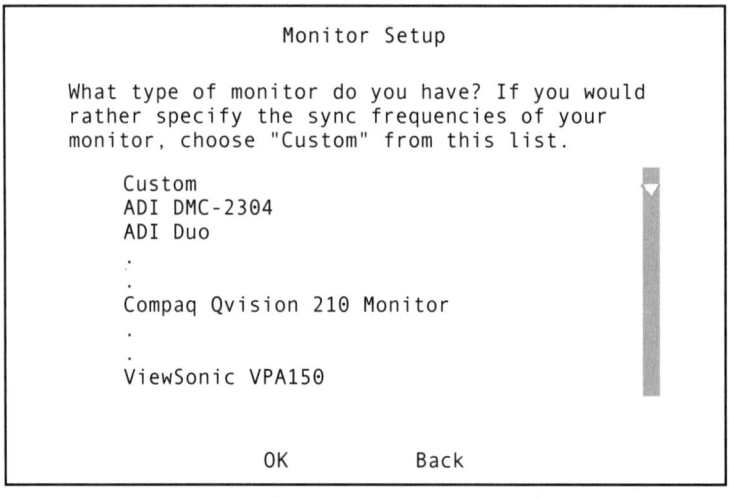

Select the name of the monitor attached to your system, <Tab> your way to OK, and press <Enter>. If your monitor is not listed, select Custom, and then <Tab> to OK and press <Enter>.

Step 7. Custom Monitor Setup

We assume that you selected Custom in the previous step. If you were able to find your monitor name in the list and selected it, then you won't see this next dialog box. You can move along to Step 10, "Setting Resolution and Color Depth."

This screen serves as a gentle warning that the configuration may now take on a slightly more complex aspect.

```
                    Custom Monitor Setup

  Now we want to set the specifications of the monitor.
  The critical parameters are the vertical refresh
  rate, which is the rate at which the whole screen is
  refreshed, and most importantly the horizontal sync
  rate, which is the rate at which the scan lines are
  displayed.

  The valid range for horizontal sync and vertical
  sync should be documented in the manual of your
  monitor. If in doubt, check the monitor database
  /usr/X11R6/lib/X11/doc/Monitors to see if your
  monitor is there.

                    OK            Back
```

The program suggests that you check the */usr/X11R6/lib/X11/doc/Monitors* file to see if your monitor and its specifications are listed there. Doing that might mean exiting Xconfigurator at this point. Assume for this exercise that you checked the file and your Brand X monitor isn't listed there. Well, you still have your owner's manual.

It's very important from this point on to understand and to enter the monitor's specifications correctly, because they represent the actual physical capabilities, and not the desired capabilities, of the monitor that you are trying to use.

Do you recognize the terms that Xconfigurator mentions here? You see that some are identical to names of specifications we discussed earlier in this chapter or to those you find in your monitor's manual, and that some *resemble* those we've discussed. Recall that we mentioned that the same concepts can have several names.

Let's look at the terms in this dialog box individually. Note that you have seen "vertical refresh rate" before, but that we called it simply "refresh rate." Did you remember that it is also called "vertical sync" (that is, vertical synchronization frequency)? Is the program tricky or inconsistent here? We won't venture any comment, because all of these terms are legitimate. But you can see why sometimes it's not always advisable to just push ahead and start making selections and plugging in numbers.

Meanwhile, your response to this advisory screen is to select OK and press <Enter>. The message is there to remind you to be ready for the rest of the process.

Step 8. Indicating Horizontal-Sync Range

This dialog box can be slightly misleading. The listing presented shows resolutions (with the industry-standard name first, followed by the corresponding line-width by screen-height specification) at certain refresh rates. Yet the text refers to horizontal-synchronization ranges. The horizontal-synchronization rates, which we have more commonly called the "line rates," are calculated for each choice by multiplying the refresh rate (that is, the Hz number) by the screen height (that is, by the second number of the resolution, such as the "480" in 640 x 480) and adding another 4% to 5% of that number for

Chapter 5: Configuring the Video

overscan. You then compare the final calculated number to the monitor's specified horizontal frequency. If it's less than the horizontal frequency, then you can be confident in choosing it.

```
              Custom Monitor Setup (continued)

    You must indicate the horizontal sync range of your
    monitor. You can either select one of the predefined
    ranges below that correspond to industry-standard
    monitor types, or give a specific range. It is VERY
    IMPORTANT that you do not specify a monitor type
    with a horizontal sync range that is beyond the
    capabilities of your monitor. If in doubt, choose a
    conservative setting.
         Standard VGA, 640 x 480 @ 60 Hz
         Super VGA, 800 x 600 @ 56 Hz
         8514 Compatible, 1024 x 768 @ 87 Hz interlaced
         .
         .
         .
         Monitor that can do 1600 x 1200 @ 76 Hz

                  OK            Back
```

If you don't know what the horizontal sync range is, return to Table 5-5 in the section titled "Monitor Performance and Capabilities" and consider using the resolution that corresponds to the monitor on your system. If you are not confident of that choice either, then your choice should reflect a very low line rate or a very early video standard, such as VGA or SVGA. Later, at some point when, perhaps, you better understand your monitor, you can reinvoke Xconfigurator and make a different choice.

For now, just select the (conservative) Super VGA standard setting, Super VGA, 640 x 480 @ 56 Hz, and then <Tab> to OK and press <Enter>.

We are confident that your adapter hardware is more high-powered than this, and we know that your monitor can handle more than this, too. But we will stick with this selection for now and make some modifications later (see Step 13, "If the Results of Xconfigurator Probe Are Not Successful"), after another probe has taken place.

Step 9. Indicating Vertical-Sync Range

This dialog box, the last one in the custom setup process, addresses the vertical-synchronization range of the monitor. The listing includes several ranges found in many popular multiple-frequency monitors. Remember, the range you select should be exactly or very close to what your monitor manual lists, and at any rate, must exceed the refresh rate you chose in the previous (horizontal-sync range) dialog box. If there has been a mix-up, <Tab> to Back and press <Enter>. You will return to the screen in the previous step to check or change your selection there.

```
                    Custom Monitor Setup (continued)

       You must indicate the vertical sync range of your
       monitor. You can either select one of the predefined
       ranges below that correspond to industry-standard
       monitor types, or give a specific range. For
       interlaced modes, the number that counts is the
       high one (e.g. 87 Hz rather than 43 Hz)

                              50 - 70
                              50 - 90
                              50 - 100
                              40 - 150

                     OK                  Back
```

Note the sentence, "For interlaced modes, the number that counts is the high one...." If you have selected interlaced 87 Hz in the previous screen, then the high number in the range selected here must exceed 87 Hz. Choosing 50-70 here would cause problems later. Select the appropriate vertical-synchronization range, and then `<Tab>` to `OK` and press `<Enter>`.

Step 10. Setting Resolution and Color Depth

Here `Xconfigurator` will again probe the system and will, as it says, set up the default resolution and color depth. Chances are that it will come up with a very conservative default resolution setting. Don't worry. You can deal with that later.

```
                    Screen Configuration

 Xconfigurator now needs to set up the default
 resolution and color depth. Most modern PCI video
 cards can be probed, and Xconfigurator will
 automatically determine the best video mode/color
 depth possible for your system. There is a chance,
 however, this could lock up your system. If you would
 prefer to give the required information instead of
 having it probed, answer "Don't Probe" to the
 following question.

         Don't Probe                      Probe
```

Choose `Probe` here and press `<Enter>`. If you don't like the results, you can always back out and choose `Don't Probe`.

Step 11. Probing with X Server Configured Thus Far

Here the program checks with you again before it probes the video hardware and sets up default resolution and color-depth settings. The feedback will be reported in a style similar to what we show in the next step.

```
            Probing to Begin

Xconfigurator will now run the X server you selected
to probe various information about your video card.
It is normal for the screen to blink several times.

                     OK
```

Press OK and press <Enter> to continue with the probe and setup.

Step 12. If Results of Xconfigurator Probe Are Successful

Assume that you know, from your manual and Table 5-5 found earlier in the chapter, that your display can handle 800 x 600. Choose Let Me Choose to do a little better than this conservative default setup and press <Enter>. This way, you won't have to edit the */etc/X11/ XF86Config* file later.

```
               Probing finished

Xconfigurator has successfully probed your video
card. The default video mode will be:

       Color Depth:   8 bits per pixel
       Resolution: 640 x 480

Do you want to accept this setting, or select
for yourself?

   Use Default        Let Me Choose          Back
```

CHAPTER 5: CONFIGURING THE VIDEO

Step 13. If Results of Xconfigurator Probe Are *Not* Successful

Sometimes the probe is not successful, no matter how conservative the default settings are. In this example, where `Xconfigurator` still cannot determine all the attributes of the video hardware (chances are the video hardware is on a board, not a card), it fails to discover how much video memory is there. That would certainly affect the resolution settings, and then it might affect calculated DCFs and comparisons to the monitor's bandwidth.

```
                         X Error

      There was an error detecting the video ram on your
      card. You should try configuring the video card
      manually.
                           OK
```

Let's take a few steps back:

a. Press OK to take you back to the Custom Monitor Setup (Continued) screen in step 9, "Indicating Vertical-Sync Range."

b. At this point, choose Back to return to the Custom Monitor Setup (Continued) screen in Step 8, "Indicating Horizontal-Sync Range."

c. At that point, choose Back again to return to the initial Custom Monitor Setup screen.

d. Choose Back again. You will see a screen that resembles the reproduction below.

149

CUSTOMIZING AND UPGRADING LINUX

```
                    Video Memory
        How much video memory do you have?
                    256 kb
                    512 kb
                    1 mb
                    2 mb
                    4 mb
                    8 mb or more

                 OK          Back
```

e. Select the amount of video memory affiliated with your video hardware (mainboard or adapter card), and then <Tab> to OK and press <Enter>.

When you back up several steps like this, you will be taken through a few extra dialog boxes—the ones that you would have encountered had you chosen Don't Probe at Step 10, "Setting Resolution and Color Depth."

Next, you will encounter the following dialog box.

```
                Clockchip Configuration
         Which Clockchip do you have?

                No Clockchip Setting (recommended)
                Chrontel 9381
                    .
                    .
                    .
                TI 3026 (autodetected)
                IBM RGB 51x/52x (autodetected)

                 OK          Back
```

For new technology, we agree with the program that No Clockchip Setting be selected. However, with older video hardware, especially

Chapter 5: Configuring the Video

those with video hardware on the mainboard, it may be worthwhile to go through the dozen or so choices.

However, for purposes of this exercise, select `No Clockchip Setting`, and then `<Tab>` to `OK` and press `<Enter>`.

Step 14. Selecting Video Modes

The number of video modes presented here by `Xconfigurator` depends on the video memory you have specified or that it has probed. Do you remember what the 8-bit, 16-bit, and 24-bit designations mean? They mean 1 byte per pixel, 2 bytes per pixel, and 3 bytes per pixel, respectively. The more memory, the more resolution choices `Xconfigurator` will present. The following screen reflects approximately 2 MB of video memory. This is also a point at which you can consult Table 5-1 in the section titled "Video Adapter Memory." The table roughly agrees with `Xconfigurator`.

```
                       Select Video Modes

          Select the video modes you would like to use.
          8 bit modes allow for 256 colors, 16 bit modes
          allow for 64k colors, and 24 bit modes allow
          for true color. Performance will be slower,
          however, the higher you go. You should select
          at least one of the elements below.

             8 bit:            16 bit:            24 bit:
            [ ] 640  x 480    [ ] 640  x 480    [ ] 640 x 480
            [ ] 800  x 600    [ ] 800  x 600    [ ] 800 x 600
            [ ] 1024 x 768    [ ] 1024 x 768
            [ ] 1152 x 864    [ ] 1152 x 864
            [ ] 1280 x 1024

                        OK              Back
```

If you have a really good monitor, you won't be able to take advantage of its capabilities unless you have adequate memory on the video card.

Likewise, if you have a video adapter with, say, a healthy 8 MB of video memory and a monitor that is only capable of 800 x 600, you will not get the higher resolutions you want.

At this point, select the appropriate resolution(s), taking into consideration video memory, nominal monitor size, and so on. You can select more than one. The X Window System will start with the very first selection, but you can switch on the fly while in X. Later you can modify your *XF86Config* file to comment out the resolutions you decide not to use.

Make your selections by using <Tab> to get to the appropriate column, and then use your down arrow key. Make the selection by pressing the <Space> bar. When all your selections have been made, <Tab> to the OK and press <Enter>.

Step 15. Starting X to Test the Chosen Configuration

If you have a good configuration, you will be very near the end of your Xconfigurator trials and tribulations. If not, then you'll get another chance to modify the *XF86Config* file and reset your video parameters.

```
                         Starting X

          Xconfigurator will now start X to test your
          configuration.


                    OK              Skip
```

To be able to select OK or Skip at this stage is convenient. If you're not sure you've configured your video correctly, then you can at least finish the basic Linux installation and plan to reconfigure your video (to use the X Window System and its assorted window managers)

CHAPTER 5: CONFIGURING THE VIDEO

later. However, be confident and select `OK`, and then press `<Enter>` to see if you've been successful.

Step 16. Can You See This Message?

```
            Can you see this message?
          Automatic time out 10 seconds.

                    Yes      No
```

If the text is in the middle of a cyan- or teal-colored display, then you can continue by selecting `Yes`. If the text appears in a ridiculous location on the display or at the bottom of the screen, then you should probably select `No` and pass through the configuration again. If you do nothing, or if you can't see the message, the program will time out shortly and automatically return you to the configuration process.

Let's assume that the box is nicely placed in the middle of the cyan-colored screen. Select `Yes` using your mouse, and you will be presented with the next dialog box.

Step 17. Do You Want to Automatically Boot into X?

At this point, we suggest that `No` be selected. If you select `Yes` and all goes well, then certainly Linux will start the X Window System immediately and will automatically boot into the X Window System every time the system is booted. If you select `Yes` and all does *not* go well, then you may be stuck with a frozen screen in a bad configuration, requiring you to take remedial action or worse.

```
Xconfigurator can set up your computer to
automatically start X upon booting. Would you like
X to automatically start when you reboot?

                    Yes      No
```

Thus, until you are satisfied with your video configuration, click No at this juncture. You can always configure X to start at bootup at some later date.

Step 18. Reviewing the Configuration File Prior to Running X

```
Configuration file has been written. Take a look at
it before running 'startx'. Note that the XF86Config
file must be in one of the directories searched by
the server (e.g. /etc/X11/XF86Conig) in order to be
used. Within the server press "Ctrl Alt +"
simultaneously to cycle through resolutions. Pressing
Ctrl Alt and backspace simultaneously immediately
exits the server (use if the monitor does not sync
for a particular mode).

For further configuration refer to
/usr/X11R6/lib/x11/doc/README.Config.

                        OK
```

This may or may not be the look of success. It's a good sign, however, that you're getting closer. The Xconfigurator program suggests here that you take a good look at the *XF86Config* before running startx, which is a very good idea. If the newly configured file works at all at this point, consider making a copy of it and storing it somewhere for safekeeping. The instructions regarding cycling through the various modes are only valid if you previously chose more than one valid video mode.

Chapter 5: Configuring the Video

The program also suggests that you exit the X Server by using the <Ctrl>-<Alt>-<Backspace> keys. This is a rather brutal approach and should be avoided. There are other proper log-out procedures available from within X. However, if something goes wrong while in X, that key sequence can be necessary.

Finally, the program suggests you refer to the *README.Config* file. While not a bad idea, the text in that file pales in comparison to the information that can be found at the Internet site *http://metalab.unc .edu/LDP/HOWTO/XFree86-video-Timings-HOWTO.html*.

At this point, click OK and you will be transported out of Xconfigurator and back to the Linux command-line prompt. You are now free to check your handiwork by typing startx at the command prompt and pressing <Enter>. Once you are in X, you can cycle through your video modes by using the <Ctrl>-<Alt>-<+> or <Ctrl>-<Alt>-<-> key sequences.

At some point in your configuration process, you may be presented with the dialog box discussed in the next step. We certainly hope not, but let's have a look at it anyway.

Step 19. Problems with Chosen Configuration

It's always a disappointment to encounter this next dialog box. You don't usually encounter it at the end of the Xconfigurator process; it often happens several steps earlier.

```
                         Error

    There is a problem with your X configuration. You
    may go back and modify your configuration or
    exit now.

              Back              Quit
```

This message usually means that your chosen video modes disagree with your video-memory specification, but it can also mean several other things. Your best bet is to go back and try again, because sometimes the problem may only be an oversight in a recent dialog box. Sometimes, however, the best strategy is to simply quit and restart, perhaps after checking your hardware via `SuperProbe` or another utility.

Quiz

1. What does the common notation 640 x 480 indicate?
2. What two descriptors indicate a monitor's display capacity or "video mode".
3. What file contains information on video and monitor configuration, and how can it be modified?
4. What utility can be used to gather information about the system video, such as chipset and memory?
5. If the `Xconfigurator` PCI probe fails to find the video hardware, what two things will need to be specified, either manually or from a provided list?
6. If Custom Monitor Setup is required, what is the horizontal-sync range, and how is it calculated?
7. What is interlacing, and what are its advantages and disadvantages?
8. If Custom Monitor Setup is required and interlacing is used, which range number should be referenced in selecting the vertical-sync range for the monitor?
9. If Custom Monitor Setup is required and probing Screen Configuration returns a lower value than your monitor supports, what should you do?

See Appendix B for answers.

Chapter 6

Configuring Printers

IN THIS CHAPTER WE ILLUSTRATE HOW TO CONFIGURE both a local and a remote printer. The example printer is an HP LaserJet 6 in both scenarios. In the local printer scenario, the printer is attached directly to the computer with a parallel cable. In the remote scenario, the printer is on a network.

The following instructions include use of `printtool`, a printer-configuration utility with a graphical user interface. Consequently, it is assumed that you have worked through the video configuration chapter (Chapter 5) and have a graphical interface available.

Basic Commands and Utilities

The three main print mechanisms are `lpr` (line printer command), `lpd` (line printer spooler daemon), and *printcap* (printer capability database). Lpr uses `lpd` to print files. When `lpd` receives a request to print a file, it checks the *printcap* file to determine if the printer requested is local or remote. If the request is for a local printer, `lpd` checks for the printer and, if it exists, sends the print job to the printer. If the request is for a remote printer, `lpd` opens a connection to the remote system and transfers both the control file and data file to the queue on the remote system. Lpd services must be installed on a computer before printing will function. You can ensure all the components for `lpd` are in place by querying Linux as follows:

```
# rpm -qal | grep -i lpd
/usr/include/sp/include/Lpd.h
/usr/include/sp/lib/LpdEntityRef.h
/usr/share/apps/ktop/pics/lpd.xpm
/usr/share/icons/kpilpdb.xpm
/etc/rc.d/init.d/lpd
/etc/rc.d/rc0.d/K60lpd
/etc/rc.d/rc1.d/K60lpd
/etc/rc.d/rc2.d/K60lpd
/etc/rc.d/rc3.d/K60lpd
/etc/rc.d/rc5.d/K60lpd
/etc/rc.d/rc6.d/K60lpd
/usr/man/man8/lpd.8.gz
/usr/sbin/lpd
/var/spool/lpd
/usr/man/it/man8/lpd.8.gz
```

When the `lpd` daemon is active, use the `lpc`, `lpq`, and `lpr` commands to manage printing. Lpc is the line printer control program. Among other things, you can use `lpc` to enable or disable a print queue, get the status of a print queue, and restart a daemon should one daemon die leaving print jobs unprocessed in a queue. Check the `lpc` man pages for the full capabilities of this utility.

Lpq is the spool queue examination program. Use it to display and manipulate jobs in a print queue:

```
lpq -l -Pprinter
```

To remove a print job from the queue, use `lpq` as follows:

```
lpq -Pprinter job_ID
```

Chapter 6: Configuring Printers

The `lpr` command is a companion to the `lpd` daemon, and it must be available; the two work together. It is possible to send a job directly to the printer without using `lpr`, but this is not recommended in a shared printing environment. Print jobs will collide when multiple users send print jobs to the same printer at the same time. The `lpr` command solves this issue by sending signals to the `lpd` daemon. All `lpr` processes communicate with a single `lpd` daemon that organizes the requests. When a job is printed with `lpr`, `lpr` assembles the data and copies it to the spooling queue. At the same time `lpr` adds to the assembly any instructions passed as arguments to the `lpr` command, which are set using environment variables and system print defaults. In addition, the `lpr` command uses the *printcap* file to determine the printer geometry (that is, the printer-to–print queue relationship) and additional instructions that may be in the *printcap* file, such as remote printing sets.

You can ensure that `lpr` is available by querying for the `lpr` package as seen in the following example:

```
# rpm -q lpr
lpr-0.50-4
```

The `lpr` command will create two files in the spool directory: a control file with the name `cfid_number`, which contains information about the print job, and the owner's name; and a data file, `dfid_number`, which is the file to be printed.

The *printcap* file is the configuration file for `lpd`. The *printcap* file is located in the */etc* directory, where all daemon configuration files reside. If you use the `printtool` utility, you will not have to configure any of these services manually, including the *printcap* file, but it is a good idea to know what this file does and how to interpret it. A typical *printcap* file is reproduced below.

```
# cat /etc/printcap
# /etc/printcap
```

```
# Please don't edit this file directly unless you
  know what you are doing!
# Be warned that the control-panel printtool requires
  a very strict format!
# Look at the printcap(5) man page for more info.
#
# This file can be edited with the printtool in the
  control-panel.

##PRINTTOOL3## LOCAL ljet4 300x300 letter {}
    LaserJet4 Default 1
lp:\
        :sd=/var/spool/lpd/lp:\
        :mx#0:\
        :sh:\
        :lp=/dev/lp0:\
        :if=/var/spool/lpd/lp/filter:
```

Each entry in the *printcap* file represents a printer on the system. This file is constructed for you by the `printtool` utility. (For further information on the *printcap* file, refer to system administration documents.) There are two things about the *printcap* file that you must keep in mind. First, if you make changes to this file either directly or using the edit function in the `printtool` utility, you have to refresh the `lpd` daemon. Second, there must be a corresponding entry in either the *hosts.lpd* or *hosts.equiv* file(s) of the target systems for remote printers. The `lpd` daemon will reject a print request from any remote system that is not listed in one of these files. We discuss these files in more detail later in the chapter. The premise here is that if the remote printer is unavailable, the job will remain in the local queue until it receives a signal that the remote queue is available. In addition, the jobs are not removed from the local queue until a signal is received from the remote system that the job is in the remote queue.

CHAPTER 6: CONFIGURING PRINTERS

Configuring Local Printing

To configure a local printer, begin by logging in as a regular user and then switching to root user. Enter `printtool` at the command line. Linux displays an Error screen about `ncpfs` (ncp file system), and it may display an Error screen about SMB. Bypass both and Linux displays the Red Hat Linux Print System Manager dialog box shown in Figure 6.1. Click the `Add` button and you'll see the Add a Printer Entry dialog box.

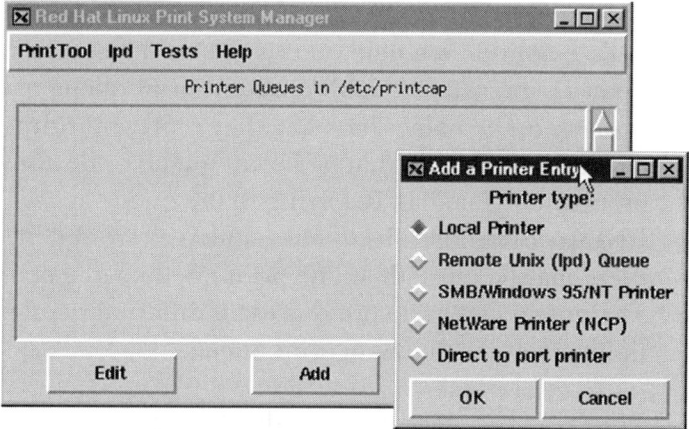

Figure 6.1. Print System Manager and Add a Printer Entry dialog boxes.

Choose `OK`, because we are configuring a local printer. An information screen may appear acknowledging that it successfully detected a parallel port. If a parallel port is not found, you may have to review your hardware configuration for IRQ conflicts or check your CMOS settings. If a parallel port is found, Linux displays the Edit Local Printer Entry dialog box shown in Figure 6.2.

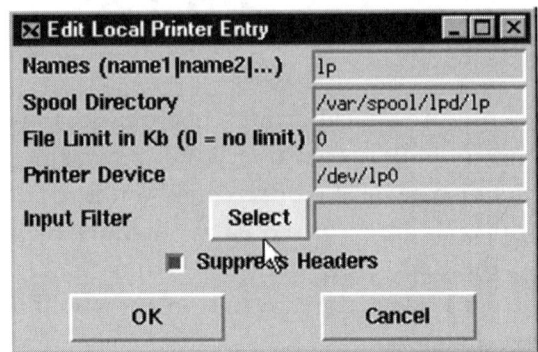

Figure 6.2. Edit Local Printer Entry dialog box.

Let's examine each field on this screen. The entries in the Names (name1|name2|...) field represent print queue names, although as expressed, the names look like they represent printers. Feel free to change the name to that of a print queue or device with which your users will be familiar. Referring to the queue as the printer name is a UNIX convention. The queue name is expressed in multiples because there may be more than one print queue name per physical queue. The queue names do not represent different queues, but rather multiple names for the same print queue.

The Spool Directory is in the */var/spool/lpd/lp* directory by default and, by convention, reflects the name of the print queue. You are allowed only one print queue per spool directory. Do not confuse the fact that you have multiple names for one print queue with the print queue representing one physical location on the hard disk called */var/spool/lpd/qname*. We recommend that you retain the spool directory name, */var/spool/lpd/lp*; it is proper form to keep the name of the spool directory the same as the name of the queue.

Each spool directory contains four files —*eq, errs, lock,* and *status*— with rw-rw-r- permissions. These permissions are important and would cause the print process to fail if they were changed. Utilities such as printtool will take care of this for you, but if you are restoring a system or manually attempting to create a print scenario, this could be an issue. The `lpd` daemon should be configured to start at system boot. This is the default behavior after installation, but you should check it anyway. During the `lpd` start-up process, the *printcap* file is read to identify the sections that apply to any printer attached to the system. The `lpd` daemon also applies any `Input Filter` directives (which we explain in a moment) that have been applied in the configuration.

The number entered in the `File Limit in Kb (0 = no limit)` field represents the size of the print queue. If you have a limited amount of space in the file system or partition containing */var*, then establishing a limit may be a good idea. The default is 0.

The entry in the `Printer Device` field represents the device found during the probe. In Figure 6.2, `/dev/lp0` is the physical device that should not be modified. It represents the parallel port on the system that you plan to use for printing. If you want to print through parallel port 2, then you will have to configure it in the CMOS, attach the printer cable to parallel port 2, and reference the device here as `/dev/lp1`. In other words, the UNIX device `lp0` represents what system administrators typically refer to as `lpt1`, and `lp1` represents what is often referred to as `lpt2`.

Selecting `Input Filter` displays the Configure Filter dialog box shown in Figure 6.3. The choices you make in this dialog box will be part of the configuration for this local printer.

Let's step through the options. First, choose the appropriate printer driver from the `Printer Type` list. Then, choose the appropriate printer resolution and paper size to be used as the default. These features can be adjusted at print time.

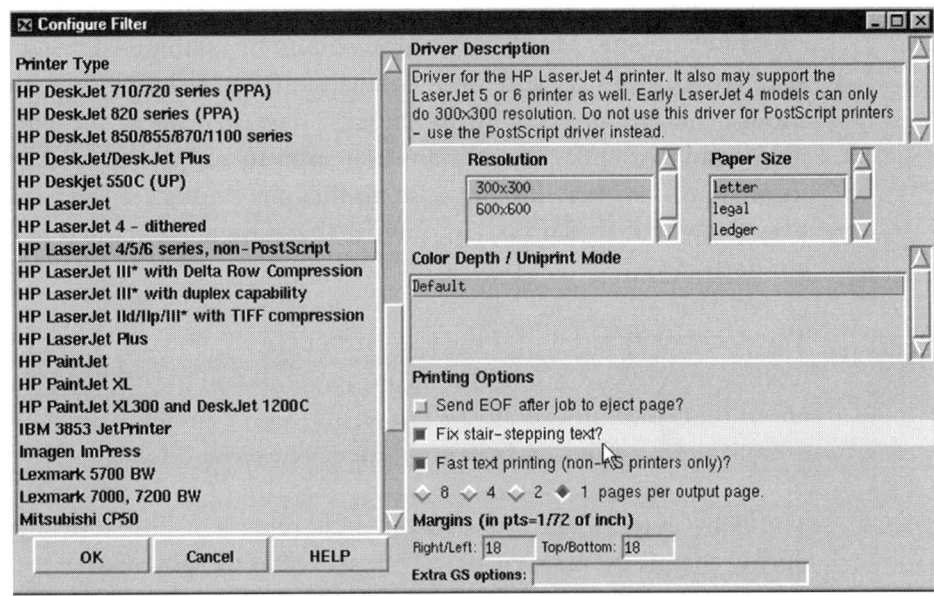

Figure 6.3. Configure Filter dialog box.

Under `Printing Options` you have the following choices:

▲ `Send EOF after job to eject page?` Choose this option to have a blank page printed after each job.

▲ `Fix stair-stepping text?` This option is important when printing across platforms. DOS and Windows files terminate lines with `EOL` (end of line) followed by `<cr>` (carriage return). This causes a stair-step appearance when the text is printed. Choose this option to remove `<cr>`, which will allow the text to print correctly.

▲ `Fast text printing (non-PS printers only)?` If you print a lot of text pages this option can improve performance, because it will print directly without checking for any filtering or sequences. If you leave this option off, an `mpage` procedure is applied. The `mpage` procedure will convert the text file to a PostScript file and then process the file with `ghostscript` (a PostScript interpreter) before printing.

CHAPTER 6: CONFIGURING PRINTERS

- ▲ 8/4/2/1 pages per output page. This is a very useful option that can save paper. What you save in paper, however, you will use in eye strain. Note that you cannot use this with the Fast text printing option we just described, because it uses the mpage procedure to create multiple pages per sheet.

- ▲ Margins (in pts=1/72 of inch). The numbers in the Right/Left and Top/Bottom fields represent your margins. The measurement used is points, not inches.

- ▲ Extra GS options. This option will work only if your printer driver is ghostscript-capable. If it is, you can enter additional ghostscript options here to influence the printing process. The available ghostscript options are documents in the literature that shipped with your printer. Color printers are good candidates for using these features.

After you have made your selections, choose OK twice and you'll be returned to the Red Hat Linux Print System Manager dialog box shown in Figure 6.4.

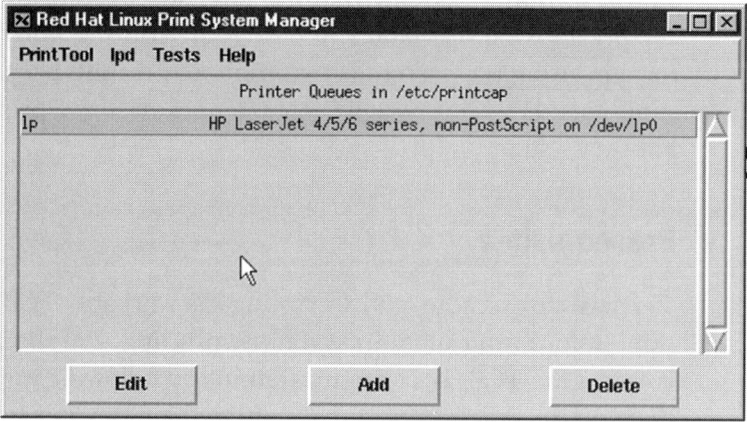

Figure 6.4. Print System Manager dialog box.

167

This dialog box can be recalled at any time to reconfigure a printer or to check your settings by choosing `PrintTool` from the menu. If you change any settings, remember to stop and start the `lpd` daemon using the `lpd` menu option. It's a good idea to test a printer after configuring it. Do this by selecting `Tests` from the menu. If the test works, send a job to the printer.

If you have multiple printers defined here, the first one listed is the default. This means that if no printer is specified when a print command is issued, the first one on this list will be used. To change the default printer, you have to manually modify the */etc/printcap* file. Be careful and make a backup copy of this file before you modify it. This file and the necessary supporting directories are created for you during the configuration process. If you are a printer configuration expert, you can create this file as well as the corresponding directories.

Configuring Remote Printing

In this section we assume that you have successfully worked through the previous exercise and you have local printing working. Setting up local printing is a prerequisite to remote printing because the latter simply sends a print request across a network to be printed on another system.

Prerequisites

The basis for remote UNIX printing is a workable TCP/IP configuration. Before you can address remote printing, you should test and confirm the TCP/IP configuration in the following way. Make sure that you can `ping` from one system to the next. You also have to confirm that the name resolution is working, which means you should be able to `ping` successfully using the host names. In the example

CHAPTER 6: CONFIGURING PRINTERS

here we are using flat TCP/IP host files. The host files on both example systems follow:

```
[root@SIM_SHOP /root]# cat /etc/hosts
127.0.0.1       localhost.localdomain localhost
192.168.6.66 SIM_SHOP    #Local Printer
192.168.6.67 SIM_LAB     #Uses remote printer on SIM_SHOP

[root@SIM_LAB /root]# cat /etc/hosts
127.0.0.1       localhost.localdomain localhost
192.168.6.67 SIM_LAB     #Uses remote printer on SIM_SHOP
192.168.6.66 SIM_SHOP    #Local Printer located here
192.166.6.36 HOSTB
```

The Configuration

Log in to the remote system, which in our case is *SIM_LAB*. Make sure that you are the root user, and then execute the `printtool` utility. Ignore the warning about NetWare printing. The Print System Manager dialog box appears (Figure 6.5).

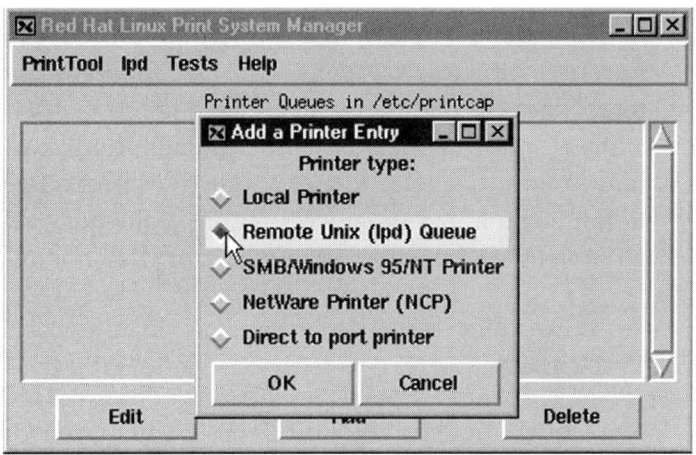

Figure 6.5. Print System Manager and Add a Printer Entry dialog boxes.

169

This time choose the `Remote Unix (lpd) Queue` option. Note the reference to `lpd` in this option. This means that we will be using the `lpd` daemon to facilitate the printing between the two computer systems. The `lpd` daemon in turn has to be configured for authentication. The `lpd` daemon references an authorization file called *hosts.lpd* upon initialization to check to see which remote hosts are authorized to print to the local queue. The only *hosts.lpd* file that needs to be configured is the one on the system with the local printer attached, which is *SIM_SHOP* in the example. This procedure is discussed later in this chapter.

Some system administrators will use the *hosts.equiv* file instead of the *hosts.lpd* file. Only one is necessary. There are two schools of thought on which file to use. The issue is that the *hosts.lpd* file provides specific authorization for the `lpd` daemon only, whereas the *hosts.equiv* file provides general authorization for additional utilities used between systems. Some system administrators do not want to give away the entire system just to facilitate a simple printing function. Others say that they require the *hosts.equiv* for a specific general function anyway and do not want an additional file to maintain.

Because the *hosts.lpd* file is a configuration file for the `lpd` daemon, its source directory is */etc*, as is the case for all daemon configuration files. Note also that the syntax requirements consist only of the IP address or host name. Remember the following rule for configuration files: You cannot refer to an IP address or host name in a configuration file that is not already resolvable to the network via flat host files, NIS (Network Information Service), or DNS (Domain Name System).

```
[root@SIM_SHOP /root]# cat /etc/hosts.lpd
SIM_LAB
```

Some of the fields in the Edit Remote Unix (lpd) Queue Entry dialog box (Figure 6.6) are the same as the ones in the Edit Local Printer

CHAPTER 6: CONFIGURING PRINTERS

Entry dialog box. The entries in these fields will be different, but the behavior may be the same. We note this as we step through each field.

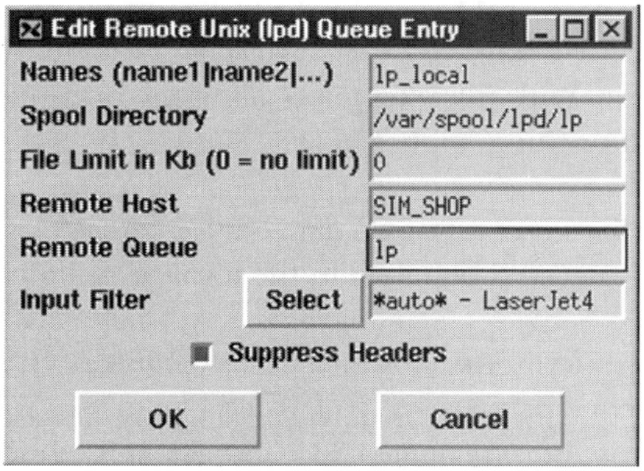

Figure 6.6. Edit Remote Unix (lpd) Queue Entry dialog box.

Let's say that we have two systems—called *SIM_LAB* and *SIM_SHOP*—networked together. We also have a printer connected directly to the *SIM_SHOP* system. Each system has a separate print queue. On *SIM_SHOP*, the print queue is called *lp* while, on *SIM_LAB*, the print queue is called *lp-local*. Users connected to *SIM_SHOP* who want to print documents on the printer connected to *SIM_SHOP* will, naturally, send their print jobs to the *lp* queue. Users connected to *SIM_LAB* who want to print documents on the same printer (that is, the printer connected to *SIM_SHOP*) will send their print jobs to the *lp-local* queue on *SIM_LAB*. Now let's look at the dialog box in Figure 6.6, which appears on the *SIM_LAB* system.

The entry in the Names (name1|name2|...) field will be the name of the queue for the system called *SIM_LAB*. All users who wish to print to the remote printer will send or forward their print jobs directly to this queue. We have called it *lp_local*, meaning local to

171

SIM_LAB. With this exception, all of the previously defined behavior for local printing applies here.

The `Spool Directory` is the corresponding directory for the queue name. We have changed it to reflect the same name as the defined queue. With this exception, all of the previously defined behavior for local printing applies here.

For the `File Limit in Kb (0 = no limit)` field, all of the previously defined behavior in the local printing case is the same here.

The entry in `Remote Host` is the name of the host with the physically attached printer that you would like to use. You can either refer to the remote host by name or IP address. It is mandatory that this host be predefined in the */etc/hosts* file before you can reference it here. This utility will try to resolve the name of this system at this time and will report an error if it is not available. We are using a flat host file here, but it could be defined via NIS or DNS as well.

The `Remote Queue` field should contain the exact name of the queue as it is defined on the remote system. You cannot rename the queue here; it is not an alias. Typically, the jobs forwarded to the above queue on *SIM_LAB* (called *lp_local* by the system users) will be moved from the *lp_local queue* on *SIM_LAB* across the network to the *SIM_SHOP* system and placed in the *SIM_SHOP lp* queue (Figure 6.7). Once the remote job is placed in the *SIM_SHOP lp* queue, it is printed. The `lpd` daemons on both systems maintain the necessary communication between systems to coordinate this effort.

The behavior of the `Input Filter` feature is defined in the same way as for local printing. However, remember that if one queue is essentially passing jobs from one spool queue to another spool queue across the network, these must be identical.

CHAPTER 6: CONFIGURING PRINTERS

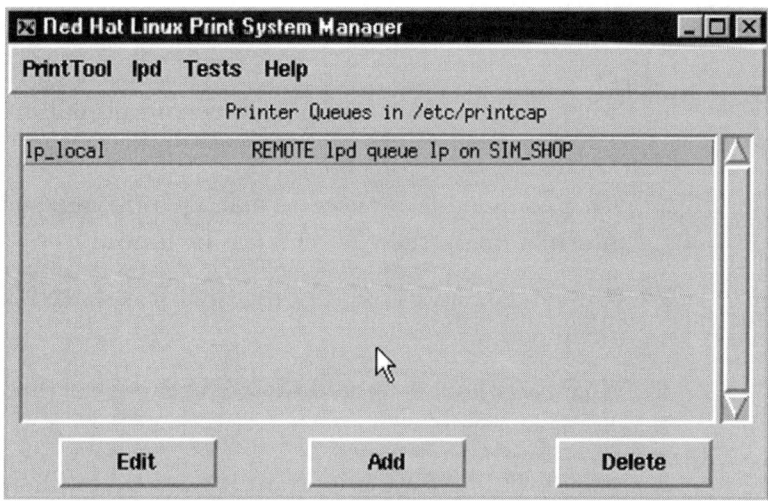

Figure 6.7. Print System Manager dialog box.

Just before you send a test page, check the lpd daemons. The lpd daemons read the configuration information only when they are started or refreshed. We have made some changes to the *hosts.lpd* and *printcap* files; therefore, the lpd daemons have to be refreshed. We recommend that you use the printtool utility to refresh the lpd daemons.

Once all the daemons have been started and refreshed, send a test print page to the remote printer. If the test is performed without a glitch, try to send a job to the printer using the lpr command.

Quiz

1. What are the three main print mechanisms in Linux, and what do they do?
2. What commands are used to manage printing, and where can information on these commands be found?
3. How do `lpr` and `lpd` work together in a shared printing environment?
4. What two files are created by `lpr` in the spool directory, and what do they contain?
5. What two things are important to remember when editing the *printcap* file, either directly or using the `printtool` utility?
6. What is the supplied Red Hat Linux tool for configuring printers?
7. Where is the spool directory located, and how many print queues may reference it?
8. What effect will restricting the permissions on the files in the spool directory have?
9. Why would you want to limit the amount of file space available for printing?
10. What two steps should be performed to test for proper printer configuration?

See Appendix B for answers.

Chapter 7

Adding, Replacing, and Upgrading RPM Packages

THIS CHAPTER IS DEDICATED TO RPM PACKAGES, software packages that can simplify a system professional's work. We begin by defining RPM and RPM packages, and showing you how to manage and query them. We discuss how to determine whether you need to add RPM packages to your system or upgrade the ones already there, and we provide installation and upgrade instructions. We focus on `XFree86` RPM packages as a prime example, because they are most common. Later in the chapter we install `XF86Setup`, a video configuration utility, using RPM packages.

This chapter serves as a precursor to Chapter 8, which covers upgrading the Linux operating system kernel using RPM packages. The principles and techniques covered in this chapter are directly applicable to that chapter. Note that when we use the term "package" in this and later chapters, we are referring to an RPM package.

RPM Definition and Package Management

RPM is an open packaging system that software vendors, developers, and others use to organize and deliver binary, source, configuration, and other files to users, programmers, and administrators. The mechanism this system uses to organize and deliver files is the RPM package. An RPM package typically contains binary, or executable, program files, along with relevant configuration and documentation files, and is used to distribute programs, updates, and upgrades.

The RPM system tracks in the RPM database all packages and associated files installed on a machine with the rpm utility. The rpm utility is a powerful tool you use to install, query, verify, update, erase, and build software packages that conform to a specific RPM format. For example, you could use the rpm utility to query the RPM database to determine if you have a particular package on your system, if it's installed, if it should be upgraded, and so on. The rpm utility is executed with the rpm command, and is available in both GUI and command-line versions.

The RPM database and binary files are built right into a distribution. This is relevant because there are dependencies among the packages themselves. These dependencies result in shared code. For example, in the new 2.2.X Linux kernels, the GNU standard C library is referred to specifically as glibc or libc6 code. All executables for this kernel version have been linked against this library. Therefore, if you attempt to install binary files from a different distribution, chances are that they will not work, at least until you install the libc5 library for backward compatibility.

CHAPTER 7: ADDING, REPLACING, AND UPGRADING RPM PACKAGES

Here is an example of the syntax you can use to install an additional XFree86 RPM package onto your system. The command and its options are explained later in the chapter.

```
rpm -ivh XFree86-76dpi-fonts.rpm
```

Prior to upgrading or installing any RPM package, the rpm man page should be mandatory reading. In particular, be sure that you understand how to uninstall and remove packages using the rpm utility, should the RPM package prove not to be what you need.

RPM Naming Convention

The RPM package-naming convention is the key to package identification.

Each package name consists of *Name-version.arch.rpm*, where *Name-version* is the current release of that package and *arch* is the platform designation, such as Intel. The standard for Intel is *i386*, although some kernel packages may indicate *i586* or *i686* and so on.

```
# ls | less
XFree86-100dpi-fonts-3.3.6-20.i386.rpm
XFree86-3.3.6-20.i386.rpm
XFree86-3DLabs-3.3.6-20.i386.rpm
XFree86-75dpi-fonts-3.3.6-20.i386.rpm
XFree86-8514-3.3.6-20.i386.rpm
   .
   .
   .
```

The packages you install must match the versions of the shared libraries available on that machine. If you try to install an RPM package that does not match the shared libraries, you will see an error on the screen. At this point, you could "force" the install. However, in this case, you must be sure that you are not affecting other RPM packages. Of course, it would be proper form to back up a system first before applying this kind of technique.

SRPM versus RPM

An SRPM file contains the original source used to build the RPM binaries. It is of interest to developers who need to modify and compile RPM packages for their systems. Many programmers will make an SRPM file available to other programmers to facilitate the free software development philosophy within the Linux community. The RPM binaries are the files that system administrators need to apply to the system.

A Package's Function and Contents

Linux users are often curious about an RPM package's function. You can use the `rpm` utility to query an RPM package about its function, as seen in the following command-line example:

```
# rpm -qip kernel-2.2.14-5.0.i586.rpm
```

```
Name         : kernel      Relocations: (not relocateable)
Version      : 2.2.14      Vendor: Red Hat Inc.
Release      : 5.0         Build Date: Wed Jun 2 30 07:09:08
   1999
Install date: (not installed)
Build Host   : porky.devel.redhat.com
Group        : System Environment/Kernel
Source RPM   : kernel-2.2.14-5.0.src.rpm
Size         : 12145883
License      : GPL
Packager     : Red Hat Inc.
               <http://bugzilla.redhat.com/bugzilla>
```

CHAPTER 7: ADDING, REPLACING, AND UPGRADING RPM PACKAGES

```
Summary     : The Linux kernel (the core of the Linux oper-
              ating system).
Description
The kernel package contains the Linux kernel (vmlinuz), the
    core of your Red Hat Linux operating system. The kernel
    handles the basic functions of the operating system:
    memory allocation, process allocation, device input
    and output, etc.
```

The `rpm` syntax follows:

`rpm   qip  <RPM package-name>`

The `rpm` query options used in this section are listed below.

▲ -q   Use the query option specifically to gather package information. Without the -q option, you would get different and unsatisfactory information, because the subsequent options would mean entirely different specifications.

▲ -i   When used with the -q option, -i asks `rpm` to display package information, including the name, version, and package description. Note that if the -q option is not specified along with the -i option, you will get different and unsatisfactory results to the `rpm` command.

▲ -p   When used with the -q option, the -p option tells `rpm` that the package is as yet uninstalled.

You can examine RPM packages using a GUI, as shown in Figures 7.1 and 7.2. Here we examine the function of a games package and the files associated with it.

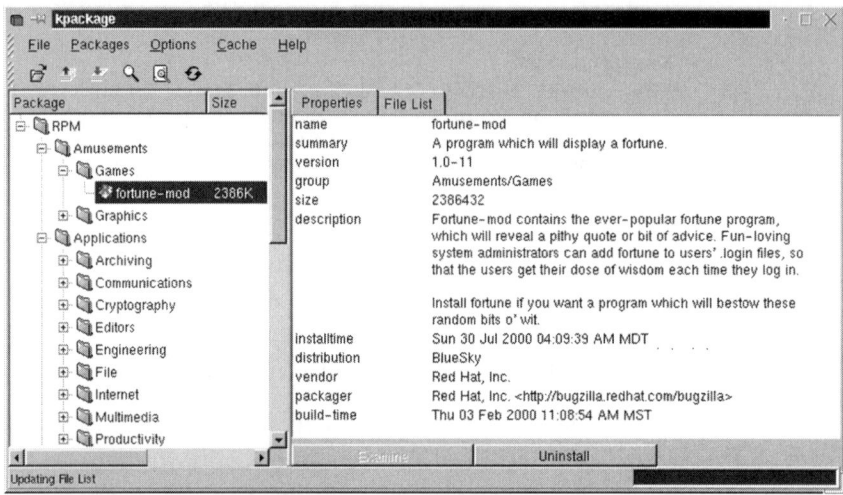

Figure 7.1. Package information displayed from a GUI.

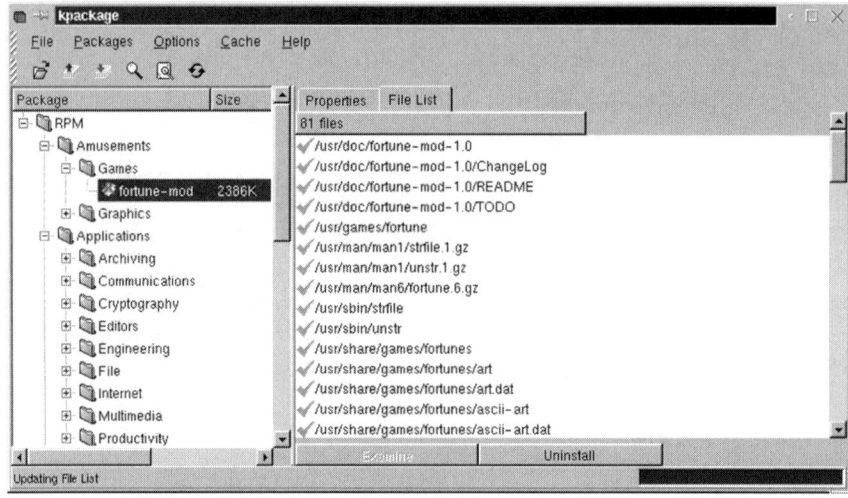

Figure 7.2. File information for an RPM package displayed from a GUI.

To practice, query the system for every RPM package of interest to you. You will see this utility at work again in Chapter 8, when we check and verify the RPM package for a new kernel.

Replacing and Upgrading the XFree86 Package

Among the most common periodic procedures a system administrator must conduct on a system are the replacement and upgrading of RPM packages. To demonstrate, we're going to replace the `XFree86` package. We chose this for two reasons: (1) because the `XFree86` package that comes with the distribution has only the most basic drivers, rather than all those you may find necessary; and (2) because the newer `XFree86` package has additional support that can help to fine-tune the video system.

We recommend that you become familiar with a trustworthy Web site and consistently use it as a source for your RPM packages. The major reason for doing so is to make it easier to track new releases by becoming familiar with the layout of the site. We recommend that you bookmark the following two Web sites: *http://www.rpm.org* and *ftp://ftp.muug.mb.ca/mirror/redhat/redhat/updates*.

The next four steps show you how to use RPM packages to add video support to a system that currently does not have the necessary RPM packages in place. For example, the standard VGA, SVGA, S3, S3V, and Mach drivers ship with the Linux distribution. However, you may need the AGX or I128 server for your system instead, in which case you may be expected to locate the necessary RPM packages, download them, and add them to the system.

Step 1. Identify RPM Packages to Replace

Sometimes more than one RPM package is involved when installing or upgrading a utility or feature. To add a new feature, you often have to upgrade an existing RPM package as well. Therefore, one of the first things that you have to do is meticulously record the versions of the RPM packages already installed on the system by using the `rpm` utility to query the RPM database. Then, compare those RPMs and their respective versions to the ones that you have found on the Internet. The versions and other requirements are almost always buried in the *README* file.

Two examples appear next. Note how we use `rpm` to query the RPM database for the `XFree86` and `XFree86-75-dpi-fonts` RPM packages.

```
# rpm -q XFree86
XFree86-3.3.6-20

# rpm -q XFree86-75dpi-fonts
XFree86-75dpi-fonts-3.3.6-20
```

You have probably noticed that querying a specific package requires that you know the name of the package. If you are uncertain of a package's name, you find it by formulating a command using `rpm` to query all packages and `grep` to display only the packages containing, for example, the text string "free". Thus, your alternative command would be as follows:

```
# rpm -qa | grep -i free
XFree86-3.3.6-20
XFree86-libs-3.3.6-20
XFree86-xfs-3.3.6-20
XFree86-75-dpi-fonts-3.3.6-20
XFree86-Mach64-3.3.6-20
```

```
XFree86-devel-3.3.6-20
Freetype-1.3.1-5
XFree86-SF86Setup-3.3.6-20
```

In the above command line, `q` stands for "query" and `a` stands for "all installed packages on the system." As for the `grep` command, the `i` option means "ignore case of text string."

If your text string is found among the package names, command results will list one or more package names found on the system. If your text string query is not even close, then the command will return nothing, and you will have to try other ideas.

In the current example, as you can see, the command tips you off to the existence of several RPM packages whose names include "free," such as the `XFree86` packages sought in the previous two example queries.

Step 2. Obtain Necessary Files and Place on System

Organizing your work is recommended. We suggest that you create a */usr/sysadmin/XFree86* directory in which to place the new RPM packages. This practice will help you to maintain an audit trail of what you have added to the system. RPM packages do not have to be placed in any specific directory. They will be added to the system by using the `rpm` command. Thus, they can be deleted from this directory after they are installed.

We assume that you have already acquired the following files via `ftp` or copied the RPM packages from their source. Our source for these RPM packages was *www.rpm.org* and *ftp://updates.redhat.com*.

```
# ls /usr/sysadmin/XFree86
XFree86-100dpi-fonts-3.3.6-20.i386.rpm
XFree86-3.3.6-20.i386.rpm
```

```
XFree86-3DLabs-3.3.6-20.i386.rpm
XFree86-75dpi-fonts-3.3.6-20.i386.rpm
XFree86-8514-3.3.6-20.i386.rpm
XFree86-AGX-3.3.6-20.i386.rpm
XFree86-FBDev-3.3.6-20.i386.rpm
XFree86-I128-3-3.6-20.i386.rpm
XFree86-ISO8859-2
XFree86-ISO8859-2-100dpi-fonts
XFree86-ISO8859-2-75dpi-fonts
XFree86-ISO8859-2-Type1-fonts
XFree86-ISO8859-7
.
.
.
```

Step 3. Make Notes on Packages to be Upgraded versus Packages to be Installed

Generally speaking, you perform upgrades first and then add new RPM packages. If a package that you are upgrading or adding requires another package, then it will advise you. In this case, you will have to locate that package and deal with it first. The following examples show how to upgrade and install an RPM package.

To upgrade an existing RPM package:

```
# rpm -Uvh XFree86-3.3.5-1.6.0.i386.rpm
# rpm -Uvh XFree86-75dpi-fonts-3.3.5-1.6.0.i386.rpm
```

To install a new (that is, new to our system) RPM package:

```
# rpm -ivh XFree86-XF86Setup-3.3.5-1.6.0.i386.rpm
```

Chapter 7: Adding, Replacing, and Upgrading RPM Packages

Command-line options are listed below.

▲ U Upgrade the RPM package.

▲ i Install the RPM package.

▲ v Verify, meaning compare information about the installed files with information about the files found in the original package stored in the RPM database, and display any discrepancies.

▲ h Hash, meaning print 50 hash marks as the package archive is unpacked to indicate its progress.

Note that the i option, here, means to install the RPM package. Previously, on page 179, we saw how the i option meant something completely different when it was used in conjunction with the q option. Then, it was only used to find information about a specified RPM package

Upgrading and installing, in that order, should prevent any potential prerequisite problems among the RPM packages.

On rare occasions, you may experience conflicts between packages; the shell may return an error message that tells you there is a conflict. In this case, you may have to force the installation of a new package. To do so, use the following syntax:

```
rpm --force <RPM package-name>
```

You should force an installation only if you are absolutely sure that the installation will not adversely affect a package dependency. That is, if one package depends on a particular version of another package or shares its code base, you shouldn't upgrade the second package by forcing its installation.

If you have a lot of RPM packages to install, consider using a wildcard. The rpm command takes wildcard arguments for file names. An example follows:

```
rpm -ivh *rpm
```

TIP: *Use the <Tab> key for command completion. Type the first part of a command, press <Tab>, and the shell may be able to fill in the rest of the command if you have typed the entire command previously and the shell still remembers it.*

Step 4. Query the RPM Database to Confirm the Upgrade

Use the rpm command to confirm the installation and upgrade. The ultimate test, however, is to confirm that the application is running correctly without problems. An example command is shown below. You can see that the command is identical to the rpm query used in Step 1.

```
# rpm -qa | grep -i free
freetype-1.2-6
XFree86-75dpi-fonts-3.3.5-1.6.0
XFree86-libs-3.3.5-1.6.0
XFree86-xfs-3.3.5-1.6.0
XFree86-SVGA-3.3.5-1.6.0
XFree86-VGA16-3.3.5-1.6.0
XFree86-3.3.5-1.6.0
XFree86-XF86Setup-3.3.5-1.6.0
XFree86-100dpi-fonts-3.3.5-1.6.0
XFree86-S3-3.3.5-1.6.0
XFree86-S3V-3.3.5-1.6.0
```

Using Packages to Install XF86Setup

In Chapter 5, we configured the video system with the Xconfigurator utility program. This time, you repeat the same exercise using an alternative GUI-like tool called XF86Setup, which we mentioned in Chapter 5 but did not discuss in detail. XF86Setup has to be installed first, however, and we can do so using a package. Figure 7.3 shows the XF86Setup tool introductory dialog.

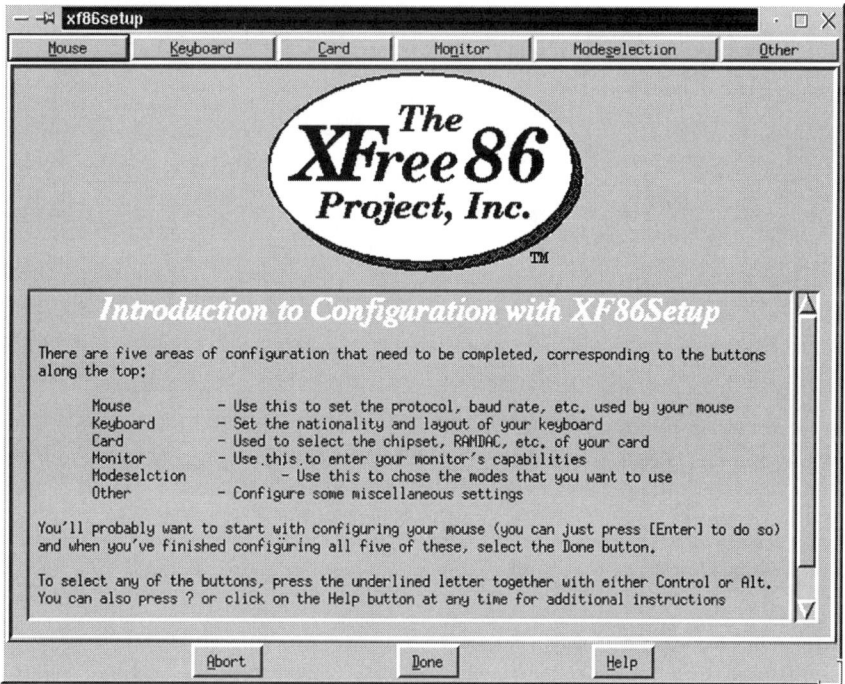

Figure 7.3. XF86Setup tool introductory dialog box.

The XF86Setup tool essentially does the same things as Xconfigurator. Both tools create a functional */etc/XF86Config* file. However, XF86Setup allows you to experiment more easily with alternate video servers. For example, instead of using the standard default

SVGA server, you can quickly choose, say, the SV3 server if it is more appropriate to your hardware. Changing from one server to a more appropriate server can make the difference between a mediocre system and a better functioning, more responsive system.

The next exercise will familiarize you with the installation of this new application using RPM packages. It will also provide you with experience in updating and adding new video support to your system by upgrading and installing the `XF86Setup` software.

CHAPTER 7: ADDING, REPLACING, AND UPGRADING RPM PACKAGES

Exercise

Replacing and upgrading `XFree86` packages are probably two of the more common system administration procedures. They are the first items that will require attention on most systems. This exercise is fairly straightforward. These instructions can be used on all versions of Red Hat Linux, as long as you ensure that the package versions are consistent with the existing version of both the distribution and the kernel levels. We demonstrate how to achieve that in the exercise. This particular example is taken from Red Hat Linux Versions 5.0, 5.2, and 6.0 because these particular versions did not have the most current `XFree86` RPM packages available which made it awkward to work with out of the box. By contrast, the Red Hat Linux Version 6.2 came with current `XFree86` RPM packages.

The following exercise is by example in the sense that the actual revision numbers on the RPM packages may vary from system level to system level. We encourage you to take good notes as you go along to ensure a successful upgrade or installation.

> **NOTE:** *The output statements listed in these exercises occurred as a result of the authors' use of the commands with an older version of Linux. Your output will likely be different, depending on which version of Linux you have installed and whether it has already been upgraded.*

1. Determine which RPM packages need replacing and their revision levels by querying the RPM database.

   ```
   # rpm -qa | grep -i xfree86
   XFree86-3.3.3.1-49
   XFree86-75dpi-fonts-3.3.3.1-49
   XFree86-libs-3.3.3.1-49
   XFree86-xfs-3.3.3.1-49
   XFree86-SVGA-3.3.3.1-49
   ```

2. Check with a reputable Web site to research and obtain the correct packages. Compare their version numbers and dates to the packages on your CD media. Use whichever ones are newer.

   If it turns out that the packages on the Web site are newer than the packages on your CD media, then you will have to download them. (In preparing this exercise, we required a copy of the S3 or S3V video server to support the S3 video chipset. So we downloaded several additional packages [seen below] from the *updates.redhat.com* `ftp` site, and we put them in a directory called */usr/sysadmin/XFree* on the Linux server that we wished to update.)

3. Proceed to create the directory in which to put the new RPM packages.

   ```
   # mkdir -p /usr/sysadmin/XFree
   ```

4. Using `ftp`, copy all the files from */usr/sysadmin/XFree* onto your server.

   ```
   # ls
   XFree86-100dpi-fonts-3.3.5-1.6.0.i386.rpm
   XFree86-3.3.5-1.6.0.i386.rpm
   XFree86-75dpi-fonts-3.3.5-1.6.0.i386.rpm
   XFree86-S3-3.3.5-1.6.0.i386.rpm
   XFree86-S3V-3.3.5-1.6.0.i386.rpm
   XFree86-SVGA-3.3.5-1.6.0.i386.rpm
   XFree86-VGA16-3.3.5-1.6.0.i386.rpm
   XFree86-XF86Setup-3.3.5-1.6.0.i386.rpm
   XFree86-libs-3.3.5-1.6.0.i386.rpm
   XFree86-xfs-3.3.5-1.6.0.i386.rpm
   ```

5. Make notes on the packages that require updating versus those to be installed. Then, proceed to install and/or upgrade the new packages onto the system using the appropriate `rpm` command.

   ```
   # cd /usr/sysadmin/XFree
   ```

CHAPTER 7: ADDING, REPLACING, AND UPGRADING RPM PACKAGES

```
rpm -Uvh XFree86-3.3.5-1.6.0.i386.rpm
rpm -Uvh XFree86-75dpi-fonts-3.3.5-1.6.0.i386.rpm
rpm -Uvh XFree86-libs-3.3.5-1.6.0.i386.rpm
rpm -Uvh XFree86-xfs-3.3.5-1.6.0.i386.rpm
rpm -Uvh XFree86-SVGA-3.3.5-1.0.i386.rpm
rpm -ivh XFree96-VGA16-3.3.5-1.6.0.i386.rpm
rpm -ivh XFree86-XF86Setup-3.3.5-1.6.0.i386.rpm
rpm -ivh XFree86-100*
rpm -ivh XFree86-S3*
```

6. Query the packages to ensure that they are placed in the system correctly.

```
# rpm -qa | grep -i xfree
XFree86-75dpi-fonts-3.3.5-1.6.0
XFree86-libs-3.3.5-1.6.0
XFree86-xfs-3.3.5-1.6.0
XFree86-SVGA-3.3.5-1.6.0
XFree86-VGA16-3.3.5-1.6.0
XFree86-3.3.5-1.6.0
XFree86-XF86Setup-3.3.5-1.6.0
XFree86-100dpi-fonts-3.3.5-1.6.0
XFree86-S3-3.3.5-1.6.0
XFree86-S3V-3.3.5-1.6.0
```

7. Execute the new XF86Setup utility and reconfigure your system video parameters.

```
# XF86Setup
```

For technical details on solving configuration issues, refer to the Chapter 5 on how to configure the video.

191

Quiz

1. What are the advantages of using RPM packages?
2. What are the capabilities of the `rpm` utility?
3. What is the RPM package-naming convention, and what does each section mean?
4. What command-line syntax is used to determine information about an RPM package prior to its installation?
5. What command-line method can be used to find RPM packages for which the name is not known?
6. What is the first step in installing or upgrading a feature or utility?
7. What is a best practice for organizing and auditing RPM package updates and installations?
8. In what order should upgrades and new installations be performed?
9. Under what circumstances should an upgrade or installation be forced?

See Appendix B for answers.

Chapter 8

Upgrading the Kernel Using RPM Packages

IN CHAPTER 7 WE COVERED THE BASICS about RPM packages. In this chapter, we upgrade a Linux operating system kernel from 2.2.14-5 to 2.2.16-3 using RPM packages. We respond to a "security advisory" released by Red Hat technical support that lists all the necessary RPM packages that require upgrading. We also provide step-by-step suggestions for handling the upgrade. Finally, we explain RAM disk support and how to modify LILO to boot from the new kernel.

You may decide to modify these suggestions to suit your needs. However, you can upgrade any kernel using these basic instructions. Only those steps related to basic preparation and system administration must be planned, and they may change from system to system.

Generally, the advantages of using RPM packages are that no compiling is necessary and that tedious little details are automated. We eventually illustrate the operational advantages of performing a kernel upgrade by using RPM packages in the exercise at the end of the chapter. A true comparison, however, will come after you perform the "scratch" kernel upgrade in the exercise in Chapter 10. As a system administrator, you may have cause to perform one upgrade or the other, or perhaps both. After performing the exercises in both Chapters 8 and 10, we think you will agree with us that using packages is much safer and more accurate. There are fewer opportunities for errors.

Some of the material in this chapter is a restatement of Chapter 7. Because we focus on the operating system kernel, however, the steps we outline will be more detailed with respect to operating practices, the directory structure, and so on.

Why Upgrade or Patch the Kernel?

The three main reasons for upgrading or patching the operating system kernel are (1) to obtain support for new hardware, (2) to obtain updated drivers, and (3) to respond to or remedy security concerns. In reality, these are the same reasons for upgrading or patching any application.

We hope to convince you in this chapter that the use of RPM packages is the best way to perform upgrades. If you are not convinced by the end of this chapter, we think you will be totally convinced by the end of Chapter 10, where we show you how to upgrade a kernel from scratch.

The Security Advisory

Examples of the first two reasons for upgrading or patching an application (obtaining new hardware support and updating drivers) appeared in Chapter 7. What about the third reason, dealing with security?

CHAPTER 8: UPGRADING THE KERNEL USING RPM PACKAGES

Let's assume that you are running Red Hat 6.2, which shipped with Linux kernel version of 2.2.14-5. At one time a document appeared at *http://www.redhat.com/corp/support/errata/RHSA-2000-037-05.html* that described a serious security issue. The document indicated that the security issue would be fixed if users upgraded to a kernel level of 2.2.16-3.

Fortunately, the document also stated that new packages to correct the vulnerability were available from *ftp://updates.redhat.com*. In this situation, you would obtain the new kernel RPM packages from the aforementioned `ftp` site and apply them to the system.

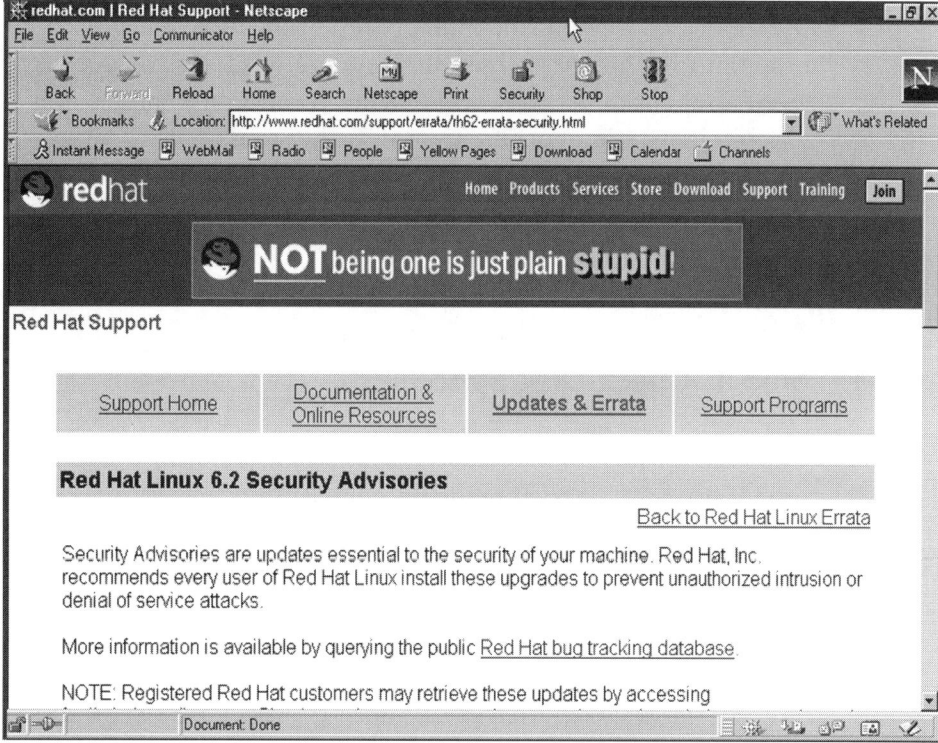

Figure 8.1. An example of a security advisory.

Figure 8.1 is an example of a recent security advisory. It is the responsibility of the system administrator to visit this site on a regular basis to check for any security advisories that pertain to your operation or server. Each security advisory is different. This figure presents the explanation at the beginning of the security advisory, and provides all the links and instructions for applying the necessary RPM packages.

Suggested Upgrade Procedure

There are many ways to upgrade your system using RPM packages. In the following, we describe one ten-step procedure. Because there are other approaches, we suggest that you use our ten steps only as a guide. Depending on how your system is configured and how it acts and interacts, you may have to modify the steps a bit.

WARNING: *Regardless of how you execute an upgrade, we definitely recommend that you back up the entire system before attempting an upgrade, especially on a production system.*

Step 1. Check Disk Space

The kernel will be built inside the */usr/src/linux/arch/ix86/boot* directory. If you have a separate file-system partition for */usr*, make sure there is at least an extra 75 MB of additional space in it. This should also be enough space for the new RPM packages as well. The kernel file itself will eventually have to be copied to the */boot* directory, and the modules will be built in the */lib* directory. These two items will use approximately 10 to 15 MB inside the root (/) file system.

The `df` command displays disk usage according to each file-system partition as follows:

```
# df
```

```
Filesystem  1k-blocks    Used  Available  Use%  Mounted on
/dev/hda1      806368   50408     714996    7%  /
/dev/hda5      272226    1550     256621    1%  /home
/dev/hda7      964500  667672     247832   73%  /usr
```

Refer to the man pages for additional information on the df command.

Step 2. Identify Packages Already Installed

Next, determine which packages are already installed on your system. Make a note of them and then compare them to the packages required to upgrade the kernel. Appearing below is an example query to identify installed packages.

```
# rpm -qa | grep -i kernel
kernel -headers-2.2.14-5.0
kernel -2.2.14.50
kernel -pcmcia-cs-2.2.14-5.0
kernel -source-2.2.14-5.0
kernel -utils-2.2.14-5.0
kernelcfg-0.5-5
```

The exact information regarding the RPM packages required to upgrade the kernel was obtained from the Red Hat Security Advisory at *http://www.redhat.com/support/errata/RHSA-2000-037-05.html,* and the *README* file extracted from the *http://www.redhat. com/corp/support/docs/kernel-upgrade.html* reference on the same advisory.

You can investigate existing packages using the rpm command. This command can be used to query the packages already installed on the system. Make sure you note their version levels as well. Naturally, you will also wish to make notes regarding the RPM packages required that are not on your system.

In Chapter 7, we discussed how the `rpm` utility can help verify what an RPM package can do for you. Here, it's important that we know that our kernel upgrade package is the right one. As illustrated in Chapter 7, the `rpm` syntax is as follows:

```
rpm -qip RPM <package-name>
```

The `rpm` query options are reiterated below.

▲ `-q` Use the query option specifically to gather package information. Without the `-q` option, you would get different and unsatisfactory information, since the subsequent options would mean entirely different specifications.

▲ `-i` When used with the `-q` option, `-i` asks rpm to display package information, including the name, version and package description. Note that, if the `-q` option is not specified along with the `-i` option, then you will get different and unsatisfactory results to the rpm command.

▲ `-p` When used with the `-q` option, the `-p` option tells `rpm` that the package is as yet uninstalled.

We'll use `rpm` with these options to verify that we have the right package.

```
# rpm -qip kernel -2.2.16-3.i686.rpm
Name         : kernel      Relocations: (not relocateable)
Version      : 2.2.16      Vendor: Red Hat, Inc.
Release      : 3           Build Date: Mon 19 Jun 2000
    05:20:2T
Install date: (not installed)
Build Host   : porky.devel.redhat.com
Group        : System Environment/Kernel
Source RPM   : kernel-2.2.16-3.src.rpm
Size         : 13183417            License: GPL
Packager     : Red Hat, Inc. <http://bugzilla.redhat.com/bug-
    zilla>
Summary      : The Linux kernel (the core of the Linux
               operating system).
```

```
Description:
The kernel package contains the Linux kernel (vmlinuz),
    the core of your Red Hat Linux operating system. The
    kernel handles the basic functions of the operating
    system: memory allocation, process allocation,
    device input and output, etc.
```

Thus far, it appears that we have found the right package.

Step 3. Organize Packages and Perform Integrity Check

Checking the integrity of the files before they are applied to the system is recommended. Again, this can be accomplished easily by using the `rpm` command. The command shown in the following example will check the internal consistency of the files to ensure that there was no damage done during the download process, as seen in the following example:

```
# ls
kernel -2.2.14-12.i686.rpm   kernel-2.2.16-3.i686.rpm
# rpm -K --nopgp kernel*
kernel -2.2.14-12.i686.rpm: rpmReadSignature failed
kernel -2.2.16-3.i686.rpm:   md5 GPG NOT OK
```

Note that the system returns a "failed" message for one of the packages, indicating that it does not match the source. In this case you should download the package again and rerun the integrity check.

Step 4. Compare Existing Packages to Downloaded Packages

This step indicates which RPM packages are to be upgraded or installed on the system. Mark all of them off before you begin. In our example, the following will be replaced by the 2.2.16-3 version of the kernel packages:

```
# rpm -q --all | grep -i kernel
kernel -headers-2.2.14-5.0
kernel -2.2.14-5.0
kernel -pcmcia-cs-2.2.14-5.0
kernel -source-2.2.14-5.0
kernel -utils-2.2.14-5.0
```

With a list of the new RPM packages and a list of the RPM packages on the system, you have to make notes on which RPM packages are to be upgraded and which are to be added, so that you can use the proper commands.

Step 5. Record Current Version

The purpose of this step is to check the current version of the kernel. You can check it by taking a look at the login-in herald, such as the one shown in the following example:

```
Red Hat Linux release 6.2 (Zoot)
Kernel 2.2.14-5.0 on an i686
login:
```

Another way of checking the current version is to use the `uname` command with the `-r` option.

```
# uname -r
2.2.14-5.0
```

A third way to check is to use the `uname` command with the `-a` option.

```
# uname -a
Linux SIM_SHOP 2.2.14-5.0 #1 Tue Aug  1 21:07:39 EST
    2000 i686 unknown
```

If you are already logged in, use the uname -a command to make note of both the version and the processor type currently on the machine. In the previous example, the processor is an i686 (that is, some type of Pentium II equivalent). If you did not know the processor type, you could simply use the i386, but why downgrade that feature when you don't have to?

Step 6. Create an Emergency Boot Diskette

The purpose of this step is to provide you with useful information in the event that something goes wrong. If you did not make an emergency boot diskette during installation, this is the easiest way to create one now.

Examine the */etc/lilo.conf* file and note the kernel image name and version currently being used. In the following example, the file contains *image=/boot/vmlinuz-2.2.14-5.0.*

```
# more lilo.conf
boot=/dev/hda
map=/boot/map
install=/boot/boot.b
prompt
timeout=50
default=linux

image=/boot/vmlinuz-2.2.14-5.0
        label=linux
        read-only
        root=/dev/hda1
```

Therefore, we can construct the syntax for the mkbootdisk command in the following way:

```
# mkbootdisk  --device  /dev/fd0   2.2.14-5.0
```

```
Insert a disk in /dev/fd0. Any information on the
    disk will be lost.
Press <Enter> to continue or ^C to abort:
```

Note that there are two dashes before the device option, but no space between them. Refer to the man pages for additional information on the mkbootdisk command.

Step 7. Proceed to Upgrade or Install Packages

If you get errors about dependencies, you will have to take care of these first and then return to the upgrade or install procedure. If the two kernel versions are too far apart, you may find that there are conflicts between packages. An error message will be returned by the shell as a result of using the rpm command. You may have to force the install. These concepts, the commands, and their options are discussed in Chapter 7.

If nonkernel packages are involved, it is important that you update those first. Then move on to the kernel-related packages. Although this step is not required for our example upgrade, an example follows.

```
# rpm -Uvh kernel-pcmcia-cs*
```

Next, update the kernel headers and kernel source packages:

```
# ls
kernel -2.2.16-3.i686.rpm
# rpm -Uvh kernel -2.2.16-3.i686.rpm
```

In any event, do not proceed to the next step until this step goes well. In addition, keep in mind that you can use the rpm command to either remove or uninstall a bad package. As always, refer to the man pages for additional information on the rpm command.

Step 8. Optional: Create RAM Disk Support File

The only criterion to meet here is: "Is this a SCSI or laptop computer that requires PCMCIA support?" If so, then you will need RAM disk support.

The easiest way to determine whether you need RAM disk support is to examine the *lilo.conf* file. There is an additional statement in the */etc/lilo.conf* file that refers to an initial RAM disk file. That reference will resemble *initrd=/boot/initrd-2.2.14.img*. Upon listing the files in the */boot* directory, you will see the *initrd-2.2.14.img* file.

The purpose of this initial RAM disk is to allow a modular kernel, such as Linux 2.2.X, to have access to modules required for the boot process as the system boots up. Thus, it resolves the old catch-22 (or, if you prefer, chicken-and-egg) scenario where you need a driver to talk to the hardware (such as a SCSI or PCMCIA driver) that is not available (yet) until the disk is up. Essentially, by creating a RAM disk file, you solve this problem by creating an additional pointer (via LILO), which in turn writes to the master boot record (MBR). In turn, the MBR will now know to use this file to boot. The necessary modules are linked within this RAM disk file.

You will have to create a new *initrd* file for the system to boot from, using the `mkinitrd` command.

```
# mkinitrd /boot/initrd-2.2.16.3.img   2.2.16-3
```

Step 9. Setting up LILO to Boot from New Kernel

In this step, you edit *lilo.conf* to point to the new kernel. Remember that if you want to boot from this new kernel all the time, place it as the first stanza in the file. That will make it the default boot item. In addition, remember to add the *initrd* file if you choose to use one. An example of a *lilo.conf file* follows:

```
# cat/etc/lilo.conf
boot=/dev/hda
map=/boot/map
install=/boot/boot.b
prompt
timeout=50
default=linux

image=/boot/vmlinuz-2.2.16-3
        label=linux
        read-only
        root=/dev/hda1
```

Then, update the MBR by running the `lilo -v` command.

```
# lilo -v
LILO version 21, Copyright 1992-1998 Werner Almes-
    berger

Reading boot sector from /dev/hda
Merging with /boot/boot.b
Boot image: /boot/vmlinuz-2.2.16-3
Added linux *
/boot/boot.0300 exists - no backup copy made.
Writing boot sector.
```

Step 10. Shut Down and Reboot to Test New Kernel

If you are successful, make note of the log-in herald. If the kernel version is correct, then you should log in and check the uname of the machine by using the `uname -a` command.

```
# uname -a
```
**Linux SIM_SHOP 2.2.16-3 #1 Mon Jul 31 19:11:44 EDT
   2000 i686 unknown**

**Red Hat Linux release 6.2 (Zoot)
Kernel 2.2.16-3 on an i686**

We recommend that you query the RPM database, check the system's disk space, create another updated boot disk, and so forth.

Exercise

The exercise is fairly straightforward. These instructions can be used on all versions of Red Hat Linux, as long as you ensure that the RPM package versions are consistent with the existing version of both the distribution and the kernel levels. This exercise is by example in the sense that the actual revision numbers on the RPM packages may vary from system level to system level. We encourage you to take good notes as you go along to ensure a successful upgrade.

1. Check to ensure that you have enough disk space for the kernel in */boot* and for the source files in */usr*.

    Before:

    ```
    # df
    Filesystem   1k-blocks    Used  Available Use% Mounted on
    /dev/hda1       806368   55140     710264   7% /
    /dev/hda5       272226    1551     256620   1% /home
    /dev/hda7       964500  667672     247832  73% /usr
    ```

    After:

    ```
    # df
    Filesystem   1k-blocks    Used  Available Use% Mounted on
    /dev/hda1       806368   55140     710264   7% /
    /dev/hda5       272226    1551     256620   1% /home
    /dev/hda7       964500  667672     247832  73% /usr
    ```

2. Identify the RPM packages already installed on your system and make a note of them. Compare them to the RPM packages that are required to upgrade the kernel.

    ```
    # rpm -q --all | grep -i kernel
    kernel -headers-2.2.14-5.0
    kernel -pcmcia-cs-2.2.14-5.0
    kernel -source-2.2.14-5.0
    kernel -utils-2.2.14-5.0
    ```

CHAPTER 8: UPGRADING THE KERNEL USING RPM PACKAGES

3. Using `ftp`, download the files into a newly created directory. We downloaded our files from *http://www.redhat.com/support/errata/RHSA-2000-037-05.html*. If this site is too busy, go to *www.redhat.com/mirrors.html* and try one of the alternate sites for the download.

   ```
   # mkdir -p /usr/sysadmin/kernel
   kernel -2.2.16-3.i686.rpm
   [/root]# rpm -K --nopgp kern*
   kernel -2.2.16-3.i686.rpm: md5 GPG NOT OK
   ```

4. Compare the packages currently on the system to the downloaded packages that are to be installed onto the system. The following packages will be replaced:

   ```
   # rpm -q --all | grep -i kernel
   kernel -headers-2.2.14-5.0
   kernel -pcmcia-cs-2.2.14-5.0
   kernel -source-2.2.14-5.0
   kernel -utils-2.2.14-5.0
   ```

   The replacement RPM package follows:

   ```
   # ls
   kernel-2.2.16-3.i686.rpm
   ```

5. Before you upgrade the kernel, check and record the current version.

   ```
   Red Hat Linux release 6.2 (Zoot)
   Kernel 2.2.14-5.0 on an i686
   login:
   ```

6. This is the last chance that you have to create an emergency boot floppy. If you have not already done so, make one now.

   ```
   # cat /etc/lilo.conf
   boot=/dev/hda
   map=/boot/map
   ```

```
install=/boot/boot.b
prompt
timeout=50
image=/boot/vmlinuz-2.2.14-5.0
label=linux
root=/dev/hda1
read-only
# mkbootdisk --device /dev/fd0 2.2.14-5.0
Insert a disk in /dev/fd0. Any information on the disk
    will be lost.
Press <Enter> to continue or ^C to abort:
```

7. Proceed to either upgrade or install the new RPM packages. You may get an error when you upgrade the kernel headers file, due to the fact that it could not remove the old */lib/modules*. This is acceptable. Make a note to yourself to clean these up later.

```
# ls
kernel-2.2.16-3.i686.rpm
# rpm -Uvh kernel -2.2.16-3.i686.rpm
```

On other versions of the kernel, you may find that there are conflicts between packages. You may have to force the install. In this exercise, forcing the install is not necessary. However, forcing the install would look like this:

```
# rpm -ivh --force kernel-pcmcia-cs-2.2.5.22.i386.rpm
kernel-pcmcia-cs
```

8. If you have a SCSI system or a laptop that needs PCMCIA support, you may have to create an initial RAM disk. As mentioned earlier, the purpose of this initial RAM disk is to allow a modular kernel, such as Linux 2.2.X, to have access to modules required for booting as the system boots up. Essentially, it copies the required module driver to the boot entity so that it is available.

```
# ls -l /boot
total 2804
lrwxrwxrwx   1 root   root        19 Jul 13 23:20 System.map -> System.map-2.2.16-3
-rw-r--r--   1 root   root    195991 Jun 19 17:19 System.map-2.2.16-3
-rw-r--r--   1 root   root       512 Jul 12 10:01 boot.0300
-rw-r--r--   1 root   root      4569 Feb  2 15:03 boot.b
-rw-r--r--   1 root   root       612 Feb  2 15:03 chain.b
-rw-r--r--   1 root   root    378376 Jul 13 23:07 initrd-2.2.16-3.img
-rw-r--r--   1 root   root       237 Jul 12 16:33 kernel.h
-rw-------   1 root   root     10240 Jul 13 23:16 map
lrwxrwxrwx   1 root   root        20 Jul 13 23:03 module-info -> module-info-2.2.16-3
-rw-r--r--   1 root   root     11773 Jun 19 17:19 module-info-2.2.16-3
-rw-r--r--   1 root   root       620 Feb  2 15:03 os2_d.b
-rwxr-xr-x   1 root   root   1603531 Jun 19 17:19 vmlinux-2.2.16-3
lrwxrwxrwx   1 root   root        16 Jul 13 23:03 vmlinux -> vmlinux-2.2.16-3
-rw-r--r--   1 root   root    620247 Jun 19 17:19 vmlinuz-2.2.16-3
```

9. From the above information you can construct the `mkinitrd` command.

   `# mkinitrd /boot/initrd-2.2.16-3.img  2.2.16-3`

10. Now set up `LILO` to point to the new kernel.

    # cat /etc/lilo.conf
    boot=/dev/hda
    map=/boot/map
    install=/boot/boot.b
    prompt
    timeout=50
    default=linux

    image=/boot/vmlinuz-2.2.16-3
    **   label=linux**
    **   read-only**
    **   root=/dev/hda1**

    # lilo -v
    LILO version 21, Copyright 1992-1998 Werner
    ** Almesberger**

    Reading boot sector from /dev/hda
    Merging with /boot/boot.b

```
Boot image: /boot/vmlinuz-2.2.16-3
Added linux *
/boot/boot.0300 exists - no backup copy made.
Writing boot sector.
```

11. Finally, shut down and test the new system.

    ```
    # shutdown -r now
    ```

12. Log in again and check the name for the correct kernel version.

    ```
    Red Hat Linux release 6.2 (Zoot)
    Kernel 2.2.16-3 on an i686
    login:
    ```

CHAPTER 8: UPGRADING THE KERNEL USING RPM PACKAGES

Quiz

1. What are the three main reasons for upgrading or patching the Linux kernel?

2. What six things should you do before installing or upgrading RPM packages?

3. What three methods can be used to check the current version of Linux?

4. What utility is used to create an emergency repair disk?

5. What is the primary consideration when installing or upgrading RPM packages?

6. In what order should dependent RPM packages be upgraded prior to kernel upgrade?

7. Under what circumstance would you create a RAM disk support file?

8. Once the kernel is upgraded, what file do you need to edit and why?

9. What post-upgrade procedures are recommended?

See Appendix B for answers.

Chapter 9
―――――――――

Configuring the Kernel

IN THIS CHAPTER, WE DISCUSS AVAILABLE TOOLS for configuring a Linux kernel. We then use make xconfig to create an *xconfig* file used by the compile process. We show the necessary and optional configurable parameters for a Linux kernel, based on hardware requirements. This chapter also makes various recommendations for handling major configuration issues for a more efficient kernel.

Generally speaking, the only people interested in configuring their own kernels are developers who are looking for code from the Internet that is newer than that offered by off-the-shelf Linux CDs, or system administrators who know exactly what they want and are moving toward a very specific set of kernel components. This chapter is presented for two reasons: (1) to give those who have not had a chance to configure a kernel a process to start with; and (2) to illustrate how you can get details on what is available via Linux kernel functions using the xconfig menus; many of these features would not be visible otherwise.

After discussing the Linux kernel configuration process, we move on to the default behavior of the most important kernel menus. Next, we identify the menu options that invoke driver details, configure basic and crucial kernel options, and create a good *xconfig* file.

Before we start, we would like to say that you should not be intimidated by what you are about to do. Only about 20% of this material is going to apply to any particular machine at once. However, the material covered in this chapter is a fine demonstration of how sophisticated Linux has become over its short history. You will see support for almost everything in these menus. We are not going to define each and every item in the menus. At any time, however, you can open a menu and read the Help prompts. The more familiar you become with these menus, the easier Linux will be to learn. Also, you should note that these choices are totally transparent if you choose to use the installation procedures for Linux shown earlier in this book (as opposed to configuring your own kernel).

We find that many people are baffled by what is and is not supported in Linux. The easy answer to these kinds of questions is to access the `make xconfig` menu and simply take a look. No changes will be made to the system until you actually perform a compile, which has to be done using `make bzImage`.

Linux Kernel Configuration Menu

The Linux Kernel Configuration start menu presented by `make xconfig` appears in Figure 9.1. We use this as a guide only. We do not use every option or combination in the following discussion. We explain the mandatory options and make various recommendations. The general rules applied here are simply to compile infrequently used features as modules to reduce resource consumption and kernel size, or compile nonoptional features such as disk-drivers and file-system support right into the kernel for performance reasons.

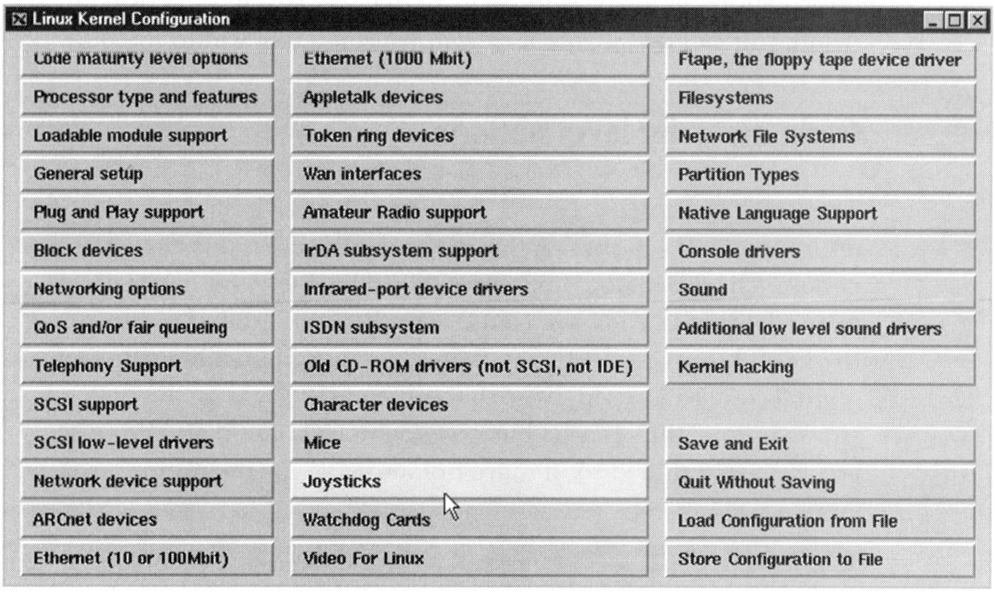

CHAPTER 9: CONFIGURING THE KERNEL

Linux Kernel Configuration		
Code maturity level options	Ethernet (1000 Mbit)	Ftape, the floppy tape device driver
Processor type and features	Appletalk devices	Filesystems
Loadable module support	Token ring devices	Network File Systems
General setup	Wan interfaces	Partition Types
Plug and Play support	Amateur Radio support	Native Language Support
Block devices	IrDA subsystem support	Console drivers
Networking options	Infrared-port device drivers	Sound
QoS and/or fair queueing	ISDN subsystem	Additional low level sound drivers
Telephony Support	Old CD-ROM drivers (not SCSI, not IDE)	Kernel hacking
SCSI support	Character devices	
SCSI low-level drivers	Mice	Save and Exit
Network device support	Joysticks	Quit Without Saving
ARCnet devices	Watchdog Cards	Load Configuration from File
Ethernet (10 or 100Mbit)	Video For Linux	Store Configuration to File

Figure 9.1. Linux Kernel Configuration start menu.

This menu looks daunting at first, but our advice is to add only those features that you will need on a continual basis. These menus will dynamically change depending on the features that you enable. For example, if you choose not to enable SCSI devices, all options pertaining to SCSI devices will be dimmed, and will thus be unavailable. For this reason, we recommend that you work through these menus in an orderly fashion, from `Code maturity level options` to `Kernel hacking`.

As we've mentioned, for this and all subsequent menus in this chapter, we will not discuss every feature. We cover only important points and issues that commonly cause problems. You will soon see that many of these features will not pertain to your kernel; hence, they can be ignored. Many are features that support hardware you probably do not have inside your system. If you encounter a situation that requires information about a specific feature that we have not discussed in any detail, you can investigate it by simply using Help within the option.

Code maturity level options

The Code maturity level options (Figure 9.2) will decide the entire scope of what you are going to configure in this kernel. If you choose y in this dialog box, you will be allowing experimental code to be used—that is, code associated with the odd-numbered version of the kernel source tree. If you choose n, you will not allow the experimental code to be used. Note that some of the areas on the dialog box (for example, the - [dash] button, Prev, and the up and down arrows) are dimmed so they are not available for the option.

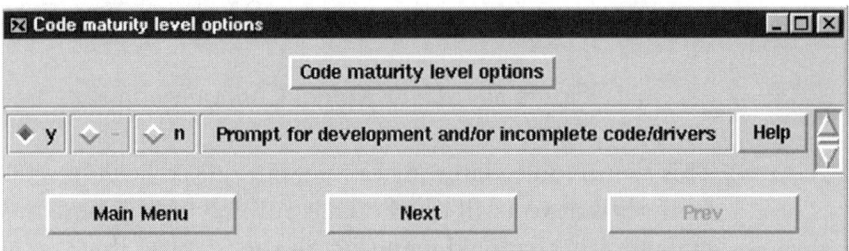

Figure 9.2. Code maturity level options dialog box.

The n choice is recommended if you are working in a production environment; y is recommended if you are installing a development system. Whatever you choose here will determine what will be available to you in the subsequent menus. Therefore, if you are trying to install a new driver but it is dimmed and seemingly unavailable, return to this Code maturity level option dialog box and change it from n to y. The otherwise unavailable driver will likely become available.

Making selections in this dialog box should be part of a larger strategy to determine which kernel version you have installed on the system. For example, all critical systems should be running kernels whose version numbers are even numbers. (We discuss kernel version numbers in Chapter 10.) Using experimental code (that is, kernels whose version numbers are odd numbers) is not recommended in critical production systems either. You should not choose the experimental code feature when using an even-numbered kernel source unless you have an overwhelming reason to do so.

Processor types and features

For performance reasons, it is recommended that you choose the correct processor for the system. If you do not know what processor you have, you can use 386, which is the default. It will work on newer systems, but it may not perform as well. The processor family used to generate the kernel that is already installed on the system is displayed as part of the log-in herald or can be displayed by using the `uname -a` command.

Choose the `Math emulation` option shown in Figure 9.3 only if your system does not have a math coprocessor chip. It adds a whopping 45 KB of overhead to your kernel. All Pentium-class machines have the coprocessor function built in; therefore, you should not have to choose this option. This option is not asking if you have math emulation. Rather it is asking, if you don't have it, do you want a software equivalent? The only systems that require this option are the older i386DX, i386SX, or i486SX systems.

Customizing and Upgrading Linux

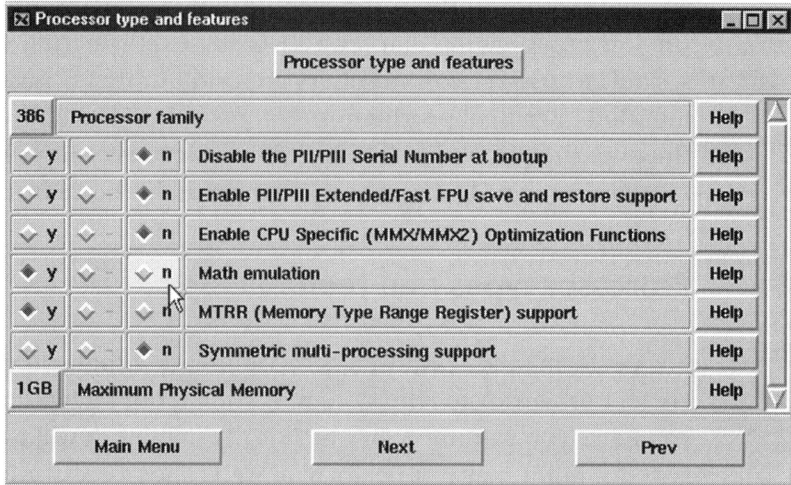

Figure 9.3. Processor type and features dialog box.

Loadable module support

Choosing Enable loadable module support (Figure 9.4) represents a kernel strategy and will determine whether you install a "monolithic" kernel or a "modular" kernel. One of the most important features of the Linux 2.X kernel is its ability to be modular. According to the modular kernel concept, certain options need only be loaded "on demand" (that is, only when they are required). When those options are not required, they are unloaded. Thus, the size of the kernel, which is loaded in RAM, is kept to a minimum, and resources are not tied up any longer than necessary. However, for performance purposes, we recommend that any feature that you expect to use regularly should be nonmodular. By choosing even one module, however, you are committing to a modular kernel. Conversely, if you choose no here, you will find that some features may not be available to you.

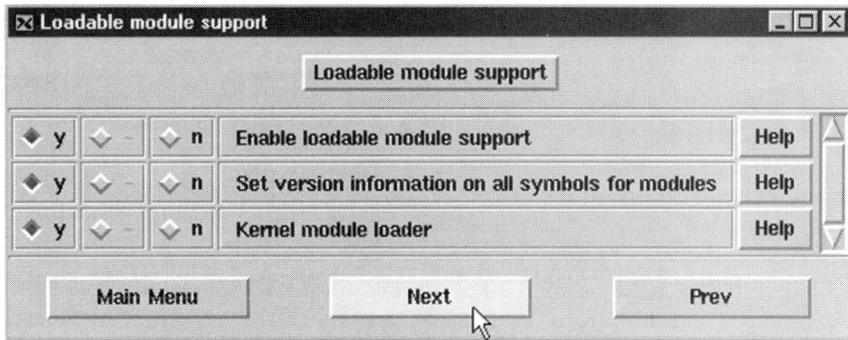

Figure 9.4. Loadable module support dialog box.

The `Set version information on all symbols for modules` option means that you can use modules from other kernel versions, as long as they are compatible.

The final option in this dialog box, `Kernel module loader`, is the `kerneld` daemon support. The `kerneld` is the daemon that actually performs the automated loading and unloading of modules.

We recommend that you choose `y` for all three options in the Loadable module support dialog box.

General setup

The General setup dialog box has many options, so we present them in three figures (9.5, 9.6, and 9.7).

Networking support Option

If you are going to have a network adapter in your system, you should answer `y` to the `Networking support` option (Figure 9.5). Answering `n` will dim the network-adapter drivers in all subsequent menus.

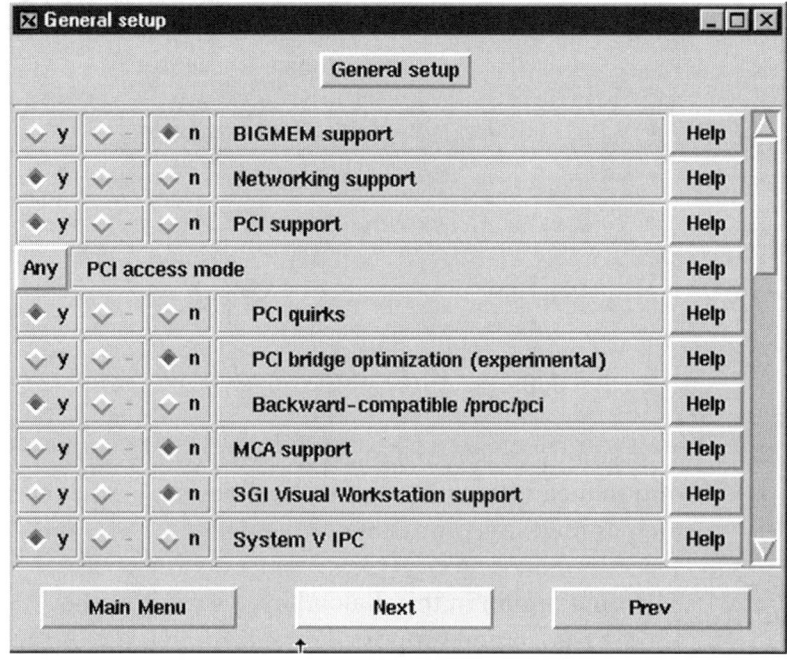

Figure 9.5. The options at the top of the General setup dialog box.

PCI support Option

PCI support (Figure 9.5) refers to the type of bus that you have. If you have a PCI motherboard, then answer y; otherwise, answer n. In other words, answer n if your bus is ISA, EISA (Extended Industry Standard Architecture), MCA (Microchannel Architecture), or VESA. If you have an ISA bus with a couple of PCI slots, answer n.

PCI access mode Option

Linux can try to determine the type of PCI devices in your system via the BIOS, by querying the device directly, or by trying other strategies. Note that the PCI access mode option (Figure 9.5) does not require the PCI support option to be selected. The PCI device can actually be inside an ISA system in a PCI slot.

CHAPTER 9: CONFIGURING THE KERNEL

PCI quirks Option

The `PCI quirks` selection (Figure 9.5) provides backward-compatible code for PCI environments with broken or obsolete BIOSes.

System V IPC Option

Indicate y for the `System V IPC` option (Figure 9.5) if you want DOS environments to work properly.

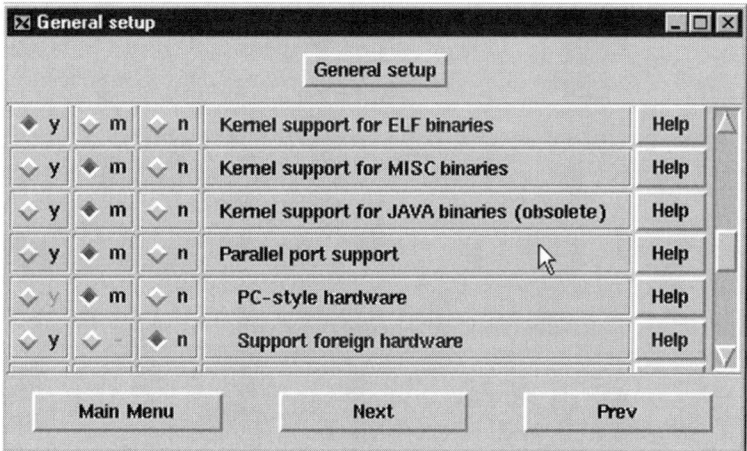

Figure 9.6. Additional options in the General setup dialog box.

Kernel support Options

It is highly recommended that you enable all three Kernel support options (for ELF, MISC, and JAVA binaries) shown in Figure 9.6 for compatibility purposes. You should enable them particularly if you have enabled `Prompt for development and/or incomplete code/drivers` back in the Code maturity level options dialog box (Figure 9.2).

CUSTOMIZING AND UPGRADING LINUX

Parallel port support Option

If you are going to use the parallel port for a printer, or other peripheral devices, then say y to the `Parallel port support` option in Figure 9.6. This is one of those options that, if set to n now, will likely cause problems later.

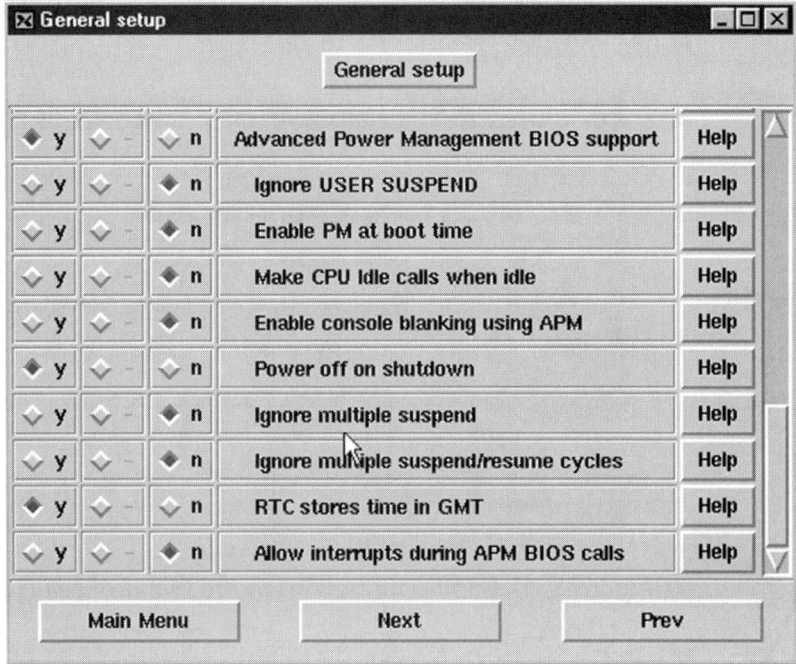

Figure 9.7. The options at the bottom of the General setup dialog box.

Advanced Power Management BIOS support Option

The `Advanced Power Management BIOS support` option (Figure 9.7) is useful for laptops. But it has nothing to do with options such as disk drive spin-downs or green monitors. Besides, those features are not governed by operating systems, but rather are built into the devices themselves.

CHAPTER 9: CONFIGURING THE KERNEL

Plug and Play support Option

You will likely benefit from enabling the `Plug and Play support`, especially to facilitate probing. You enable it through the dialog box shown in Figure 9.8.

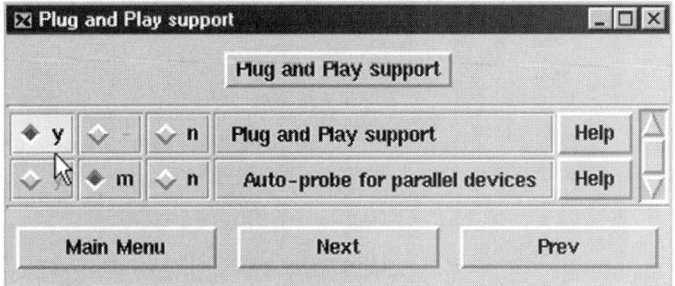

Figure 9.8. Plug and Play support dialog box.

Block devices

The Block devices option requires many subsequent choices. We present these choices in Figures 9.9 through 9.14.

Normal PC floppy disk support Option

If you want to use your floppy disk drives with Linux, you have to select the `Normal PC Floppy disk support` option, shown in Figure 9.9.

223

CUSTOMIZING AND UPGRADING LINUX

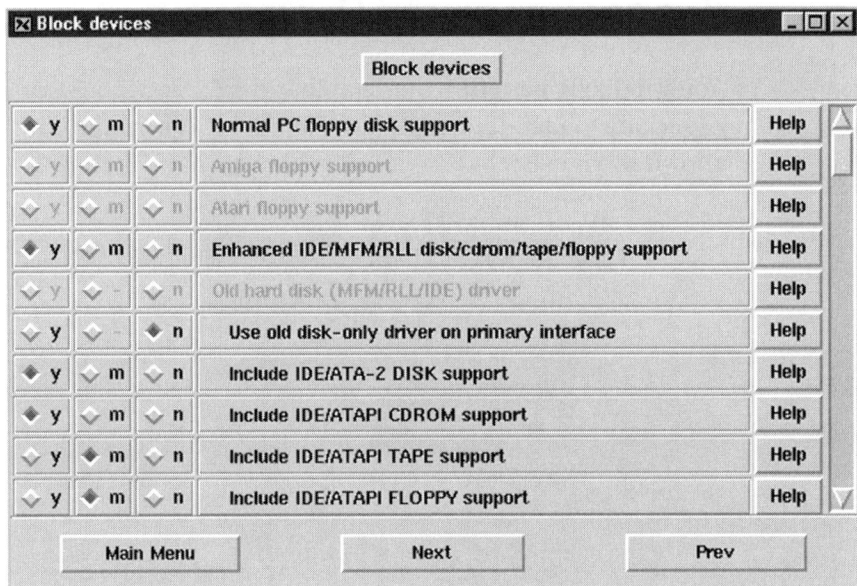

Figure 9.9. Options at the top of the Block devices dialog box.

Enhanced IDE/MFM/RLL disk/cdrom/tape/floppy support Option

If you have any type of IDE drive in your system, select y for this Enhanced IDE option, shown in Figure 9.9. This driver is preferred over the one listed a few features below it: Include IDE/ATA-2 DISK support. If the system is 100% SCSI, you can select n. You could also enter m here; this means that if you need this type of support later, you can load it as a module.

Include IDE/ATA-2 DISK support Option

Originally, IDE technology supported two drives: one was the master and one was the slave. Multiple IDE-drive support came later. The Include IDE/ATA-2 DISK support option (Figure 9.9) applies to an older version of an IDE driver that may be required for systems with dated IDE technology. If you have an up-to-date system, try the

CHAPTER 9: CONFIGURING THE KERNEL

Enhanced IDE/MFM/RLL disk/cdrom/tape/floppy support first, and only try this option if the Enhanced option does not work.

Include IDE/ATAPI Options

For the Include IDE/ATAPI CDROM support, Include IDE/ATAPI TAPE support, and Include IDE/ATAPI FLOPPY support options (Figure 9.9), we offer the same comment as above.

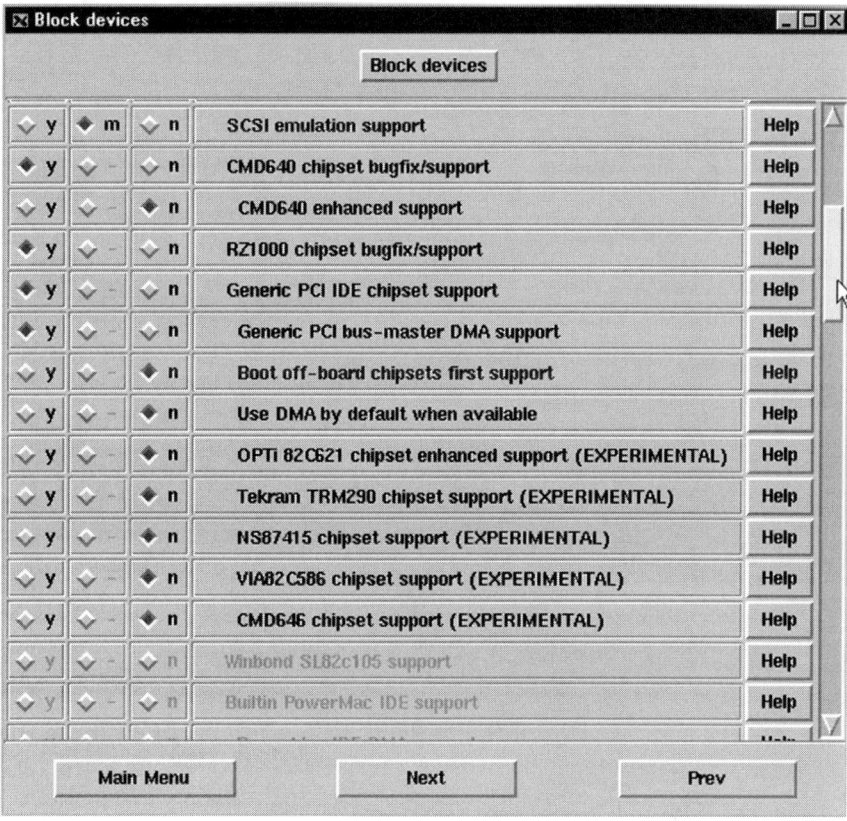

Figure 9.10. Additional options in the Block devices dialog box.

225

SCSI emulation support Option

Many new devices on the market today, such as CD-ROM writers and certain backup devices, are IDE devices, but they emulate a SCSI device. We recommend that you choose m for the SCSI emulation support (Figure 9.10) if you have such devices, unless kernel size is an issue.

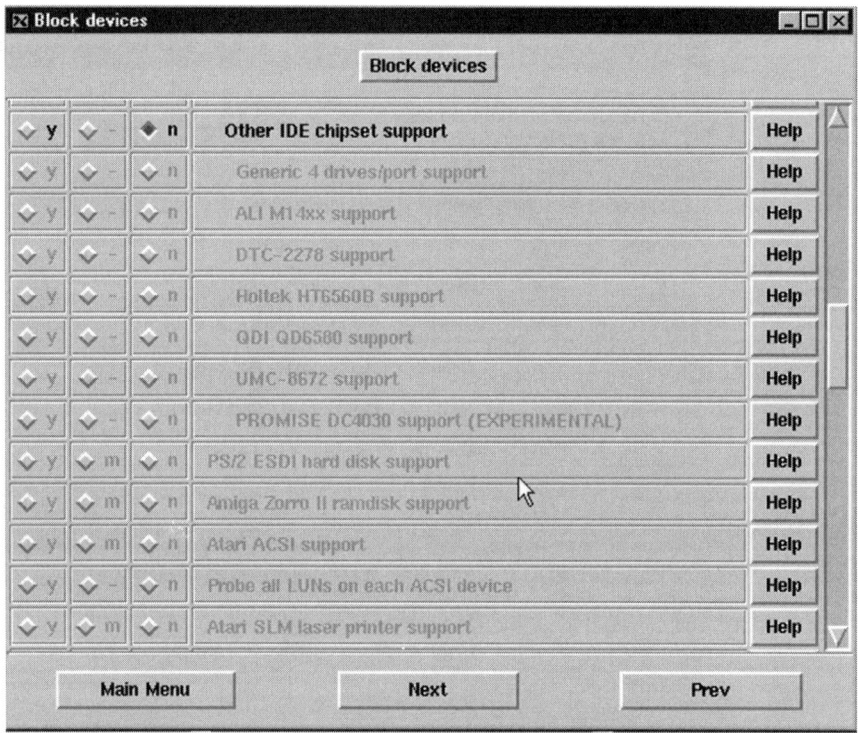

Figure 9.11. Block devices dialog box, continued.

Other IDE chipset support Option

If you are having a lot of trouble getting the older IDE drives to be recognized, try enabling Other IDE chipset support (Figure 9.11). In some cases, it can make a difference.

CHAPTER 9: CONFIGURING THE KERNEL

Some of these support options are for odd stuff. Someday, when you have nothing else to do, you can become familiar with these by browsing all the Help option panels. We recommend that you just make a mental note of the options here.

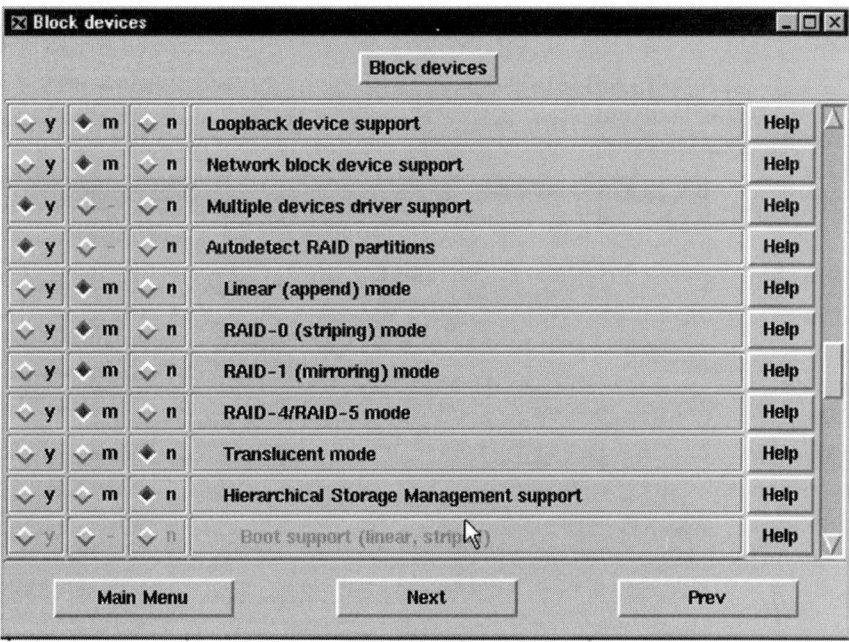

Figure 9.12. Block devices dialog box, continued.

Loopback device support Option

Activating the Loopback device support option (Figure 9.12) is required for the Common Desktop Environment. Saying y here will also allow you to use a regular file as a block device. This is useful if you want to check an ISO 9660 file system before burning a CD, or if you want to use floppy images without first writing them to floppy, as well as many other things. We recommend you choose y or m here.

Network block device support Option

The Network block device support option in Figure 9.12 is not your network adapter and driver information. Network-adapter and driver support is in the next section.

Multiple devices driver support Option

If you plan on bridging, striping, or mirroring disk sets, you had better select y for Multiple devices driver support (Figure 9.12).

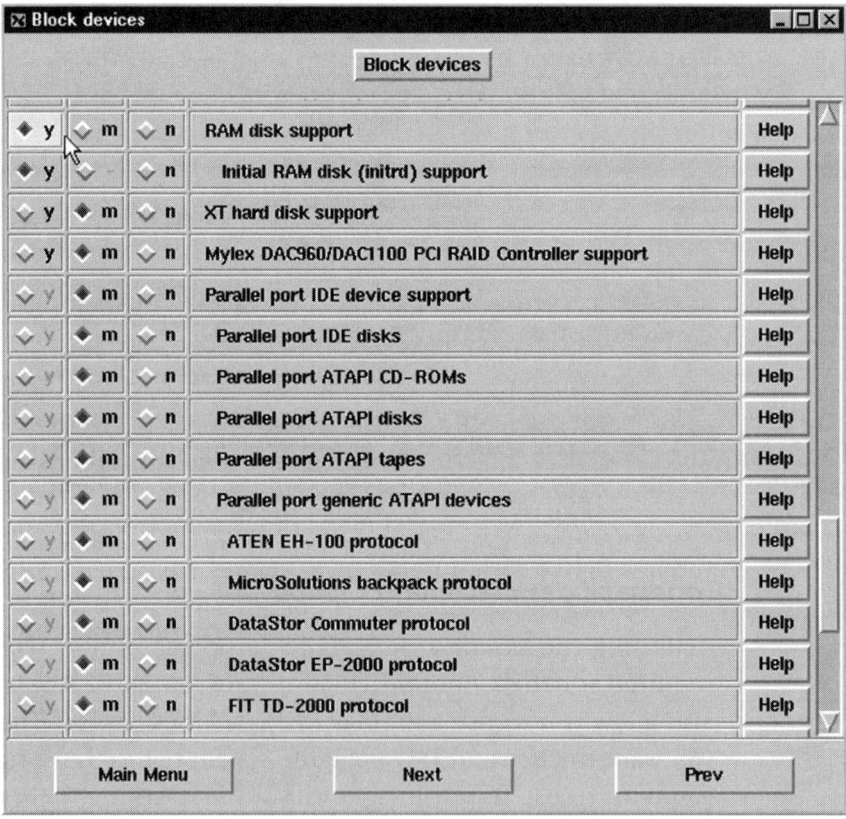

Figure 9.13. Block devices dialog box, continued.

CHAPTER 9: CONFIGURING THE KERNEL

RAM disk support Option

If you have either a SCSI device or a laptop requiring PCMCIA support, we recommend that you answer y to the RAM disk support option (Figure 9.13). Otherwise, you will not be able to create a RAM disk file using the mkinitrd command to accommodate booting the system with preboot module requirements, such as SCSI drivers or PCMCIA support.

The SCSI support option is discussed a bit later. If you intend to install SCSI support then, you better select RAM disk support now.

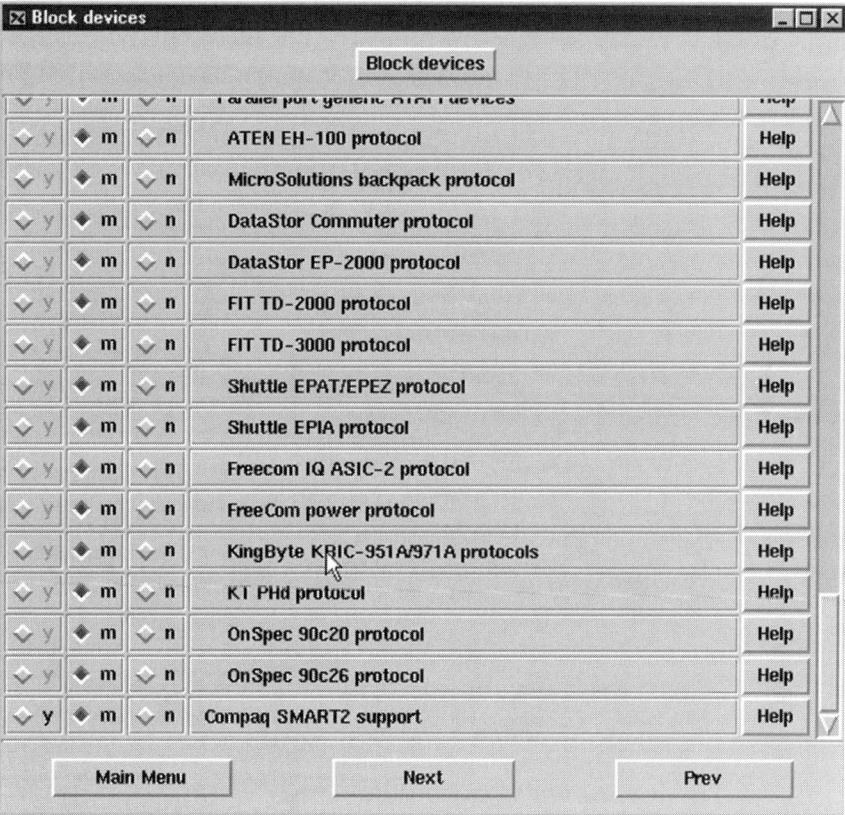

Figure 9.14. Options at the bottom of the Block devices dialog box.

Here you find relatively esoteric support programs and protocols. Just have a look at them and move on. If you are curious, check out their respective Help buttons.

Networking Options

It is a good idea to have a clear strategy or knowledge of which networking features will be required and installed on your system (see Figure 9.15). To arbitrarily enable all options is inappropriate and insecure. We are not going to delve into definitions of TCP/IP at this juncture. It is assumed, however, that your system will participate as a typical host on a network.

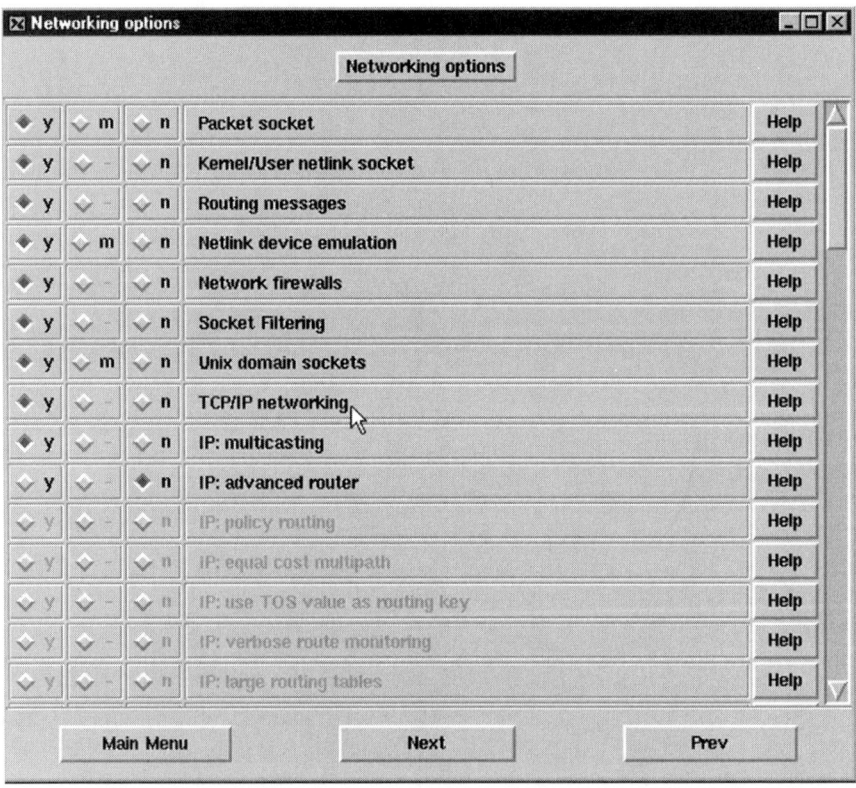

Figure 9.15. Networking options dialog box.

UNIX domain sockets Option

The `UNIX domain sockets` option in Figure 9.15 is required for X protocol and daemon communication support. We recommend that you answer y here to enable basic TCP/IP support.

TCP/IP networking Option

Select `TCP/IP networking` (Figure 9.15) to enable all the basic IPv4 TCP/IP protocols.

Network Device Support

Network device support is another large group of options. We present them in Figures 9.16 through 9.18.

Network device support Option

Select the `Network device support` feature (Figure 9.16) if you have an adapter card to configure. Answering n will dim all possibilities for network adapter choices.

Dummy net driver support Option

The `Dummy net driver support` option (Figure 9.16) is useful if you are going to be enabling either SLIP (serial-line IP) or PPP (point-to-point protocol) support. Neither of these protocols will work if you do not answer either y or m here.

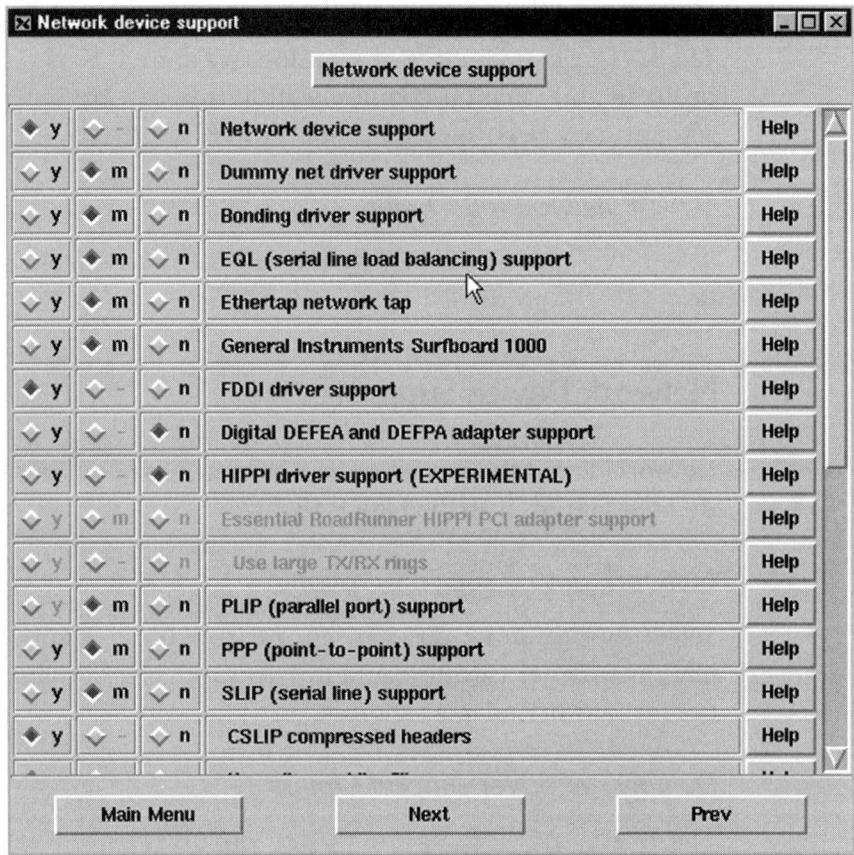

Figure 9.16. Network device support dialog box.

Ethernet (10 or 100Mbit) Option

Select Ethernet (10 or 100 Mbit) option (Figure 9.17) if you have an Ethernet adapter in your system. Then proceed to locate the driver that matches your adapter. If your driver does not show up here, you may have to return to your source tree and add a patch file to include your driver.

CHAPTER 9: CONFIGURING THE KERNEL

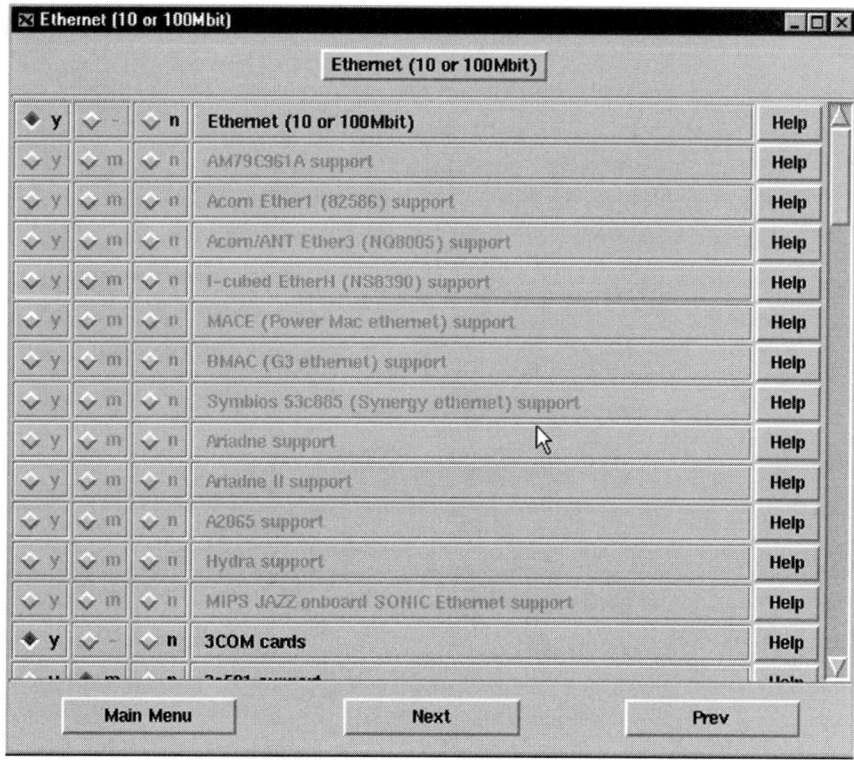

Figure 9.17. Network device support—Ethernet configuration.

At this point you can continue down the list and choose either y or m to indicate the drivers that you wish to have compiled into the system.

Customizing and Upgrading Linux

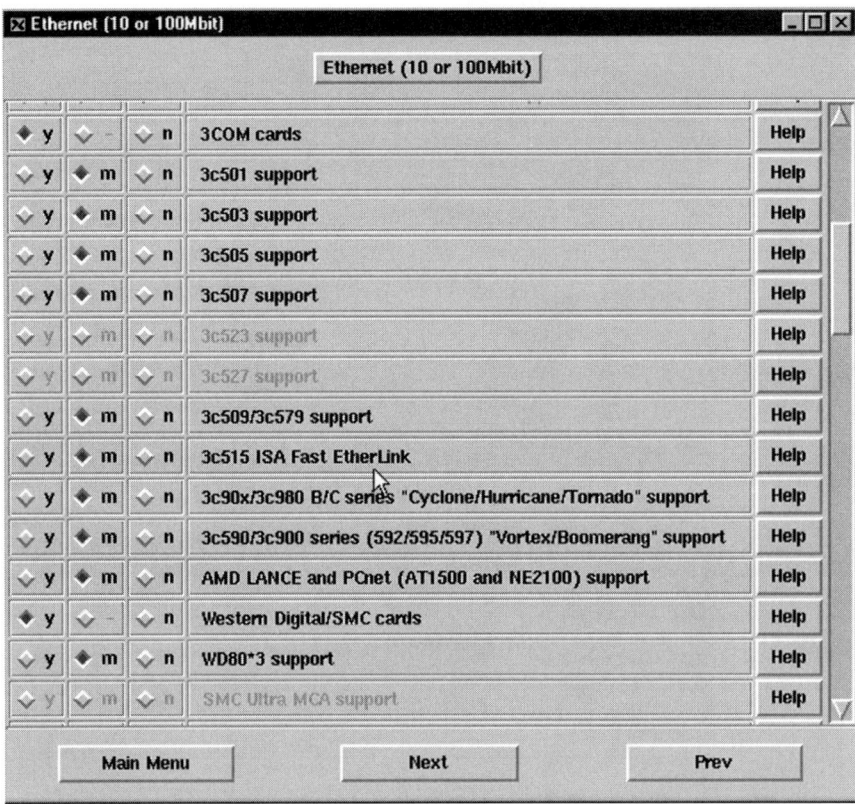

Figure 9.18. Network device support—Ethernet configuration, continued.

These are not common network devices, but they do exist. You may encounter them in your travels (or perhaps "travails" would be more appropriate).

CHAPTER 9: CONFIGURING THE KERNEL

SCSI Support

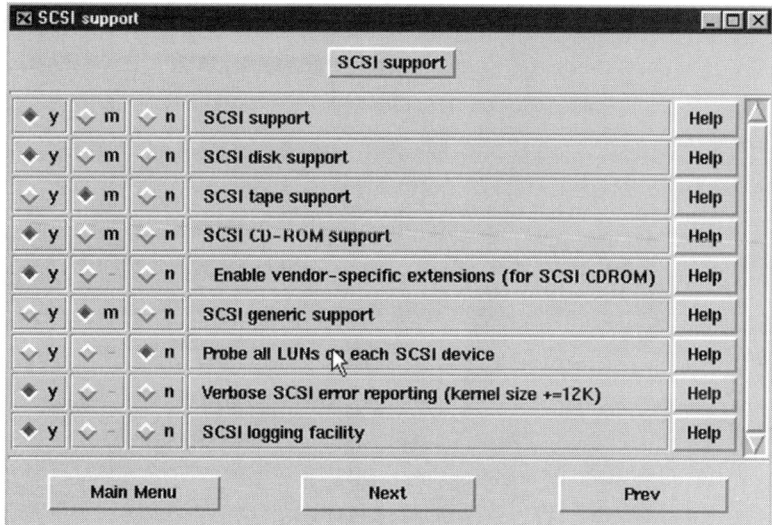

Figure 9.19. SCSI support dialog box.

If you are planning to use SCSI devices on your system, then you should select y or m for the SCSI support option in Figure 9.19 (y is the preferred selection).

If you choose SCSI support, then you have to be sure you selected RAM disk support earlier (see "Block Devices" section). Doing so ensures that the necessary SCSI modules and utilities will be loaded at boot time, so that patches and upgrades can be applied if and when necessary or desired.

SCSI low-level drivers

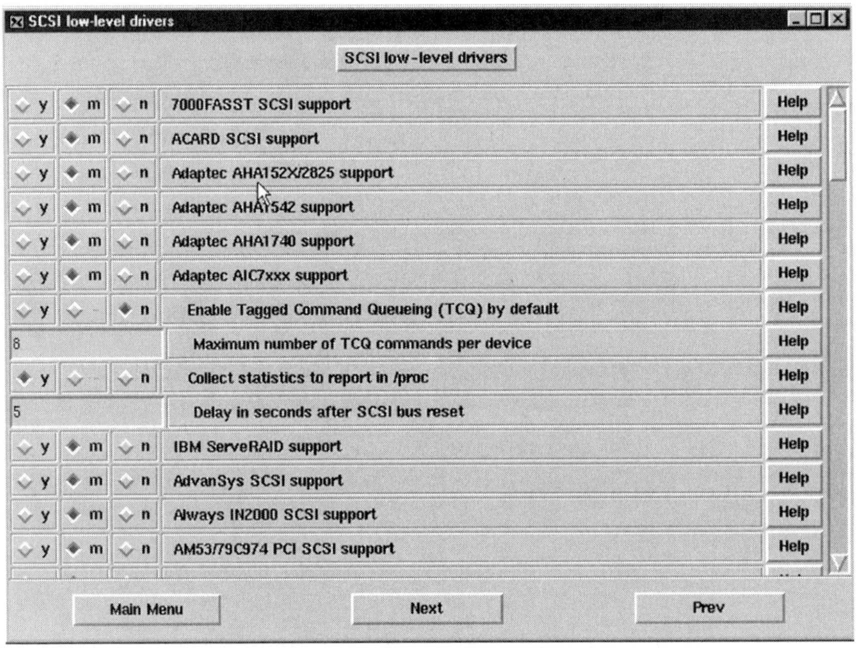

Figure 9.20. SCSI low-level drivers dialog box.

If you chose y for SCSI support in the previous section, then you must advise the installation program of the type of SCSI adapter or bus installed in your system. Choose the appropriate equipment from the list. A partial list is shown in Figure 9.20.

CHAPTER 9: CONFIGURING THE KERNEL

Filesystems

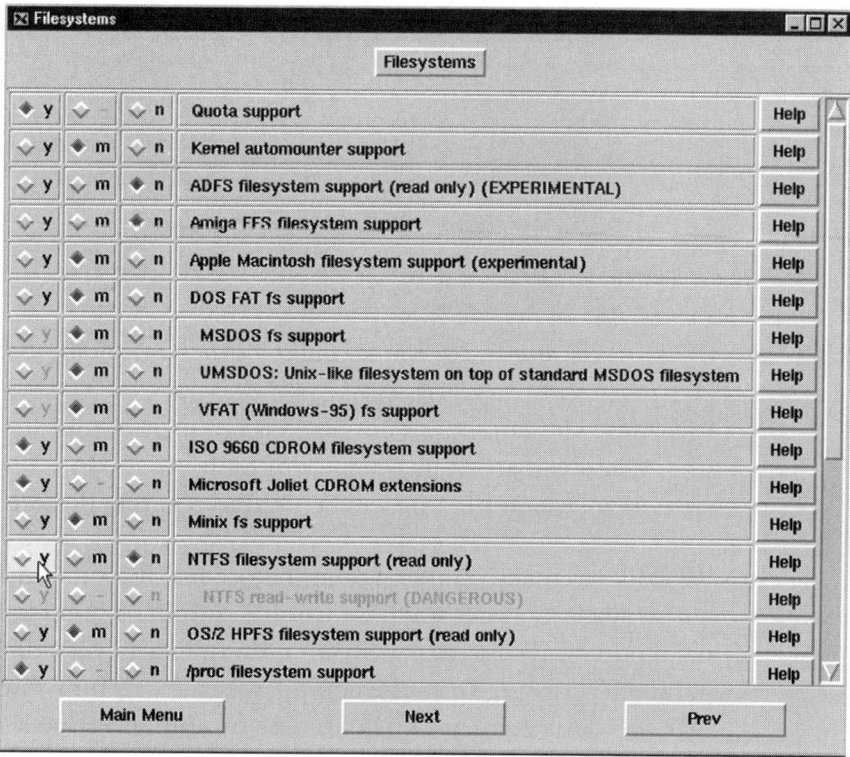

Figure 9.21. Filesystems dialog box.

If you choose to add `NTFS filesystem support (read only)` to the kernel (see Figure 9.21)— whether monolithic or modular—you will be able to access files on a Windows NTFS file system while Linux is up and running.

Save and Exit

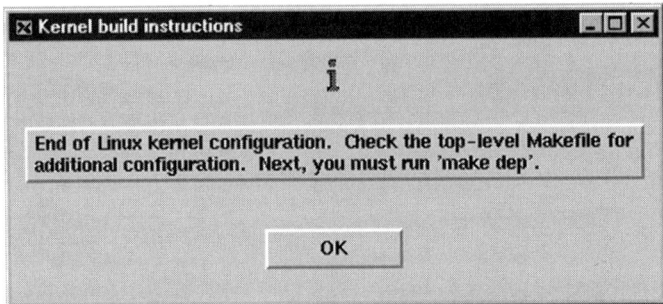

Figure 9.23. Kernel build instructions dialog box.

Save and exit! This may seem obvious but many people do forget this step. When you are at this point, this entire procedure should have created an *xconfig* file that will be used to compile the kernel.

We'd like to make one final point before moving on to the next chapter. If, at a later time, you have trouble running a command, configuring a port, and so on, ask yourself if there may be a configurable parameter missing from the compiled kernel. By now you realize that files on your system are no guarantee of support in the kernel.

Quiz

1. What two groups of professionals will need to perform kernel configuration?

2. What two general guidelines can be applied to kernel configuration?

3. Which configuration options will appear dimmed on menus?

4. What does the `Code maturity level` option determine?

5. What does the `Loadable module support` option determine?

6. When should you enable the `RAM disk support` option?

7. Which two `Networking` options should be enabled to provide basic TCP/IP support?

8. If the system is going to support either SLIP or PPP connections, which option needs to be enabled?

9. What is the final step in kernel configuration, and what does it create?

See Appendix B for answers.

Chapter 10

Installing a New Kernel by Building a New Source Tree

CHAPTER 8 FOCUSED ON INSTALLING a new Linux kernel by installing an upgraded RPM package, and Chapter 9 covered the basics of configuring a new kernel. In this chapter, the focus is on installing a new kernel beginning from the very basics—that is, beginning with the downloading of the kernel in `tar` file format from a source Web site on the Internet. Then we create all the new directories and symbolic links to prepare for the new source tree, and configure, compile, and implement the new kernel.

You may have to modify steps presented in this chapter based on the particular version of code that you are planning to use. This is probably the most complex task that you will ever have to perform on Linux, and it requires some knowledge of basic system-administration tasks such as creating new directories and symbolic links. We do not make the assumption that you can do this without assistance, and thus provide example syntax throughout.

You may have read about a utility called `zlilo`. This utility attempts to configure LILO to boot your new kernel, and although theoretically useful, it can fail the test for multiple kernels which is what we are trying to achieve.

We are going to assume that you have an existing functional system, and we are going to have you preserve your existing kernel configuration file using the `make oldconfig` method. This will allow you to get through this exercise without committing mental suicide. Once you have mastered the many kernel configuration options, we suggest using `make xconfig`.

As we proceed, we are going to encourage you to occasionally use modules as opposed to compiling an option right into the kernel. The results of this will show up when you test your new system after it is compiled. For example, if you choose to make your networking modular, you have to use a tool such as Red Hat, System, Control Panel to access your Ethernet interface to actually activate it or read the man pages on `insmod`. If nothing else, it will illustrate both the positive and negative aspects of using modules. If this becomes very confusing for you, you can simply go back and change your configuration to compile the feature into the kernel as opposed to being modular. However, having said this, if you use the `make oldconfig` method and use your previous *.config* file, then the new kernel should behave similarly to the old kernel.

Finding a New Kernel

To install a kernel from scratch, we'll start by obtaining a `tar` file from a reputable Web site and then creating the necessary file structures to recompile the kernel and rebuild the system. The most popular Web site to begin from is the Linux public archive at *http://www.kernel.org*, which is shown in Figure 10.1. However, as you

CHAPTER 10: INSTALLING A NEW KERNEL BY BUILDING A NEW SOURCE TREE

can see from the figure, there are other "mirror" sites from which the kernel files can be downloaded, which may be faster.

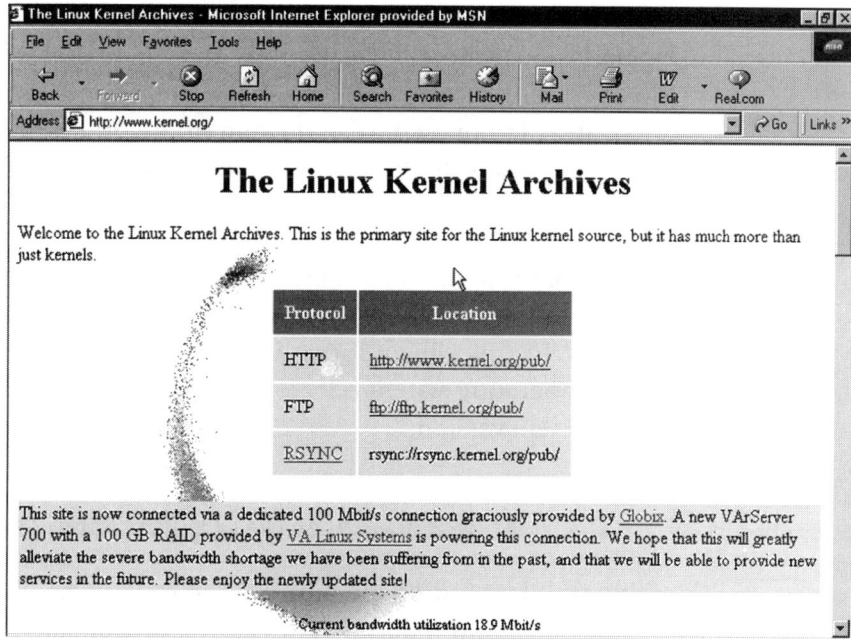

Figure 10.1. Linux public archive and mirror sites.

Installing a New Kernel

Installing a new kernel using a `tar` file we've downloaded from the Internet (as close to scratch as we can get in the Linux world) requires more expertise than using RPM packages. There are more than a dozen things that you must remember to do. We take you through this process over the course of the next 18 steps. Performing these tasks will also demonstrate how the operating system is assembled and introduce its internal operations.

Step 1. Record Current Kernel Level and Create Boot and Rescue Diskettes

The first component of this step, recording kernel information, is important because there is some information here that you will need to help you decide how to handle some of the compilation parameters. Repeating the procedure at the end of the process and comparing the two will indicate that the files were indeed properly upgraded or handled.

In the example command lines below, the command uname tells Linux to display system information. The -a option tells Linux to display all of the following information: hardware type, network-node host name, operating system release, operating system name, and operating system version.

```
# uname -a
Linuxhost1 2.2.14-5.0 #1 Wed Mar 7 20:53:41 MST 2000 i586 unknown
```

We recommend recording the output from the uname -a command. Record the exact information on the kernel version and the architecture, which in the example case is i586.

If you have not already done so, create a boot and rescue disk set now.

```
# mkbootdisk --device /dev/fd0 2.2.14-5.0
Insert a disk in /dev/fd0. Any information on the disk will be
   lost.
Press <Enter> to continue or ^C to abort:
```

If the existing version of Linux is older than Linux 6.1, you may also need to use the following two commands:

```
# mount /mnt/cdrom
# dd if=/mnt/cdrom/images/rescue.img of=/dev/fd0 \ bs= 1440k
```

CHAPTER 10: INSTALLING A NEW KERNEL BY BUILDING A NEW SOURCE TREE

We also recommend, purely for academic reasons, that you document the links and directories in the boot directory before you start because all of this is going to change after the new kernel is installed.

```
# cd /boot
# ls -l
Total 2481
lrwxrwxrwx  1 root root         21 Jul 14 08:39 System.map ->
   System.map-2.2.14-5.0
-rw-r--r--  1 root root     202709 Mar 07 18:58 System.map-2.2.14-5.0
-rw-r--r--  1 root root        512 Jul 13 11:39 boot.0300
-rw-r--r--  1 root root       4568 Feb 02 15:03 boot.b
-rw-r--r--  1 root root        612 Feb 01 15:03 chain.b
-rw-r--r--  1 root root        237 Jul 13 17:52 kernel.h
drwxr-xr-x  2 root root      12288 Jul 13 11:22 lost+found
-rw-------  1 root root      10240 Jul 13 11:39 map
lrwxrwxrwx  1 root root         22 Jul 13 11:31 module-info -> module-
   info-2.2.14-5.0
-rw-r--r--  1 root root      11773 Mar 07 18:58 module-info-2.2.14-5.0
-rw-r--r--  1 root root        620 Feb 02 15:03 os2_d.b
-rwxr-xr-x  1 root root    1638964 Mar 07 18:58 vmlinux-2.2.14-5.0
lrwxrwxrwx  1 root root         18 Jul 13 11:31 vmlinuz -> vmlinuz-
   2.2.14.5.0
-rw-r--r--  1 root root     640052 Mar 07 18:58 vmlinuz-2.2.14-5.0
```

Step 2. Obtain the Source Code in tar File Format

Figure 10.2 illustrates a listing that might be found at a typical Linux kernel source mirror site. Note that these `tar` files have a very specific naming convention that provides information on the state of the Linux kernel. For example, a kernel source `tar` file that has a minor-version number that is an odd number is deemed to be a development release and may contain bugs. On the other hand, a `tar` file whose minor-version number is an even number is considered to be a better, more stable release.

245

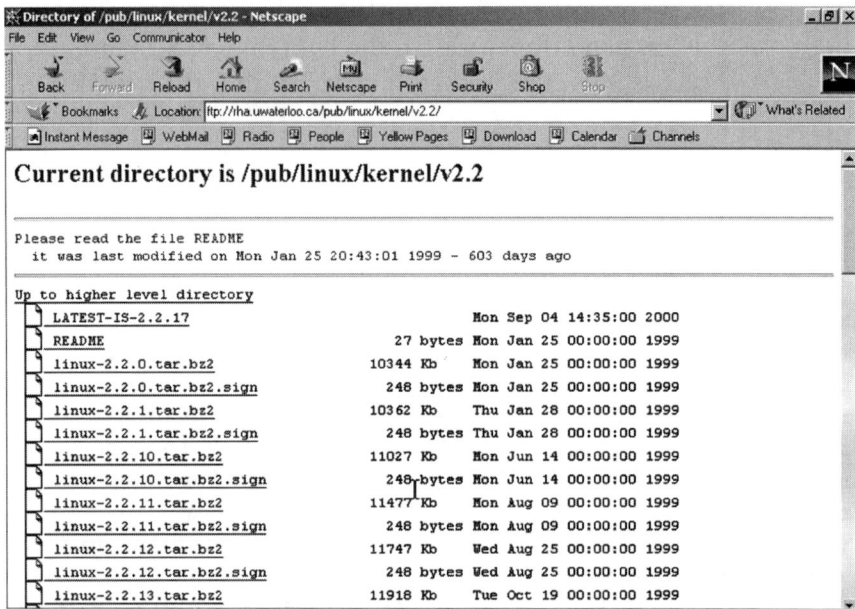

Figure 10.2. Typical listing at a Linux kernel source mirror Web site.

Let's have a closer look at the numbering convention. The format is: major-version number, minor-version number, revision number, and `tar` file type. The major-version number rarely changes. We have been using the same major version of the kernel for several months now. The minor-version number is an indication of stability. As we mentioned above, if the number is even, then the kernel is a more stable "production" version of the kernel. Odd-numbered minor numbers indicate that the kernel is still under development. These minor-version–number releases can cause problems for novice users. Development kernels are necessary for developers. The revision number indicates the patch level of the respective kernel. These can change frequently.

Red Hat is very particular about deeming a version to be production quality. At this writing, the following is stated on *www.kernel.org*: the latest stable version of Linux is 2.4.0-test4; the latest beta version of

Linux is 2.3.26; and the latest prepatch (alpha) version appears to be 2.3.27-6.

The files are going to be in *.tar*, *.tar.gz*, or *.tar.bz2* format. The *gz* and *bz2* files are files compressed with `gzip` and `bzip2`, respectively, which means you need the `gzip` and `bzip2` utilities to unzip them.

Put the `tar` file into the */usr/src* directory. However, do not unpack the files yet. At this point, simply note that when you unpack these files, you have to use the appropriate syntax.

For the *.tar.gz* files, you can use the following:

```
tar zxpvf linux-x.y-z.tar.gz
```

For the *.tar* files, use:

```
tar xpvf linux-x.y.z.tar
```

For the *.tar.bz2* files, use:

```
bzip2 linux-x.y.z.tar.bz2
```

We explain the commands and their respective options in Step 5.

Step 3. Check Space Requirements for New Kernel and New Source Tree

You will need an additional 55 MB or so if you want to add the new kernel and source tree without touching the existing one. We recommend that you try to create a new "parallel" structure so that you do not interfere with the existing kernel structure for now. Once the new kernel is up and running satisfactorily, then you can remove the existing structure. In extreme circumstances you can just overwrite the existing structure with the new kernel. This strategy is not recommended, however.

To check available space, use the df command as follows:

```
# df
Filesystem   1k blocks   Used    Available   Use%   Mounted on
/def/hda5     2909420   728596    2033028     26%   /
/dev/hda2       23333     2482      19647     11%   /boot
/dev/hdc       656134   656134          0    100%   /mnt/cdrom
```

Step 4. Preserve Old Source Tree

In this step we discuss preserving the old source tree by renaming the directories and removing the links to the old Linux source tree.

First, check to see that you put the new `tar` file (in the following example, we see the new `tar` file is called *linux-2.4.0-test4.tar.gz*) in the */usr/src* directory.

```
# cd /usr/src
# ls -l
total 21216
lrwxrwxrwx 1 root   root             12 Jul 13 11:27 linux ->
    linux-2.2.14-5.0
drwxr-xr-x 4 root   root           4096 Jul 13 11:27 linux-2.2.14
-rw-rw-r-- 1 linda  linda      21686364 Jul 14 15:54 linux-2.4.0-
    test4.tar.gz
drwxr-xr-x 7 root   root           4096 Jul 13 11:25 redhat
```

Note that when you unpack this file, it will automatically create or overwrite the existing directory called *linux*. The *linux* directory under */usr/src* is quite often just a link anyway. Because we do not want the existing directory overwritten, we need to unlink it.

Either remove the link or rename the existing directory to keep it separate (we suggest using the command **# rm linux**). It is customary to rename the *linux* directory using the current kernel revision number, which you can get by executing the `uname -r` command. In the above example, you can see we'll need to do this. So, let's change the name of the *linux-2.2.14 directory* to *linux-2.2.14-5.0* by using the following command:

```
# mv linux-2.2-14 linux-2.2.14-5
```

Now, we should have */usr/src* directory with no directory named *linux* in it. When the `tar` file is unpacked, it will create a new directory called *linux*.

Step 5. Unpack Archived tar Files

Now you can unpack the archived `tar` file named *linux-2.4.0-test4.tar.gz*. We will use the `tar` command. The `tar` program is an archiving utility that stores files in a compressed format.

We will use `tar` with several of its options, as follows:

- ▲ x Extract files from an archived `tar` file.

- ▲ p Preserve all the permission/protection information appended to the files in the archive file.

- ▲ v List individual files as they are unpacked ("verbose" option).

- ▲ f Indicate which archive `tar` file to unpack.

- ▲ z Filter archive through `gzip` as `tar` unpacks the *.tar.gz*-formatted `tar` file.

First, copy or move the file to the */usr/src* directory. Then, because we are unpacking a *.tar.gz* file, we use all the options:

```
# cd /usr/src
# tar zxpvf linux-2.4.0-test4.tar.gz
```

Otherwise, if we had a *.tar* file, we would only use four of the options as follows:

```
# tar xpvf linux-2.4.0-test4.tar
```

Step 6. Create Link to New Linux Source Tree

This step is more of a recommendation than a mandatory task, but taking it will make the next few utilities behave differently. Do not create a link after this point because it will be difficult. For example, the next few `make` commands will place and organize module and script information based on the link created here.

First, rename the directory named *linux* to *linux-new_revision_number* (in our case, it will be *linux-2.4.0*) by using the following command:

```
# mv linux linux-2.4.0
```

We want the generic *linux* directory, when called by the compile procedures, to link to the proper directory *linux-2.4.0* and not to *linux-2.2.14-5*. So, we enter:

```
# ln -s linux-2.4.0 linux
```

To check whether the links are correct, we list the directory contents:

```
# ls -l
Total 21220
lrwxrwxrwx   1 root root           11 Jul 13 13:38 linux -> linux-2.4.0
drwxr-xr-x  18 root root         4096 Jul 13 10:43 linux-2.2.14-5
drwxr-xr-x  14 1046 101          1046 Jul 13 13:38 linux-2.4.0
-rw-r--r--   1 root root     21686384 Jul 13 13:30 linux-2.4.0-test4.
   tar.gz
drwxr-xr-x   7 root root         4096 Jul 13 10:36 redhat
```

We are now ready to remove any old *.o* files.

Step 7. Check for .o Files and Dependencies in Source Tree

The `mrproper` command is a script that will find all old object code (that is, *.o*) files that correspond to the version 2.2.14-5 code, and sys-

CHAPTER 10: INSTALLING A NEW KERNEL BY BUILDING A NEW SOURCE TREE

tematically remove them from */usr/src/linux*. This script has to be run from the new */usr/src/linux* directory. It will also remove information from a series of other related directories as well. This script will make note of the name of the path and apply it to its logic.

For example, if you leave the *linux* directory name as *linux* without a link, the `mrproper` command will clean up module information in */usr/src/linux/include/linux/modules*. On the other hand, if you have relinked the directory as recommended above, it will clean up */usr/src/linux-2.4.0-test4/include/linux/modules,* which is what you want.

You can see how changing your strategy for naming or linking this directory after this step will confuse the process.

Let's invoke `make mrproper` now. Please note two things: you need to be in the */usr/src/linux* directory to run `make mrproper`; and there will likely be a lot of output that will vary from what we show you here. Each system is configured differently, which results in different responses to this command.

```
# cd /usr/src/linux
# make mrproper
make[1]: Entering directory '/usr/src/linux/arch/i386/boot'
rm -f tools/build
rm -f setup bootsect zImage compressed/vmlinux.out
rm -f bsetup bbootsect bzImage compressed/bvmlinux.out
make[2]: Entering directory '/usr/src/linux/arch/i386/boot/
   compressed'
rm -f vmlinux bvmlinux_tmp_*
make[2]: Leaving directory '/usr/src/linux/arch/i386/boot/compressed'
make[1]: Leaving directory '/usr/src/linux/arch/i386/boot'
rm -f kernel/ksyms.lst include/linux/compile.h
find . -name '*.[oas]' -type f -print | grep -v |xdialog/ | xargs rm -f
rm -f core 'find . -type f -name 'core' -print'
rm -f core 'find . -name f -name'.*.flags' -print'
rm -f vmlinux System.map
rm -f tmp*
rm -f drivers/char/consolemap_deftbl.c drivers/video/promcon_tbl.c
```

```
rm -f drivers/char/conmakehash
rm -f drivers/pci/devlist.h drivers/pci/classlist.h drivers/pci/
   gen-devlist
rm -f drivers/sound/bin2hex drivers/sound/hex2hex
rm -f drivers/atm/fore200e_mkfirm drivers/atm/
   {pca,sba}*{.bin,.bin1,.bin2}
rm -f net/khttpd/make_times_h
rm -f/net/khttpd/times.h
rm -f submenu*
rm -rf modules
```

Step 8. Check Software Requirements

Inside your new */usr/src/linux/Documentation* directory is a file called *Changes*. You have to read this file and locate a stanza of information called "Current Minimal Requirements." This is a listing of software revisions that you must have before attempting to compile a new kernel.

All software entities and their respective revision levels are listed here, as are the various commands (for example: `gcc -version`, `ld -v`, `chsh -v`, and so on) that you can enter at the command line to check the respective version numbers. An excerpt of a sample file and stanza is shown next.

```
# cd /usr/src/linux/Documentation
# cat Changes | less
Intro
=====
This document is designed to provide a list of the minimum levels of
software necessary to run the 2.4 kernels, as well as provide brief
instructions regarding any other "Gotchas" users may encounter when
trying life on the Bleeding Edge. If upgrading from a pre-2.2.x
kernel, please consult the Changes file included with 2.2.x kernels
for additional information; most of that information will not be
repeated here. Basically, this document assumes that your system is
already functional and running at least 2.2.x kernels.

This document is originally based on my "Changes" file for 2.0.x
kernels and therefore owes credit to the same people as that file
```

CHAPTER 10: INSTALLING A NEW KERNEL BY BUILDING A NEW SOURCE TREE

(Jared Mauch, Axel Boldt, Alessandro Sigala, and countless other users all over the 'net).

The latest revision of this document, in various formats, can always Be found at http://cyberbuzz.gatech.edu/kaboom/linux/Changes-2.4/ <http://cyberbuzz.gatech.edu/kaboom/linux/Changes-2.4>.

Following is the "Current Minimal Requirements" stanza of this file:

```
Current Minimal Requirements
============================
Upgrade to at *least* these software revisions before thinking you've
encountered a bug! If you're unsure what version you're currently
running, the suggested command should tell you.

Again, keep in mind that this list assumes you are already functionally
running a Linux 2.2 kernel. Also, not all tools are necessary on all
systems; obviously, if you don't have any PCMCIA (PC Card) hardware,
for example, you probably needn't concern yourself with pcmcia-cs.

- Gnu C2.7.2.3#         gcc --version
- binutils2.9.1.0.22#   ld -v
- util-linux2.10g   #   chsh -v
- modutils2.3.10#       insmod -v
- e2fsprogs1.18#        /sbin/tune2fs --version
- pcmcia-cs3.1.13#      cardmgr -V
- PPP  2.4.0b1#         pppd --version
- isdn4k-utils3.1beta7# isdnctrl 2>&1|grep version
```

If you do not meet the current software requirements (that is, if the results of entering the recommended commands provide software version numbers that are lower than those listed in the *Changes* file), you are expected to obtain the software and add it to your system. The software should be available in the form of RPM packages and can be added using the same procedure as the one we used for the XFree86 RPM packages in Chapter 7.

We cannot emphasize enough the importance of this step. It takes time and patience, but it will ensure a successful installation. This can be a very difficult and time-consuming part of creating your new kernel. If the instructions set out for you inside this new *Changes* file are not implemented, then you will be wasting valuable time from this point forward. Now, in some cases, you may not require each and every one of these new pieces of code, but only the ones that are applicable to your specific configuration (for example, your PC may not require PCMCIA-CS support). In our experience, this is the task that, when ignored or undertaken without due attention, causes most upgrades to fail. If you are lucky, it just will not compile. If you are unlucky, it will compile something weird into your code, and it will drive you nuts from this time forward.

Step 9. Configure Kernel

This is probably the most involved task, and you have to get it right. We do not provide steps here because we have already dedicated Chapter 9 to it. At this point, you should refer to Chapter 9.

You can return to configuring the kernel as many times as you need to, until you feel you have it right. We recommend that you first run `make oldconfig` (from the *linux-2.2.14-5* directory, in this case), which will show you the differences between the old and new kernels. The `make oldconfig` command will attempt to configure the new kernel from the old configuration file; it will prompt you only for the new features. To use `oldconfig`, you have to preserve your previous configuration options. To do this, you have to copy your previous */usr/src/linux-2.2.14-5.0/.config* file to the new */usr/src/linux* directory. If you discover that you have no *.config* file, go to the directory containing the old source files (in this case, the *linux-2.2.14-5* directory) and run `make config` at least once to generate a *.config* file in that directory. Then you can copy it over. We have used this technique in the exercise at the end of this chapter. You can also use this as a check to determine if all new features added to the kernel are going to be available. As soon as you see this information, you should go immediately to `make xconfig` to continue configuration of the kernel.

CHAPTER 10: INSTALLING A NEW KERNEL BY BUILDING A NEW SOURCE TREE

We've already alluded to the fact that you also can use `make config` instead of `make xconfig`. You can even use `make menuconfig`. All these utilities do the same thing, but `make config` and `make menuconfig` require more effort and patience to see what is going on, because the presentations are text and overwhelming to the novice. We recommend that you use `make xconfig` until you have this step down to a "mad science."

Step 10. Prepare for Compilation: make dep and make clean

The `make dep` command takes the *.config* file and builds a corresponding dependency tree. If this command does not return an error code of 0, return to `make xconfig` (if that's the utility you used originally; otherwise, use the two others mentioned in the previous section) and rectify any errors before proceeding to the next task.

The `make clean` command removes all files related to any previous compiles to ensure that you do not mingle or inherit previously compiled information.

Alas, many system managers tend to proceed past this point without reading their error messages. We recommend that the results of running these scripts be redirected to a file, or that error lines be `grep`'d and examined before proceeding. In the next example, the program complains about missing directories for some drivers that we do not wish to have anyway. These will not prevent us from compiling, but had we needed these drivers and missed these lines, we would have been in trouble, at least for a while. In other words, you can compile a kernel containing errors as long as you know the exact nature of the errors and you are certain that they are irrelevant.

An example of the `make dep` command follows. Note that you must execute it from the */usr/src/linux* directory, or it will not work.

```
# cd /usr/src/linux
# make dep > /tmp/dep.out
newport.c:11: asm/gfx.h: No such file or directory
newport.c:12: asm/ng1.h: No such file or directory
newport.c:14: asm/newport.h: No such file or
    directory
config.c:423: #error "HiSax: No cards configured"
adb.c:28: asm/prom.h: No such file or directory
adb.c:29: asm/adb.h: No such file or directory
adb.c:30: asm/cuda.h: No such file or directory
adb.c:31: asm/pmu.h: No such file or directory
adb.c:33: asm/hydra.h: No such file or directory
```

You will notice that you get much more output than we've listed here. OK, now let's get ready to invoke make clean.

As you did with the make dep command, execute the make clean command from the */usr/src/linux* directory, or it will not work.

```
# cd /usr/src/linux
# make clean >/tmp/clean.out
```

Step 11. Compile Kernel: make bzImage

This step compiles the kernel and can take a while depending on the processing power of your system. We have seen this process take up to an hour. Be patient and be prepared.

The commands for using zImage and bzImage follow. Note that you have to be in the */usr/src/linux* directory to execute them, or they will not work.

```
# cd /usr/src/linux
# make zImage
```

CHAPTER 10: INSTALLING A NEW KERNEL BY BUILDING A NEW SOURCE TREE

or

```
# make bzImage
```

The difference between the two is simply the compression algorithm used to compress the file. No configuration issues will arise other than it may take a bit longer to uncompress a *bzImage* file than it will a *zImage* file during boot. The bzImage utility is an improvement over zImage only in terms of compression ratio.

This procedure will not overwrite the existing kernel. The new kernel will be placed in the */usr/src/linux/arch/i386/boot* directory and will be called *bzImage*, as shown in Figure 10.3.

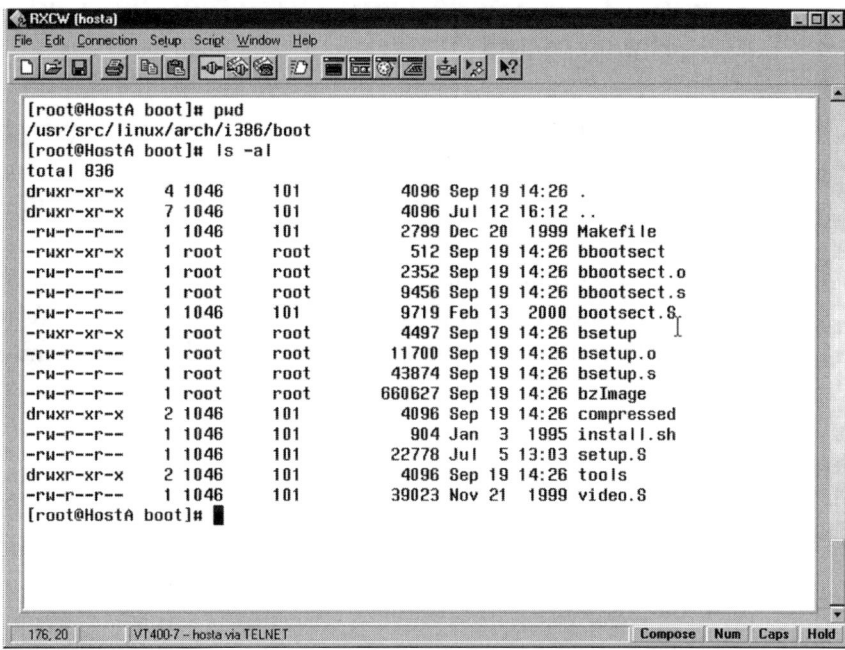

Figure 10.3. The new kernel file, bzImage, is added to the already-existing kernel files in the directory.

A limitation of Intel machines requires the kernel to be decompressed at start-up time within the first 600–700 KB of memory. Otherwise, you may get an error indicating that the kernel is too large. If you get a message like that, use `bzImage` instead of `zImage` to compile a smaller kernel, so that you can work around this limitation.

TIP: *If you want to make a boot disk (without the root file system or LILO), insert a floppy diskette in your A: drive, and execute the* `make disk` *command. Now you have a diskette with the kernel on it to test without changing your system. When the kernel is what you want, then proceed to put this new kernel in place on your machine for future use.*

Step 12. Make Modules: make modules and make modules_install

Assume that during the `make xconfig` procedure (see the beginning of this chapter), you chose to use the modules you need for `make modules` and `make modules_install`. Executing these commands in this step will overwrite your existing module information if you do not rename the directory. The modules reside in the */lib/modules* directory as */usr/modules/<kernel_release>*. We recommend that you rename the directory prior to issuing these commands. (Note that you must execute the `make modules` and `make modules_install` commands from the */usr/src/linux* directory, or they will not work.)

```
# cd /lib/modules
# mv 2.2.14-5.15 2.2.14-5.old
# cd /usr/src/linux
# make modules
# make modules_install

# ls -l /lib/modules/
total 8
```

```
drwxr-xr-x 11 root root 4096 Jul 13 17:52 2.2.14-5.0 .old
drwxr-xr-x  6 root root 4096 Jul 14 21:39 2.4.0-test4
# uname -r
2.2.14-5.0
```

The `make modules` command creates the modules. The `make modules_install` command installs the modules in the directory. The new modules should be in a directory named with the version number of the kernel you just compiled.

If errors occur, you have probably chosen some conflicting modules. To resolve these issues, go back to the `oldconfig` or `xconfig` stage and rework the kernel options again—and again, as many times as you need to. At some point in this process, you may want to resort to paper and pen to map out an objective that does not contain conflicts. To do this, you should use the Help option within the kernel configuration tool to carefully research each item that you are adding to or removing from the new kernel. We are also assuming that you still have access to the original *.config* file which corresponds to the previous kernel version. The scientific method works well here. Consider changing only one thing at a time to find out where the break is.

Step 13. Copy bzImage Kernel and System.map Files to Correct Directories

The new *bzImage* kernel file in */usr/src/linux/arch/i386/boot* should be copied to the */boot* directory. We recommend that you rename this file, so that it does not overwrite the old kernel file, and then relink it.

```
# cd /usr/src/linux/arch/i386/boot
# cp bzImage /boot/vmlinuz-2.4.0-test4
# cd /boot
# rm vmlinuz
# ln -s vmlinuz-2.4.0-test4   vmlinuz
# ls -l /boot
```

Note that the second command in the preceding listing copies and renames simultaneously, so that the older version is not clobbered. In addition, the fifth command gives it the generic name *vmlinuz* which LILO will use to refer to it.

You will also have to replace *System.map*, although some systems have a static *System.map* file in which case you are okay here. We have assumed that you have a symbolic link named *System.map* which has to be modified and copied.

When the kernel was compiled, a new *System.map* file was created that must also be put in place. Otherwise, when you reboot, the kernel will give you a "missing System.map" error.

The new *System.map* file will be in the top-level directory called */usr/src/linux*. This file should have the same creation time and date as the *bzImage* file. Again, we recommend that you rename the *System.map* file and create a link to it, so as not to overwrite the old *System.map* file.

```
# cd /usr/src/linux
# cp System.map /boot/System.map-2.4.0-test4
# cd /boot
# rm System.map
# ln -s System.map-2.4.0-test4 System.map
total 3667
lrwxrwxrwx  1 root root        16 Jul 14 22:15 System.map ->
    System.map-2.4.0-test4
-rw-r--r--  1 root root    202709 Mar 07 18:58 System.map-2.2.14-5.0
-rw-r--r--  1 root root    406161 Jul 14 22:12 System.map-2.4.0-test4
-rw-r--r--  1 root root       512 Jul 13 11:39 boot.0300
-rw-r--r--  1 root root      4568 Feb 02 15:03 boot.b
-rw-r--r--  1 root root       612 Feb 02 15:03 chain.b
-rw-r--r--  1 root root       237 Jul 13 17:52 kernel.h
drwxr-xr-x  2 root root     12288 Jul 13 11:22 lost+found
-rw-------  1 root root     10240 Jul 14 21:48 map
lrwxrwxrwx  1 root root        22 Jul 13 11:31 module-info -> module-
    info-2.2.14-5.0
```

```
-rw-r--r--   1 root    root      11773 Mar 07 18:58 module-info-2.2.14-5.0
-rw-r--r--   1 root    root        620 Feb 02 15:03 os2_d.b
-rwxr-xr-x   1 root    root    1638964 Mar 07 18:58 vmlinux-2.2.14-5.0
lrwxrwxrwx   1 root    root         13 Jul 14 22:05 vmlinuz -> vmlinuz-
   2.4.0-test4
-rw-r--r--   1 root    root     640052 Mar 07 18:58 vmlinuz-2.2.14-5.0
-rw-r--r--   1 root    root     798939 Jul 14 21:43 vmlinuz-2.4.0-test4
```

Step 14. Optional: Create RAM Disk File

The purpose of using an initial RAM disk file is to allow a modular kernel to have access to modules that it might need to boot from before the kernel has access to the device where the modules normally reside. Not all systems require you to make an `initrd` or RAM disk file, but for older kernel versions and older hardware, this can be paramount. For example, we have an old SCSI system that cannot find the drive unless we preload the Adaptec 1520 controller. (We hope that you have better equipment, but this system of ours refuses to die. We have appropriately named it Christine.) To make the RAM disk, which you'll call *initrd-2.4.0-test4.img*, you use the `mkinitrd` command with the new kernel as its argument, as seen in the example below.

```
# cd /boot
# mkinitrd /boot/initrd-2.4.0-test4.img  2.4.0-test4
# ls -l init*
-rw-r--r-- 1 root root 278788 Jun 1 15:08 initrd-
   2.4.0-test4.img
```

When finished, you will have a RAM disk file in the */boot* directory called *initrd-2.4.0-test4.img*, which you will point to from the */etc/lilo.conf* file. In the next section we provide an example of a *lilo.conf* file that uses an `initrd` statement.

Step 15. Modify /etc/lilo.conf File to Point to New Kernel without and with a RAM Disk File

Change directory to /etc. We reproduce the contents of the lilo.conf file here:

```
# cd /etc
# cat lilo.conf
boot=/dev/hda
map=/boot/map
install=/boot/boot.b
prompt
timeout=50
image=/boot/vmlinuz-2.2.14-5.0
label=linux
root=/dev/hda1
read-only
```

Using your favorite text editor, make the following changes to your lilo.conf file if you are not using a RAM disk:

```
# cat /etc/lilo.conf
boot=/dev/hda
map=/boot/map
install=/boot/boot.b
prompt
timeout=50
linear
default=;linux_new

image=/boot/vmlinuz-2.4.0-test4
    label=linux_new
    read-only
    root=/dev/hda5

image=/boot/vmlinuz-2.2.14-5.0
    label=linux
```

```
read-only
root=/dev/hda5
```

Make the following changes to your *lilo.conf* file if you are using a RAM disk:

```
# cat /etc/lilo.conf
boot=/dev/sda
map=/boot/map
install=/boot/boot.b
prompt
linear
timeout=50
image=/boot/vmlinuz-2.2.14-5.0
label=linux-2.2.14-5.0
root=/dev/sda1
initrd=/boot/initrd-2.2.14-5.0.img
read-only
image=/boot/vmlinuz-2.4.0-test4
label=linux-2.4.0-test4
root=/dev/sda1
initrd=/boot/initrd-2.4.0-test4.img
read-only
```

Before you exit this section, make sure that the files you are pointing to in the `image=` statements are in the boot directory. The `lilo -v` command should tell you, but only you know if you copied the correct one.

Step 16. Update Master Boot Record

Now run `lilo -v` to update the MBR with the new LILO information. Remember that if you make any changes to the */etc/lilo.conf* file you have to rerun `lilo -v` to update the master boot record.

```
# lilo -v
LILO version 21, Copyright 1992-1998 Werner
    Almesberger

Reading boot sector from /dev/hda
Merging with /boot/boot.b
Boot image: /boot/vmlinuz-2.4.0
Added linux_new
Boot image: /boot/vmlinuz-2.2.14-5.0
Added linux *
/boot/boot.0300 exists - no backup copy made.
Writing boot sector.
```

Step 17. Shut Down and Test System: Rescue If Necessary

Shut down and reboot the system with the following command:

```
# shutdown -r now
```

To boot a system that has a Linux version equivalent to those older than Red Hat Linux 6.1 or 6.2, you will likely need two diskettes: a boot diskette and a rescue diskette. If you have Red Hat Linux 6.1 or 6.2 and the system will boot from a CD-ROM, then you only need the Linux CD. If booting from the CD-ROM drive isn't an option, then you'll need the boot diskette.

Because Step b below has to be taken quickly, read this procedure over before you begin!

a. Boot Linux from the boot diskette (that is, the one with the boot image), unless your system is capable of booting from the CD.

b. Quick! When the `boot:` prompt appears, type `rescue`, which will load the kernel from the diskette or the CD, whichever is applicable in this situation.

c. Follow the prompts. You may need to replace a boot disk with a rescue disk when prompted to do so, depending on your configuration.

d. When you get a shell prompt, you can try to mount your drives.

e. Create an empty mount point.

```
# mkdir    /mnt/linux
# mount  -t  ext2  /dev/hda1    /mnt/linux
```

Good luck!

If you are really desperate to boot, you can also try to boot from the Linux installation CD-ROM.

If you are super desperate to boot, you can try to do so from DOS via accessing the CD-ROM and using the `autoboot` option under the *dosutils*.

Step 18. Check New Kernel

There are three ways to check on your new kernel. First, make sure the new log-in herald reflects the new kernel revision. Then, when you are logged in, issue a `uname -a` command and make sure that it, too, reflects the new revision. At this point, you should proceed to check all applications to ensure that they are responding correctly and as expected. If all three of these checks work, congratulations are in order.

Exercise

This exercise may or may not be straightforward. Like previous exercises, the specifics are particular to our example system (wherein we upgrade from kernel version *2.2.14-5.0* to *2.4.0-test4*, the most current kernel level as of this writing), but the steps for other systems are the same. Again, we encourage you to make all the necessary notes as you go along to ensure a successful upgrade. If you are an experienced system administrator, you will no doubt know to add additional backup steps and procedures to this list.

1. Begin by recording the current level of your kernel and the system architecture type you currently have (for example, i386 or i586).

    ```
    # uname -a
    Linux host1 2.2.14-5.0 #1 Wed Jun 2 09:02:27 EDT 2000
        i586 unknown
    ```

2. Create a boot diskette. But first, check to see that the kernel points to the root device.

    ```
    # rdev /boot/vmlinuz
    Root device /dev/hda1
    ```

3. Format a floppy diskette.

    ```
    # fdformat    /dev/fd0H1440
    Double-sided, 80 tracks, 18 sec/track. Total capacity
        1440 kB.
    Formatting ... done
    Verifying ... done
    ```

4. Copy your good kernel to the diskette.

    ```
    # cd /usr/src/linux/arch/i386/boot
    # dd  if=bzImage  of=/dev/fd0
    ```

```
1117+1 records in
1117+1 records out
# mkbootdisk --device /dev/fd0   2.2.14-5.0
```

5. Ensure that your system's BIOS is set to look at the floppy drive first, or you can simply use `mkbootdisk`.

```
# uname -r
2.2.14-5.0
# mkbootdisk --device /dev/fd0   2.2.14-5.0
Insert a disk in /dev/fd0. Any information on the disk
    will be lost.
Press <Enter> to continue or ^C to abort:
```

Your boot diskette is created.

6. Create a rescue diskette.

```
# mount /mnt/cdrom
# dd  if=/mnt/cdrom/images/rescue.img  of=/dev/fd0
    bs=1440k
```

7. Obtain the required `tar` file and put it into the */usr/src* directory. The file used in this exercise was obtained from the *www.kernel.org* Web site. Using `ftp`, copy the file to your system.

```
# cd /usr/src
# mv /root/linux-2.4.0-test4.tar.gz /usr/src
```

8. Make sure that there is enough space in the */* and */usr* directories for the new source tree. Note that this is almost a 1:1 relationship because these 1-K blocks are really 1024 K, which means you need approximately 1000 1-K blocks for a megabyte. Given that we have 404933 1-K blocks available in */usr*, we have 404 MB of free space.

```
# df
Filesystem   1k-blocks     Used Available  Use% Mounted on
/dev/hda        398124    42294    335269   11%  /
/dev/hda6        99507      102     94266    0%  /home
/dev/hda5       944271   490553    404933   55%  /usr
```

9. Because there is enough space available, we are going to preserve the old Linux source tree by renaming the directories and removing the link to the old source tree. This will allow the new *linux* directory to be created without writing on top of the existing tree.

Before

```
# ls -l
total 14789
lrwxrwxrwx  1 root root    11 May 31 20:22 linux ->
    linux-2.2.14-5
drwxr-xr-x 17 root root 1024 May 31 20:19 linux-2.2.14-5
drwxr-xr-x  7 root root 1024 May 27 04:12 redhat
#
# rm linux
```

After

```
# ls -l
total 14788
-rw-r--r--  1 root  root 15079540 May 31 20:04 linux-
    2.4.0-test4.tar.gz
drwxr-xr-x 17root  root     1024 May 31 20:19 linux-
    2.2.14-5.0
drwxr-xr-x  7 root  root     1024 May 27 04:12 redhat
```

10. Unpack the *tar.gz* file.

```
# tar zxpvf linux-2.4.0-test4.tar.gz
# ls -l
total 14789
drwxr-xr-x 14 1046 console 1024 Apr 20 18:16 linux
-rw-r--r--  1 root root 15079540 May 31 20:04 linux-
    2.4.0-test4.tar.gz
drwxr-xr-x 17 root root     1024 May 31 20:19 linux-
    2.2.14-5.0
drwxr-xr-x  7 root root     1024 May 27 04:12 redhat
```

11. Create a link to the new Linux source tree for consistency.

```
# ln -s linux-2.4.0-test4 linux
```

CHAPTER 10: INSTALLING A NEW KERNEL BY BUILDING A NEW SOURCE TREE

12. Make sure that there are no stale *.o* files and dependencies in the source tree.

    # `make mrproper`

    You should now have the source tree installed.

13. Check for software requirements. Upgrade your software to a version whose number is higher than those displayed in the */usr/src/linux/Documentation/Changes* file, before imagining that you have encountered a bug! Your *Changes* file may or may not be the same as what is shown below. Meanwhile, if you are unsure of the version you are running, the command suggested in your *Changes* file should tell you. Remember, if the software listed doesn't apply to your configuration, don't worry about the version requirement(s).

    ```
    # cd /usr/src/linux/Documentation
    # cat Changes | less
    - Kernel modutils       2.1.121      ; insmod -V
    - Gnu C                 2.7.2.3      ; gcc --version
    - Binutils              2.8.1.0.23   ; ld -v
    - Linux libc5 C Library 5.4.46       ; ls -l /lib/libc*
    - Linux libc6 C Library 2.0.7pre5    ; ls -l /lib/libc*
    - Dynamic Linker (ld.so)1.9.9        ; ldd --version or
                                           ldd -v
    - Linux C++ Library     2.7.2.8      ; ls -l /usr/lib/
                                           libg++.so.*
    - Procps                1.2.9        ; ps --version
    - Procinfo              16           ; procinfo -v
    - Psmisc                17           ; pstree -V
    - Net-tools             1.52         ; hostname -V
    - Loadlin               1.6a
    - Sh-utils              1.16         ; basename --v
    - Autofs                3.1.1        ; automount --
                                           version
    - NFS                   2.2beta40    ; showmount --
                                           version
    ```

```
- Bash           1.14.7    ; bash -version
- Ncpfs          2.2.0     ; ncpmount -v
- Pcmcia-cs      3.0.13    ; cardmgr -V
- PPP            2.3.8     ; pppd --version
- Util-linux     2.9t      ; chsh -v
```

As outlined in Step 8 of the main text of this chapter, you have to read this file and locate a stanza of information called "Current Minimal Requirements." This is where we obtained the above listing of software revisions that have to be installed before attempting to compile a new kernel.

Each software entity and its revision level is listed here, as well as the command that you can enter at the command line to check the version. For example, to check to see if your kernel modutils are at 2.1.21, you type in `insmod -V` at the command line and interpret the results. If your software does not meet the current version requirements, you are expected to obtain the required software and add it to your system. The software should be available in the form of RPM packages, which can be added using the same procedure as the one we used for the `XFree86` RPM packages in Chapter 7.

14. Configure the kernel. If you are going to use the `oldconfig` option, remember to copy your *.config* file from the old kernel directory to the new */usr/src/linux*. Refer back in this chapter for the specific methodology.

```
# cd /usr/src/linux
# make oldconfig
```
or
```
# make xconfig
```
Then
```
# make dep
```
and

```
# make clean
```

and

```
# make bzImage
```

and

```
# make modules
# make modules_install
```

15. Copy the newly compiled kernel to the */boot* directory. Modify the necessary file links so that they point to the new kernel and kernel support directories for *System.map*.

```
# cd /usr/src/linux/arch/i386/boot
# cp bzImage /boot/vmlinuz-2.4.0-test4
# cd /usr/src/linux
# cp System.map /boot/System.map-2.4.0-test4
# cd /boot
# rm linuz
# ln -s vmlinuz-2.4.0-test4 vmlinuz
# rm System.map
# ln -s System.map-2.4.0-test4 System.map
```

16. Modify the */etc/lilo.conf* file to add the new stanza that points to the new kernel. Remember that if you make a change to the */etc/lilo.conf* file, you must rerun `lilo -v` to update the master boot record.

Before

```
# cat lilo.conf
boot=/dev/hda
map=/boot/map
install=/boot/boot.b
prompt
timeout=50
image=/boot/vmlinuz-2.2.14-5.0
label=linux
```

```
root=/dev/hda1
read-only
```

After

```
# cat /etc/lilo.conf
boot=/dev/hda
map=/boot/map
install=/boot/boot.b
prompt
timeout=50
default=linux_new
image=/boot/vmlinuz-2.4.0-test4
        label=linux_new
        root=/dev/hda1
        read-only
image=/boot/vmlinuz-2.2.14-5.0
label=linux
root=/dev/hda1
read-only
```

17. Run `lilo -v` to update the master boot record.

    ```
    # lilo -v
    ```

18. Shut down and test the system.

    ```
    # shutdown -r now
    ```

19. Check the log-in herald to make sure that the new kernel version is reflected there and check the name.

    ```
    # uname -a
    ```

Congratulations! You are now running a new Linux kernel.

CHAPTER 10: INSTALLING A NEW KERNEL BY BUILDING A NEW SOURCE TREE

Quiz

1. What two things should be done on the current system before starting to install a new kernel?
2. What do the different parts of the *.tar* file name represent?
3. What do even-numbered minor-version numbers indicate?
4. How much additional space is required to build a new kernel and source tree while leaving the current one intact?
5. What step needs to be performed to preserve the old source tree?
6. What information does the *Changes* file include that is essential to know before compiling?
7. What command should be run after kernel configuration, and what does it indicate?
8. What is the difference between using `zImage` and `bzImage` to compile the kernel?
9. What changes need to be made to *lilo.conf* after the kernel has been compiled?
10. The `lilo -v` command needs to be run after modification of the *lilo.conf* file. Why?

See Appendix B for answers.

Appendix A

Patching Kernels

PATCHING A KERNEL IS NOT NECESSARILY DIFFICULT to do, but you do have to remember innumerable dependencies. If you have control of your kernel level and are very good at kernel compiling from source code, you may want to try kernel patching. Some Linux experts consider it a tremendous time-saver to download only 20 MB of patches to move from kernel version of 2.2.12 , for example, to 2.2.16 .

To patch your kernel, you need to know the precise version of the kernel that is currently installed, and then download the cumulative patches. The term "cumulative patches" means that you have to research all patches released since your kernel version up to the newer version you select. Assuming the currently installed kernel is version 2.2.12, and you wish to upgrade to 2.2.16, you would have have to download the following files:

▲ *patch-2.2.13.gz*

▲ *patch-2.2.14.gz*

▲ *patch-2.2.15.gz*

▲ *patch-2.2.16.gz*

The first file, containing the 2.2.13 kernel patch, is the required patch for moving from 2.2.12 to 2.2.13. Remember that the patches are upgrades. In other words, a patch numbered 2.2.12 is an upgrade from 2.2.11, not a patch for 2.2.12.

Unlike the kernel source tree, the above patch files do not have to reside in any specific directory. Thus, you can place them wherever you wish. To execute the patches, however, you must be the root user, and you have to execute them from the */usr/src* directory. Use the following command lines to execute each patch. Remember that you must execute patches in order. Review the `man` pages for information on the numerous available options for the `patch` command. The available options for the `patch` command correlate directly to the innumerable dependencies mentioned previously.

```
# cd /usr/src
# gunzip  -c   /directory/patchfile   |   patch -p0
```

The only option we regularly use is -p0, which tells the system not to modify any file name path references inside the patch file. This option has nothing to do with intrapath levels and related matters.

In its most simple form, a patch may merely replace an old file with a new file. In its more complex form, the concept of patching is very much like comparing two files using the `diff` command. In practice the code in the patch file is compared with the code on your system. The `patch` command attempts to locate code differences and then proceeds to replace old code with new and additional code. The command routine deals with code in chunks. Thus, you may notice exceptional activity on your system when you apply one of these complex patches, because `patch` scans forward and backward trying to find context matches in the code. If this process fails, the command reworks the code again, applying a fuzz factor. As it processes the code, it will report back all successes and failures.

APPENDIX A: PATCHING KERNELS

You can locate the context matches by using the `find` command to identify the files containing comments. Examples follow:

```
# find   /usr/src/linux -follow -name "*.rej" -print
# find   /usr/src/linux -follow -name "*#"    -print
```

In the event that these files are clean, you have a newly patched kernel. If not, you have to read all of the files. If any of the patches fail, you have to determine the reason for the failure. We recommend that you download the kernel source package or the new source code.

Appendix B

Quiz Answers

Chapter 1

1. Failure to determine system-hardware specifications.
   New equipment for which there are not yet drivers available.

2. Video.
   Monitor.

3. All technical hardware references.
   The newest drivers and utilities for your hardware.
   All system hardware specifications.

4. Determine existing system-hardware specifications.
   Replace unsupported hardware (if necessary).

5. DOS-based, including single bootable disk utilities.
   Windows-based, including `winmsd` and Device Manager.

Chapter 2

1. Process management.
   Memory management.

2. Both swap files and swap partitions provide for the paging of memory out of physical RAM to the hard disk.
Swap partitions must be created during installation or require repartitioning after installation. Swap files can be created at any time.
A swap partition is a dedicated partition on the hard disk; a swap file is a file created on a nondedicated partition.

3. Two times the physical RAM of the system is the rule of thumb, but the applications and intended system use may require changes to this amount.

4. Primary—only four per drive.
Extended—only one per drive, will reduce the number of primary partitions to three plus one extended.
Logical— twelve per drive, within the one extended partition.

5. `fdisk`, `Disk Druid`, `FIPS`, and Partition Magic.

6. With the exception of OS/2 (which can create multiple types of partitions), each operating system's disk-partitioning tool should be used to create the partition for that OS. The recommended order is Windows 9*x*, Windows NT/2000, OS/2, Linux.

7. a. Power on invokes BIOS which starts POST.
b. BIOS reads MBR and invokes the boot manager.
c. Boot manager reads partition table and identifies active partition.
d. Boot manager reads boot sector of active partition.
e. Boot sector reads OS kernel into RAM, OS kernel is uncompressed.
f. OS kernel checks hardware and installs drivers.

8. LILO is the LInux LOader or boot manager program. It can be placed on a floppy disk, in the MBR, or on the Linux partition.

9. Single boot (Linux only)—MBR.
Multi-boot—first sector of root partition.

APPENDIX B: QUIZ ANSWERS

10. Press the <Tab> key at the LILO `boot:` prompt. Select the operating system from the list of available operating systems presented by LILO.

Chapter 3

1. CD-ROM and boot floppy disk.

2. The controller's IRQ and base address; drive geometry for systems that do not specify it in the CMOS.

3. Hexadecimal with the prefix 0x.

4. Install or upgrade a system running Red Hat Linux 2.0 or later.
   Install or upgrade a system running Red Hat Linux 2.0 or later in text mode.
   Enable rescue mode.
   Enable expert mode.

5. Selecting the device driver manually from a list.
   Specifying the device options manually.

6. Check to see if the BIOS is limited or if there is a misconfigured master/slave jumper issue.

7. Master followed by slave, `hdx` where *x* is a letter of the alphabet beginning with *a*.

8. Using the `makeboot` utility.

Chapter 4

1. The NFS server and the target system must use TCP/IP to communicate.
   The NFS server must share binary files that are on a hard disk or CD-ROM.

CUSTOMIZING AND UPGRADING LINUX

> The target system must mount the shared drive.
> Some configuration files must be modified.

2. Insert the Linux CD-ROM.
   Log in as a regular user and `su` to root.
   Record the IP address and netmask of the server.
   Add an entry for the CD-ROM to the server's */etc/fstab* file.
   Mount the CD-ROM as file system.
   Export the CD-ROM file system to access without security.

3. Create the required floppies for installation.
   Boot the system from the Linux boot disk.
   Select the NFS Image option from installation.
   Provide networking information for the system.
   Provide the information about the NFS installation server.
   Install Linux.

Chapter 5

1. This is the screen resolution designated as the width in pixels by the number of lines.

2. The color depth and screen resolution (for example: 16 bit, 800x600).

3. `XF86Config` can be modified manually or by using `Xconfigurator`, `xf86config`, `XF86Setup`, or `xvidtune`.

4. `SuperProbe`.

5. Video-adapter type; monitor type.

6. The horizontal-sync rate or line rate is the monitor refresh rate multiplied by the screen height with an additional 4% to 5% added for overscan. This number should be less than the monitor's specified horizontal frequency per the manufacturer.

APPENDIX B: QUIZ ANSWERS

7. Interlacing is the process by which a monitor performs two line scans, each scanning every other line, to complete a frame. The advantage of interlacing is it allows the system to overcome certain limitations such as bandwidth or limited DCF. The disadvantages are flickering and reduced image quality.

8. The higher number in the range.

9. Probe will always return a conservative value. Screen Configuration values can be changed by selecting the `Let Me Choose` option in the Probing Finished dialog box.

Chapter 6

1. `lpr` sends process commands to `lpd`, assembles and processes the
   print data.
   `lpd` organizes and processes and requests from `lpr`, handles remote printing requests.
   `printcap` is the configuration file for `lpd`.

2. `lpc`, `lprm`, and `lpq`; information on these can be found in the `man` pages for the commands.

3. `lpr` assembles the data and copies it to the spooling queue, adding in any specific instructions and configuration information. It then communicates the process requests to `lpd` for organization.

4. `cfid_number`: information about the print job and the owner.
   `dfid_number`: the data file to be printed.

5. The `lpd` daemon must be refreshed with the new information and, if adding an additional printer, the entry must be included in either the *host.lpd* or *host.equiv* file of the target system so that `lpd` recognizes the remote system.

6. `printtool`.

283

7. *var/spool/lpd*

   There can be only one print queue per spool directory, but there may be multiple names for the print queue.

8. The print process will most likely fail without the correct level of permissions.

9. If there is a limited amount of space on the hard disk or partition containing the spooler directory, there should be corresponding limits on the amount of available space for the spooler.

10. Send a test page to the printer, and then send a job to the printer using `lpr`.

Chapter 7

1. Automation of common administrative steps.
   Upgrades and updates for software.
   Single container for executable, documentation, and configuration information.

2. The `rpm` utility is a package manager that allows you to install, query, verify, update, erase, and build software packages.

3. `name-version.arch.rpm`, where `name-version` refers to the name and release version of the package, `arch` is the architecture platform for which the package was compiled, and `rpm` is the standard rpm file extension.

4. The syntax is `rmp -qip <RPM package name>`, where `-q` gathers package information (query); `-i`, when used with the `-q` option, displays package information; and `-p`, when used with the `-q` option, tells `rpm` that the package is as yet uninstalled.

5. `rpm -qa | grep -i <text string sought>`

APPENDIX B: QUIZ ANSWERS

6. Documentation of the existing RPM packages and version levels on the system as well as the required RPM packages and version levels for the upgrade or installation.

7. Placing all RPM packages to be installed or updated in a separate directory created for that purpose. Packages may be deleted from that directory once they are installed.

8. It is a best practice to perform all required and desired upgrades before installing new packages. If a new RPM package requires other existing packages to be upgraded before it can be installed, it will prompt for that task to be completed. Upgrading first will eliminate most prerequisite problems.

9. If the upgrade or installation is required, but you receive a shell error message that there is a conflict and you are absolutely sure that installation of the RPM package will not cause version-based dependency problems with other packages already on the system.

Chapter 8

1. To obtain support for new hardware.
   To obtain updated drivers for existing hardware.
   To respond to security issues.

2. Check to make sure there is enough disk space available.
   Inventory the RPM packages and versions already on the system.
   Check the integrity of the RPM packages to be installed or updated.
   Compare downloaded and existing RPM packages.
   Record the current version of Linux.
   Create an emergency repair disk.

3. Check the log-in herald.
   Use the uname command with the -r option.
   Use the uname command with the -a option.

4. `mkbootdisk`.

5. Availability of and correct versioning of RPM-package dependencies.

6. Non-kernel packages should be upgraded first, then kernel packages.

7. The system requires SCSI or PCMCIA support at boot.

8. The *lilo.conf* file must be edited to point to the new kernel. If you wish the new kernel to be the default boot selection, it should be placed as the first stanza of the *lilo.conf* file.

9. Querying the RPM database.
Checking system-disk space.
Create an updated boot disk/repair disk.

Chapter 9

1. Developers who want to work with the newest code and administrators who want a specific set of kernel components.

2. Specify infrequently used features be compiled as modules and mandatory features be compiled directly into the kernel.

3. Those for which the kernel components have not been enabled.

4. Whether or not beta code will be allowed to be compiled into the kernel.

5. Whether a modular or monolithic kernel will be installed and whether or not compatible modules from other kernels can be used. A modular kernel allows for loading and unloading of modules on demand, whereas a monolithic kernel has all options in the kernel.

6. When you have SCSI or PCMCIA devices that need to be available when the system boots.

7. The UNIX domain sockets and TCP/IP networking options.

APPENDIX B: QUIZ ANSWERS

8. Dummy `net driver support` option.

9. Save and Exit, and it creates an *xconfig* file for kernel compilation.

Chapter 10

1. Recording of the current kernel level and creating of boot and rescue disks.

2. The first number is the major version, followed by the minor version, revision number, and `tar` file type.

3. Even numbers indicate more stable production versions of the product.

4. 55 MB or more.

5. The existing *linux* directory needs to be renamed or unlinked.

6. The "Current Minimal Requirements" stanza of the file includes those changes in the form of software revisions that must be completed before the kernel is compiled.

7. The `make dep` command should be run to create the dependency tree. Any error-return value other than 0 indicates a configuration problem that needs to be resolved before compiling the kernel.

8. The compression algorithms are different. The `bzImage` utility compiles a smaller kernel.

9. It needs to be modified to point to the new kernel and RAM disk (if required).

10. To update the master boot record (MBR) with the new information.

Index

A
a.out binary support 221
ATA-2 DISK support 224
authentication configuration
   IDE system 80
   SCSI system 54
auto-completion of commands 186

B
bandwidth (monitor) 122–123
bandwith requirements 124
binary support 221
BIOSes, broken or obsolete 221
boot disks, creating
   DOS/Windows 29–30
   for a new kernel 244
   IDE system 84–85
   SCSI system 57–58
   UNIX 31–32
boot managers
   definition 15
   OS/2 Boot Manager 17
   Partition Magic 17
   See also LILO (LInux LOader)
boot.img disk 97
booting the system
   boot manager 15
   POST (power on self-test), 14
   target of network installation 97
   with LILO (LInux LOader) 19
   without LILO (LInux LOader), 19
   See also LILO (LInux LOader)
bootnet.img disk 97
bootstrap loaders. *See* boot managers
bridging support 228
bus type, specifying 220

C
CD-ROM, installing Linux from. *See* installing Linux from a CD-ROM; installing Linux on a network; installing Linux on a SCSI system; installing Linux on an IDE system
CD-ROM not detected 65
CD-ROM support 224
chipsets 107
code maturity level, specifying 216
color depth (monitor)
   definition 105–106
   setting 147
commands
   auto-completion of 186
   lpq 160
   lpr 161
   make clean 255
   make dep 255–256
   make modules 258–259
   make modules_install 258–259
   make oldconfig 254
   mkbootdisk 201
   mkinitrd 229
   mrproper 250
   patch 276
   rpm 186

tar 249
uname 200
compiling a kernel 256
component list, example 5
components, selecting for installation
   IDE system 80–82
   SCSI system 54–55
CRT (cathode ray tube) 112

D

dd utility 31
dead keys 40
dependency trees, creating 255–256
device naming 164
Disk Druid 12
disk paging 10
disk partitioning
   Disk Druid 12
   extended partitions 10
   fdisk 12
   FIPS 12
   for multiple operating systems 13
   IDE system 71, 72–75
   logical partitions 10
   MBR (master boot record), 13–14
   on a blank disk 13
   operating system compatibility 13
   Partition Magic 12
   partition tables 13–14
   primary partitions 10
   SCSI system 44–45
   tools for 12
disk partitioning, examples
   multiple file systems 22–24
   multiple partitions 22–24
   one operating system 21
   one partition 21
   planning partitions 25
display capacity 106
DOS support
   enabling 221
   pre version 5.0 21
dot clocks 110

dot pitch 126–128
drive geometry
   specifying for IDE systems 65
   specifying for SCSI system 34–35
drive naming conventions 65
dummy net driver support 231

E

ELF binary support 221
emergency boot diskette, creating 201
eq files 164
errs files 164
/etc/fstab file 94
Ethernet support 232
exercises
   hard-disk-partition planning 25
   installing a kernel from scratch 266–272
   installing Linux, hardware requirements 7
   monitor configuration 138–156
   upgrading 189–191
   upgrading a kernel 206–210
   Xconfigurator 138–156
   XF86Config file, modifying 138–156
experimental code, allowing 216
expert mode, enabling
   IDE system 67
   SCSI system 38
extended partitions 10

F

fast text printing, enabling 166
fdisk 12
file size (printer), limiting remote printers 172
file size (printer), limiting local printers 165
file systems
   partitioning for multiple 22–24
   specifying 237
FIPS 12
flicker 114, 115, 131
floppy disk support 223
floppy disks, creating for network
      installation 97
forcing an installation 185

INDEX

G
ghostscript, enabling 167
GNOME desktop
  IDE system 70
  SCSI system 40
GUI install panel
  IDE system 67
  SCSI system 37

H
hard disk attributes, viewing
  IDE system 72
  SCSI system 44–45
hard-disk partitioning 11
hard-disk-partition planning
  exercise 25
  quiz 25
hard disk partitions. *See* disk partitioning; swap partitions
hardware requirements 2–4
horizontal frequency 123–125
horizontal scan frequency (HSF) 114
horizontal sync pulse (HSP) 114, 116–118
horizontal synchronization frequency 114
host name, specifying
  IDE system 77
  SCSI system 51
HSF (horizontal scan frequency) 114
HSP (horizontal sync pulse) 114, 116–118

I
ICP Vortex controller issues 35
IDE chipset support 226
IDE drive geometry 65–66
IDE support 224
image data transfer rate 108, 109
input filters, enabling
  for remote printers 172
  local printers 165
install log, creating
  IDE system 82–83
  SCSI system 56

installing a kernel as an upgrade. *See* patching a kernel; RPM packages, upgrading a Linux kernel
installing a kernel from scratch
  .o files, finding 250
  boot disks, creating 244–245
  compile duration 256
  compiling the kernel 256
  configuring the kernel 254
  current level, determining 244
  dependency trees, creating 255–256
  downloading files for 242
  exercise 266–272
  LILO file changes 262–263
  linking to new source tree 250
  make clean command 255
  make dep command 255–256
  make modules command 258–259
  make modules_install command 258–259
  make oldconfig command 254
  MBR (master boot record), updating 263
  mrproper command 250
  new configuration vs. old 254
  old compile files, cleaning up 255
  pointing to the new kernel 262–263
  preserving the old source tree 248
  quiz 273
  RAM disk, creating 261
  rescue diskettes, creating 244–245
  rescue procedure 264
  software requirements, checking 252–254
  source tree dependencies, finding 250
  space requirements, checking 247
  System.map, replacing 260
  tar command 249
  tar files, obtaining 246–247
  tar files, unpacking 249
  testing the new kernel 264–265
installing LILO (LInux LOader) 18
installing Linux from a CD-ROM
  boot disk, creating in DOS/Windows 29–30
  boot disk, creating in UNIX 31–32
installing Linux on a network
  booting the target system 97

CD-ROM, accessing 95–96
CD-ROM, exporting file system 95–96
CD-ROM, mounting 95
floppy disks, creating 97
installation method, choosing 98
logging in 94
mounting 95
network information, specifying 98–99
network requirements 92
NFS (Network File System) 91–93
NFS client preparation 96–100
NFS server information, specifying 98–99
NFS server IP address, recording 94
NFS server netmask, recording 94
NFS server preparation 93–96
ownership 93
quiz 101
security 93
installing Linux on a SCSI system
   authentication configuration 54
   boot disk, creating 57–58
   components, selecting 54–55
   disk partitioning 44–45
   expert mode, enabling 38
   GNOME desktop 40
   GUI install panel 37
   hard disk attributes, viewing 44–45
   host name, specifying 51
   ICP Vortex controller issues 35
   inputting information 33
   install log, creating 56
   installation complete 62
   installation type, selecting 40–41
   KDE desktop 40
   keyboard, selecting 39–40
   language, selecting 38–39
   LILO configuration 48–49
   monitor configuration 58–61
   mouse configuration 51–52
   overlapping files 56–57
   progress indicator 57
   quiz 90
   rescue disks 38
   rescue mode 38
   root password, setting 53
   SCSI configuration 42–44
   starting the install program 33
   TCP/IP configuration 50
   text mode, enabling 37
   time zone configuration 52
   video adapter 56
   Welcome! screen does not appear 34
   Welcome! screen, description 36–38
   X Window System, starting 61
installing Linux on an IDE system
   authentication configuration 80
   boot disk, creating 84–85
   CD-ROM not detected 65
   components, selecting 80–82
   disk partitioning 71, 72–75
   drive naming conventions 65–66
   expert mode, enabling 67
   GNOME desktop 70
   GUI install panel 67
   hard disk attributes, viewing 72
   host name, specifying 77
   IDE drive geometry 65–66
   inputting information 64
   install log, creating 82–83
   installation complete 88
   installation type, selecting 70
   KDE desktop 70
   keyboard, selecting 69
   language, selecting 68–69
   LILO configuration 75–76
   monitor configuration 85–87
   mouse configuration 78
   new installation vs. upgrade 71
   overlapping files 83
   progress indicator 83
   quiz 90
   rescue disks 68
   rescue mode 68
   root password, setting 79
   starting the install program 63
   TCP/IP configuration 77
   text mode, enabling 67
   time zone configuration 78

INDEX

video adapter 82
Welcome! screen, description 66–68
X Window System, starting 87–88
installing Linux, hardware requirements
  component list, example 5
  current hardware configuration,
    determining 4
  exercise 7
  on new hardware 2–3
  on old hardware 3–4
  quiz 8
installing Linux upgrades. *See* RPM packages
installing XF86Setup 187–188
interlacing video displays 129–132

K

KDE desktop
  IDE system 70
  SCSI system 40
kernel, configuring
  a.out binary support 221
  ATA-2 DISK support 224
  binary support 221
  BIOSes, broken or obsolete 221
  bridging support 228
  bus type, specifying 220
  CD-ROM support 224
  code maturity level, specifying 216
  DOS support 221
  dummy net driver support 231
  ELF binary support 221
  Ethernet support 232
  experimental code, allowing 216
  file systems, specifying 237
  floppy disk support 223
  IDE chipset support 226
  IDE support 224
  kerneld daemon support, enabling 219
  laptop power management 222
  loadable module support, enabling 218
  loopback device support 227
  make xconfig tool 213
  math emulation, enabling 217
  MFM support 224

mirroring support 228
MISC binary support 221
mixing versions 219
mkinitrd command 229
modular kernels 218
monolithic kernels 218
network block device support 228
networking options 230–234
networking support 219
parallel port support 222
PCI access mode option 220
PCI quirks option 221
PCI support option 220
plug and play support 223
processor types, specifying 217
quiz 239
RAM disk support 229
RLL disk support 224
saving the configuration 238
SCSI emulation support 226
SCSI support 235–236
start menu 214–216
striping support 228
system V IPC option 221
tape drive support 224
TCP/IP, enabling 231
UNIX domain sockets option 231
kernel, upgrading. *See* patching a kernel; RPM
  packages, upgrading a Linux kernel
kerneld daemon support, enabling 219
keyboard, selecting
  IDE system 69
  SCSI system 39–40
KHz (kilohertz), definition 114

L

language, selecting
  IDE system 68–69
  SCSI system 38–39
laptop power management 222
LILO (LInux LOader)
  booting with 19
  booting without 19
  configuring 20

293

definition 17
file changes for new kernel 262–263
installation location 18
managing 20
LILO (LInux LOader) configuration
　IDE system 75–76
　SCSI system 48–49
　zlilo utility 242
line rates
　calculating 109, 125
　definition 114
　selecting 144
linear mode 48
linking to new source tree 250
Linux, installing. *See* installing Linux
LInux LOader (LILO). *See* LILO (LInux LOader)
loadable module support, enabling 218
lock files 164
logging in for network installation 94
logical partitions 10
loopback device support 227
lpd 169
lpd files 159
lpq command 160
lpr command 159, 161

M

make dep command 255–256
make modules command 258–259
make modules_install command 258–259
make oldconfig command 254
make xconfig tool 213
managing LILO (LInux LOader) 20
margins, setting 167
master boot record (MBR). *See* MBR (master boot record)
math emulation, enabling 217
MBR (master boot record)
　definition 13
　disk partitioning 13–14
　repairing 20
　updating for new kernel 263
memory requirements (video) 104

MFM support 224
microseconds, definition 116
milliseconds, definition 118
mirroring support 228
MISC binary support 221
mkbootdisk command 201
mkinitrd command 229
modelines 119–121
modular kernels 218
Monitor 124
monitor configuration
　exercise 138–156
　IDE system 85–87
　online resources for 128
　quiz 157
　SCSI system 58–61
　XFree86 Video Timings HOWTO 128
monitor performance, factors affecting
　age 121–122
　bandwidth 122–123
　dot pitch 126–128
　horizontal frequency 123–125
　line rate calculations (VESA) 125
　vertical frequency 125
monitors
　bandwidth requirements, table of 124
　color depth
　　definition 105–106
　　setting 147
　CRT (cathode ray tube) 112
　display capacity 106
　flicker 114, 115, 131
　horizontal synchronization frequency 114
　HSF (horizontal scan frequency), 114
　HSP (horizontal sync pulse) 114, 116–118
　interlacing 129–132
　maximum resolution by monitor size 128
　modelines 119–121
　phosphor 112
　phosphor persistence 114
　refresh rate 115
　resolution
　　definition 106
　　setting 147

INDEX

scan lines 113
screen refresh rate. *See* VSF
shadow mask 112
sync pulsing 115
synchronization 112–116
vertical refresh rate 115
vertical sync range, selecting 146–147
vertical synchronization frequency 115
video frame 112–116
video modes
    definition 106
    selecting 151–152
    table of 107
VSF (vertical scan frequency) 115
VSF (vertical synchronization
    frequency) 108
VSP (vertical sync pulse) 115, 118–119
monolithic kernels 218
mouse configuration
    IDE system 78
    SCSI system 51–52
mrproper command 250

N

naming conventions
    IDE drives 65
    RPMs 177–178
    tar files 245–247
    version numbers 245–247
network block device support 228
Network File System (NFS)
    installing Linux on 91–100
    See also installing Linux on a network
network, installing Linux on. *See* installing
    Linux on a network
networking options 230–234
networking support 219
NFS (Network File System), installing Linux.
    See installing Linux on a network

O

.o files, finding 250
onboard memory clock 110
operating systems, multiple 13

OS/2 Boot Manager 17
overlapping files
    IDE system 83
    SCSI system 56–57
ownership, NFS 93

P

package conflicts 185, 202
package dependencies 55
packages. *See* RPM packages
paper size, specifying 165
parallel port support 222
partition boot record. *See* MBR (master boot
    record)
Partition Magic 12, 17
partition tables 13–14
partitions. *See* disk partitioning; swap partitions
patch command 276
patches. *See* RPM packages
patching a kernel 275–277
PCI access mode option 220
PCI quirks option 220
PCI support option 220
pcmcia.img disk 97
phosphor 112
phosphor persistence 114
pixels, definition 105
plug and play support 223
POST (power on self-test), 14
PPP, enabling 231
primary partitions 10
print queue name, specifying 171–172
print queues, managing
    deleting jobs from 160
    lpq command 160
Print System Manager
    configuring local printers 163
    configuring remote printers 169
printcap 159
printcap file 161
printer configuration, quiz 174
printer drivers, specifying 165
printers
    lpd files 159

295

lpr command 159, 161
  printcap 159
  printcap file 161
  sending jobs to 161
printers, configuring locally
  device naming 164
  eq files 164
  errs files 164
  fast text printing, enabling 166
  file size, limiting 165
  ghostscript, enabling 167
  input filters, enabling 165
  invoking Print System Manager 163
  local printer, specifying 163
  lock files 164
  margins, setting 167
  paper size, specifying 165
  printer device, specifying 165
  printer drivers, specifying 165
  printing multiple pages per sheet 167
  resolution 165
  separator pages 166
  Spool Directory 164
  stair-step text, fixing 166
  status files 164
printers, configuring remotely
  confirming TCP/IP configuration 168
  file size, limiting 172
  input filters, enabling 172
  invoking Print System Manager 169
  prerequisites 168–169
  print queue name, specifying 171, 172
  printtool utility 169
  remote host authorization, determining 170
  remote host, specifying 172
  spool, directory 172
  test page, sending 173
printtool utility 169
processor type
  determining 201
  specifying 217

Q

quizzes
  configuring the kernel 239
  hard-disk-partition planning 25
  installing a kernel from scratch 273
  installing Linux on a network file system 101
  installing Linux on a SCSI system 90
  installing Linux on an IDE system 90
  installing Linux, hardware requirements 8
  monitor configuration 157
  printer configuration 174
  upgrading a kernel 211
  upgrading RPM packages 192

R

RAM disks 203, 229, 261
RAM, swap space requirements 11
RAMDAC 107
rawrite program 29
Raymond, Eric S. 128
Red Hat Package Managers. *See* RPM packages
refresh rate (monitor) 115
remote host (for printers)
  authorization, determining 170
  specifying 172
repairing LILO (LInux LOader), 20
rescue diskettes
  IDE system 68
  new kernel 244
  SCSI system 38
rescue mode
  IDE system 68
  SCSI system 38
rescue procedure 264
resolution (monitor)
  definition 106
  maximums by monitor size 128
  setting 147
RLL disk support 224
root password, setting
  IDE system 79
  SCSI system 53
RPM vs. SRPM 178

INDEX

rpm command 186
RPM packages
  contents of 178–181
  definition 176
  installing XF86Setup with 187–188
  matching version numbers 177
  naming conventions 177–178
  online source for 181
  rpm utility 176
  upgrading, quiz 192
RPM packages, upgrading
  confirming the upgrade 186
  exercise 189–191
  forcing an installation 185
  identifying replacement targets 182–183
  package conflicts 185
  package names, determining 182, 183
  package versions, determining 182
  replacement files, obtaining 183
  rpm command 186
  upgrades vs. additions 184–186
  with wildcards 186
RPM packages, upgrading a Linux kernel
  booting from new kernel 203
  checking disk space 196
  current RPMs, identifying 197–199
  current version, determining 200
  dependency errors 202
  emergency boot diskette, creating 201
  exercise 206–210
  integrity check 199
  marking RPMs for upgrade 199
  mkbootdisk command 201
  organizing RPMs 199
  package conflicts 202
  processor type, determining 201
  quiz 211
  RAM disk, creating 203
  reasons for upgrading 194–196
  security advisory 194–196
  testing the new kernel 204
  uname command 200
rpm utility 176

S

scan lines 113
SCSI controller, forcing recognition of 34
SCSI emulation support 226
SCSI low-level drivers 236
SCSI support 235
security, NFS 93
security advisory 194–196
separator pages, enabling 166
shadow mask 112
SLIP, enabling 231
software packages. *See* RPM packages
source tree dependencies, finding 250
spool directory
  local printers 164
  remote printers 172
SRPM vs. RPM 178
stair-step text, fixing 166
startx script 122
status files 164
striping support 228
SuperProbe 135–136
supp.img disk 97
swap files
  creating 10
  vs. swap partitions 10
swap partitions vs. swap files 10
swap space requirements 11–12
sync pulsing 115
synchronization, video displays 112–116
system V IPC option 221
System.map, replacing 260

T

tape drive support 224
tar command 249
tar files
  obtaining 246–247
  unpacking 249
TCP/IP configuration
  confirming 168
  IDE system 77
  SCSI system 50
TCP/IP, enabling 231

text mode, enabling
   IDE system 67
   SCSI system 37
time zone configuration
   IDE system 78
   SCSI system 52

U

uname command 200
UNIX domain sockets option 231
upgrading a kernel. *See* patching a kernel; RPM packages, upgrading a Linux kernel

V

versions
   mixing 219
   odd vs. even numbers 245
   production vs. experimental 246
vertical scan frequency. *See* VSF (vertical synchronization frequency)
vertical frequency 125
vertical refresh rate 115
vertical sync pulse (VSP) 115, 118–119
vertical sync range, selecting 146–147
vertical synchronization frequency (VSF) 108, 115
VESA 109, 125
VGA memory clock 110
video
   chipsets 107
   dot clock 110
   horizontal sync ranges. *See* line rates
   IDE system 82
   image data transfer rate 108
   line rate calculations (VESA) 109, 125
   line rates
      definition 114
      selecting 144
   memory requirements 105
   onboard memory clock 110
   pixels, definition 105
   RAMDAC 107
   VGA memory clock 110
   SCSI system 56
   See also monitor; XF86Config file

video adapter
   IDE 82
   SCSI 56
video adapter bus 107–110
video adapter memory 104
video configuration exercise 138–156
   See also monitor configuration; XF86Config file
Video Electronics Standards Association. *See* VESA
video frame 112–116
video modes
   definition 106
   selecting 151–152
   table of 107
VSF (vertical synchronization frequency) 108, 115
VSP (vertical sync pulse) 115, 118–119

W

Welcome! screen does not appear 34
Welcome! screen, description
   IDE system 66–68
   SCSI system 36
wildcards, and RPM upgrades 186

X

X Window System, starting
   IDE system 87–88
   SCSI system 61
Xconfigurator
   creating an XF86Config file 137
   exercise 138–156
   Select Video Modes 106
   using to configure XF86Config 134
   See also XF86Config file; XF86Setup
XF86Config file
   chipset, determining 135–136
   configuring 134
   creating 137
   modifying, exercise 138–156
   sections of 133
   SuperProbe 135–136
   uses for 133–134
   video information, getting 135–136

INDEX

video memory, determining 135–136
video mode timing information 119–120
video resolution information 119
X server 133–135
XFree86 133–135
See also Xconfigurator

XF86Setup
  installing 187–188
  using to configure XF86Config 134
  See also Xconfigurator
XFree86, replacing packages, exercise 189
xvidtune, using to configure XF86Config 135

GEARHEAD PRESS

Gearhead Press is committed to delivering technical information to IT professionals who challenge themselves to learn new technologies and advance their skills. To provide you with quality learning tools, we've taken the unprecedented step to publish only authors who are professional technical trainers.

The Expertise of a Professional Trainer in Every Book

Professional technical trainers are subject-matter experts, skilled developers and network engineers, and effective communicators. As authors, technical trainers will develop books that reflect a combination of skill, knowledge, and years of classroom experience that is highly valued and sought after by corporations and professionals worldwide.

Three Series to Meet Your Needs

We currently offer three series to help you grasp new topics, acquire functional or network administration skills, and develop integrated solutions to real-world business challenges. Each series offers a distinctive editorial approach and learning style.

- **In the Trenches:** A fast-paced series of books, written by authors who have been "in the trenches" as IT professionals themselves, that will introduce you to a new technology, help you become proficient, and serve as long-lasting references.
- **Virtual Workshop Gold:** A full-color series of books, each with a unique blend of information, examples, exercises, and review questions for self-paced, hands-on learning and reference.
- **Point to Point:** A series that invites you to join a project and implement a technology in a real-world environment, contending with problems such as legacy systems, planning, product integration, implementation, system maintenance, and more.

Gearhead Press books are available at
bookstores, online retailers, or at www.gearheadpress.com

THE GEARHEAD GROUP

Gearhead Press • Gearhead Curriculum • Gearhead Training • Gearhead Online

UPCOMING BOOKS FROM GEARHEAD PRESS

In the Trenches: Installing and Administering Linux by Linda McKinnon and Al McKinnon helps IT professionals leverage prior experience on Windows NT-, NetWare-, and UNIX-based networks to develop Linux-specific installation and system administration skills.

$49.95 (U.S.)
ISBN 1-930713-00-2
Available October 2000

In the Trenches: Windows 2000 Automated Deployment by Ted Malone and Rolly Perreaux is a blueprint for administrators who want to save time and money installing and upgrading software by using the new automated-deployment tools included in Windows 2000 Professional.

$49.95 (U.S.)
ISBN 1-930713-06-1
Available January 2001

Virtual Workshop Gold: Web Application Programming with PHP by Matt Bridges uses a unique blend of reference information, exercises, and online resources to teach programmers in a Windows or Linux environment how to develop real-world, data-driven Web applications using PHP 4.0.

$59.95 (U.S.)
ISBN 1-930713-07-X
Available February 2001

Virtual Workshop Gold: Windows 2000 Programming
by Donis Marshall contains experience-based insights, examples and exercises to instruct developers in system-level, API programming using Microsoft's Platform Software Development Kit (SDK), showing Visual Basic, MFC and J++ programmers how to build faster and more robust Windows applications.

$59.95 (U.S.)
ISBN 1-930713-05-3
Available March 2001

Point to Point: Migrating to Microsoft Exchange 2000
by Stan Reimer invites readers to join the IT team at North American Airlines — a model company with multiple Windows NT 4.0 domains and several Exchange Servers spread across multiple sites — as they embark on the migration path from Exchange 4.0 or 5.x to Exchange 2000.

$49.95 (U.S.)
ISBN: 1-930713-08-8
Available March 2001

Visit us at www.gearheadpress.com for detailed descriptions, tables of contents, author bios, and sample chapters, plus access to online resources!

Gearhead Press
Delivering technical information to IT professionals

Gearhead Press is a division of the Gearhead Group

GEARHEAD TRAINING

Gearhead Training travels to Fortune 100 and other companies worldwide, educating corporate IT developers and network engineers about leading-edge technologies and products. We work with companies to meet their technology and business goals by helping their IT staffs:

- Update their technical skills
- Be productive by using products and technologies more effectively
- Learn new tools and technologies

Gearhead trainers are certified IT professionals who have honed their expertise "in the trenches," first as practitioners and then as trainers.

As leaders in the IT community, Gearhead trainers:

- Earn multiple certifications from leading vendors, including Microsoft, Novell, Compaq, IBM, and SUN Microsystems, as well as various Linux certifications.
- Convey technical information succinctly, anticipate students' problems, and respond to questions by drawing upon real-world anecdotes and examples.
- Write white papers, author books, give presentations at conferences, and contribute articles to leading trade and industry journals.

Choose from our catalog or develop a custom course

Each Gearhead Training course has been carefully developed and fine-tuned to ensure that our clients and students achieve their training goals. In addition, we develop customized courses with curriculum based on the specific technologies and products an IT team is using (or planning to use), its current processes, and its overall strengths and weaknesses. Whether you choose a course from our catalog or customize one, we guarantee a productive training experience for all.

Contact us today for information about current course offerings, or to explore customized training solutions.

Gearhead Training
A division of the Gearhead Group
www.gearheadtraining.com

GO ONLINE
WITH GEARHEAD PRESS

Gearhead Press supplements each book it publishes with a valuable collection of technical information and resources. When you purchase a Gearhead Press book, you can gain free, 24/7 access to its numerous resources. Simply log on to our Web site, www.gearheadpress.com, and enter the code 010B7C5.

Go online and take advantage of:

- Online Help Desk (Q&A) to obtain answers to pressing questions and expert advice
- White Papers to gather information on vendors' technologies and products
- Tech Notes to help you make maximum use of technologies and products
- Updates on new functionality and features, workarounds, patches, and more
- Example Code to use as a guide, or to modify to meet your needs
- Chat Sessions where you can interact with Gearhead Press authors, editors and other IT experts
- Supplemental Exercises, which you can practice to develop new skills faster
- Professional Networking Opportunities, including links to user groups, associations, trade journals, and more
- Gearhead Press News for information on new books, series, and resources available to address your needs

Bookmark this Web site and visit it frequently.
We're continually posting new information and we welcome your comments.

Gearhead Press

Delivering technical information to IT professionals
www.gearheadpress.com

LICENSE AGREEMENT

This book includes a copy of the Publisher's Edition of Red Hat Linux from Red Hat, Inc., which you may use in accordance with the license agreement accompanying the software. The Official Red Hat Linux, which you may purchase from Red Hat, includes the complete Official Red Hat Linux distribution, Red Hat's documentation, and may include technical support for Official Red Hat Linux. You also may purchase technical support from Red Hat. You may purchase Official Red Hat Linux and technical support from Red Hat through the company's web site (www.redhat.com) or its toll-free number **1-888-REDHAT1.**